TRANSFORMATIONS OF THE NEW GERMANY

Studies in European Culture and History

edited by

Eric D. Weitz and Jack Zipes
University of Minnesota

Since the fall of the Berlin Wall and the collapse of communism, the very meaning of Europe has been opened up and is in the process of being redefined. European states and societies are wrestling with the expansion of NATO and the European Union and with new streams of immigration, while a renewed and reinvigorated cultural interaction has emerged between East and West. But the fast-paced transformations of the last fifteen years also have deeper historical roots. The reconfiguring of contemporary Europe is entwined with the cataclysmic events of the twentieth century, two world wars and the Holocaust, and with the processes of modernity that, since the eighteenth century, have shaped Europe and its engagement with the rest of the world.

Studies in European Culture and History is dedicated to publishing books that explore major issues in Europe's past and present from a wide variety of disciplinary perspectives. The works in the series are interdisciplinary; they focus on culture and society and deal with significant developments in Western and Eastern Europe from the eighteenth century to the present within a social historical context. With its broad span of topics, geography, and chronology, the series aims to publish the most interesting and innovative work on modern Europe.

Series titles

Fascism and Neofascism: Critical Writings on the Radical Right in Europe
Edited by Angelica Fenner and Eric D. Weitz

Fictive Theories: Towards a Deconstructive and Utopian Political Imagination
Susan McManus

*German-Jewish Literature in the Wake of the Holocaust: Grete Weil, Ruth Klüger,
and the Politics of Address*
Pascale R. Bos

Exile, Science, and Bildung: The Contested Legacies of German Intellectual Figures
Edited by David Kettler and Gerhard Lauer

Transformations of the New Germany
Edited by Ruth A. Starkman

*The Turkish Turn in Contemporary German Literature: Toward a New Critical Grammar of
Migration*
Leslie A. Adelson

*Terror and the Sublime in Art and Critical Theory: From Auschwitz to Hiroshima to
September 11*
Gene Ray

TRANSFORMATIONS OF THE NEW GERMANY

EDITED BY

RUTH A. STARKMAN

palgrave
macmillan

TRANSFORMATIONS OF THE NEW GERMANY
© Ruth A. Starkman, 2006.

First published in 2006 by
PALGRAVE MACMILLAN™
175 Fifth Avenue, New York, N.Y. 10010 and
Houndmills, Basingstoke, Hampshire, England RG21 6XS
Companies and representatives throughout the world.

PALGRAVE MACMILLAN is the global academic imprint of the Palgrave Macmillan division of St. Martin's Press, LLC and of Palgrave Macmillan Ltd. Macmillan® is a registered trademark in the United States, United Kingdom and other countries. Palgrave is a registered trademark in the European Union and other countries.

ISBN 1–4039–6795–4

Library of Congress Cataloging-in-Publication Data

Transformations of the new Germany / edited by Ruth A. Starkman.
    p.cm.—(Studies in European culture and history)
    Includes bibliographical references and index.
    ISBN 1–4039–6795–4 (alk. paper)
    1. Germany—Intellectual life. 2. Political culture—Germany—History—20th century. 3. Germany—Social conditions—1990– 4. Jews—Germany—History—1945– 5. National socialism—Psychological aspects. 6. Germany—Ethnic relations. I. Starkman, Ruth A. II. Series.

DD290.26.T73 2005
943.088—dc22   2004059901

A catalogue record for this book is available from the British Library.

Design by Newgen Imaging Systems (P) Ltd., Chennai, India.

First edition: February 2006

10 9 8 7 6 5 4 3 2 1

Printed in the United States of America.

CONTENTS

About the Contributors

Russell A. Berman is professor of German Studies and the Department of Comparative Literature at Stanford. He is the author of numerous articles and books including *Enlightenment or Empire: Colonial Discourse in German Culture*, 1998.

Martin Blum is associate professor of Critical Studies at the University of British Columbia, Okanagan, he has published widely on popular culture in East Germany.

Stephen Brockmann is associate professor of German Studies at Carnegie Mellon University. His book *Literature and German Reunification* was published by Cambridge University Press, 1999, he is the author of many articles on Germany, unification and normalization of German culture.

Gottfried Korff is professor of anthropology at the Ludwig-Uhland-Institute for Empirical Cultural Studies in Tübingen.

Hermann Kurthen is assistant professor of sociology at the State University of New York, Binghamton. He is coeditor of *Anti-Semitism and Xenophobia in Germany after Unification* Oxford, 1997, as well as many other essays on German and citizenship.

Jonathan Laurence is assistant professor of political science at Boston College. He was a fellow at Harvard's Minda de Gunzburg Center for European Studies. His research focuses on Muslim and Jewish relations in Germany and France.

Alison Lewis is associate professor of German at the University of Melbourne and has published widely on East German literature.

Nora Räthzel is professor of sociology at the University of Umea in Sweden and has published widely on race and citizenship in Germany.

Klaus Scherpe is professor of modern German literature, Cultural and Media Studies at Humboldt University and has published widely on modernism/ postmodernism/ culture/ race and globalization.

Patricia Simpson is assistant professor of German at Montana State University, she has published widely on East German culture.

Ruth A. Starkman teaches social and political philosophy at the University of San Francisco.

Brett Wheeler was assistant professor of German in the School of Foreign Service at Georgetown University.

Acknowledgements

This book evolved from a grant and seminar originally funded by the DAAD. Berkeley's Townsend Center and Center for German and European Studies also provided generous support. During the editing process, I benefited from the advice of friends, colleagues and press editors, whose suggestions and reports ultimately determined the book's final outcome. I would like to thank Brett Wheeler and Fritz Tubach, who originally worked on the project. Peter Tokofsky did all the major editing and made many important decisions in its first versions. Russell A. Berman was also very encouraging from the beginning, and, of course, I am most grateful to my series editors Eric D. Weitz and Jack Zipes for their faith and interest in the project.

Chapter 8 appears by permission from Routledge press, it originally appeared in Social Identities 1/2 (1995). Chapter 10 appears by permission from Berghahn Books, it is a revised version of an article by the same title that appeared in *German Politics and Society* (summer 2001).

FOREWORD: INTERDISCIPLINARITY OR CULTURAL STUDIES

Russell A. Berman

Most interdisciplinary studies would be expected to include a series of chapters each with a different disciplinary perspective; e.g., the literature of German unification, the art of German unification, the politics, the economics, the anthropology of German unification and so on: a sort of summative interdisciplinarity would add together the contributions from distinct, separate, and stable types of scholarship that share one and only one facet—their topic of inquiry, German unification. The result could well be a multiperspectival account of the single object (or, more likely, different specific objects—books, paintings, and so on, all temporally associated with the same singular event), but wherein each contribution would retain an allegiance to its professional provenance and be measured by the standards and norms of its site of origin. The essays would speak and listen less to each other than merely display the results of monodisciplinary scholarship in an interdisciplinary setting; the boundaries between the disciplines themselves would not have become fluid and one might even be tempted to lend credence to the hostile argument that the displacement from the authentic disciplinary context could diminish the rigor of the criteria by which scholarly work might be judged: the essays on literature that political scientists like may not be up to snuff in specialized journals of literary study. Summative interdisciplinarity runs the risk, therefore, of being less than disciplinary and therefore only second-rate.

This volume is put together very differently. A few of the authors in this volume have degrees in German Studies (a.k.a. Germanic Languages and Literatures, and the name change is crucial for reasons to be explained), but the volume does not introduce them as such. We are precisely not given a volume organized in terms of: part one—literature; part two—sociology; part three—art, and so on. Instead, small groups of essays are clustered around different kinds of materials all associated with the phenomenon of

German unification, while no single material is reserved exclusively for a particular discipline. In fact, it is impossible, in many cases, to assign neat and traditional disciplinary identities to the single essays; this holds good more for some than for others, but it holds for all to some extent and points toward a new, non-summative interdisciplinarity. Or is it perhaps no longer interdisciplinarity at all, but rather the emergence of a new discipline, with a new definition of the object of scholarly inquiry as well as new conventions of scholarly quality? This would suggest, however, that the divisions between older disciplines were beginning to blur and that some academic walls have opened up.

Crossing borders, opening walls? A volume devoted to the two topics of interdisciplinarity and unification runs the risk of inviting too much fraternization (or is it just flirtation?) with the shared metaphor. The method and the masses sound as if they have a lot in common. Overcoming disciplinary borders, we study the borders, overcome; refusing the separation of scholarly fields, we turn to the end of national separation. Both levels—scholarship and society, the ivory tower and the Brandenburg Gate—participate in a pathos of defragmentation and dedifferentiation: *Wir sind ein Volk* (We are one people) and therefore we rush to the interdisciplinary demonstration of unity. The underlying trope is one of totality— separation, national or disciplinary, is intolerable and unstable—and only unity seems to have the vitality to prevail in the end. Yet no matter how strong the shared rhetoric may be, a scholarship bound to norms of accuracy or consistency would quickly have to point out how the German Democratic Republic (GDR), ending in a love feast of unity began in a forced one as well, the unification that became the *Sozialistische Einheitspartei*, just as the popular nationalist condemnation of the division in the nation in 1989 was clearly the rhetorical heir, at least, to the older Communist condemnation of the division in the working class. What irony: for the seminal Marxist philosopher Georg Lukács, the central category of Marxism was totality, while the Marxist regime of the GDR collapses in the face of an appeal to a national totality, and all this in a postmodern context where any invocation of totality or identity or universals is deeply suspect. Did the GDR fail because it was totalitarian or, because it was the wrong totality or, because it was not totalizing enough?

Interdisciplinarity and unification—clearly no one can argue a simple causal relationship in either direction. The opening of the Wall did not initiate the transformation of the discipline, since interdisciplinarity in German Studies long pre-dates the events of 1989 (indeed it is more reasonable to argue that *Germanistik* was interdisciplinary from the start and the foreshortening of its domain to literary works of art has been an episodic exception); and the reverse, a suggestion attributing 1989 to the impact of a Western culture associated with interdisciplinarity makes no sense at all. Interdisciplinarity .and unification: no chicken and egg story here. Nevertheless, a relationship between the two terms does exist, and it is more than an arbitrary connection between a particular method ("interdisciplinarity") and a particular topic ("unification"). In other words, in several important ways, the profound transformation in the object ("Germany") does indeed induce changes or, at least, amplify particular tendencies in the scholarship ("German Studies"), and this is both crucial and not surprising.

Since its institutionalization in the early nineteenth century, the study of German literature has understood literature to be constitutively implicated in the pursuit of nationhood. Literature became a privileged topic precisely because it was viewed as the vehicle that provided an ideal and cultural unity to the nation in the absence of a shared political identity: as long as there was no German state unifying the people, at least there was the ideal realm of culture and literature. Literary history was, therefore, national history, because literature was assumed to give expression to the nation and because literary works, or at least romantic and postromantic works, aspired to a national popularity: the question of popular culture has been there from the start, since in at least some accounts, culture, qua genuinely national culture, is necessarily popular. Whether works were empirically popular is, of course, quite another matter, and the precise character of the nation and its imputed nuances could certainly vary wildly from the left to the right: the Prussianizing patriots in the universities of the Bismarck era had little sympathy for the enthusiasm for German idealism promoted by a left Hegelian, like Heine. Yet in all versions of the cultural discourse both literary production and scholarship treat literature and nationhood as fundamentally inseparable—culture and context—and the structure of national literary history was, therefore, understood to be equally teleological as the one imputed to national history. Consequently major events in German national history have reverberated strongly through the study of German culture.

This holds true for the complex turn toward positivist philology in the wake of the unification of 1871, just as it holds for the collaboration of the Germanists after 1933 as well as for the imaginations of an other, better Germany by the exiled intellectuals. It is the postwar paradigm, however, which is of particular interest here since that was also the paradigm of the Cold War and the division of Germany. What was the fate of the Nazi's *deutsche Wissenschaft* in the era, which began in 1945 and came to an end in 1989? In the East, of course, the study of literature was politicized in terms of the orthodox Marxism of Soviet-style Communism (nonconforming Marxisms were denounced just as much as Western scholarship, or probably even more so). In the West, the situation was more complex. The extreme politicization of the Third Reich induced a reaction, a general skepticism toward all ideologies and a flight from the political, which, certainly, could draw on longer standing antipolitical traditions in Germany. An eagerness to (phrased positively) learn from the Americans or to (phrased critically) please the occupation forces led to a strong reception of the New Criticism and therefore an increased focus on the literary work of art, divorced from social, political, or even national contexts. This odd and uniquely West German combination of cultural conservatism and modernist autonomy aesthetics began to crumble during the 1960s when a heightened political atmosphere generated a scholarship oriented more toward the social history of literature and which utilized increasingly sophisticated theoretical models, leading to concerns with the legitimacy and contingency of literary institutions.

It is important to understand that the social historical turn was not only a response to the ahistoricism of the so-called *Werkimmanenz*—the German corollary to New Criticism—but also uncovered buried capacities within the Germanistik tradition: the discipline that, historically, has been about the nation, ought to ask questions about national history, or rather the one overriding question for postwar youth—Why fascism?—which was precisely the question which the conservative professoriate of the Adenauer era assiduously avoided or, more precisely, repressed. For the one side, the nation was present as a category only through its denial since it was such an embarrassment; for the other, national memory was a vehicle for politicized judgment. What both sides shared, however, was the privileging of the work of literature; the celebrated "death of literature" in 1968 was on the contrary, never a death of literary studies. Evidently, the fundamental paradigm during the era of Germany's division involved the extraordinary importance of the literary work, whether it was treated, on the one hand, formalistically by the old New Critics or, more recently, by the neo-formalist deconstructors or, on the other hand, politically by critics of ideology or theoreticians of institutions.

This literary privilege had many sources, but a key one, certainly, was the competition between East and West German literature. As in the early nineteenth century, literature was the terrain where national unification could be played out or fought over, and judgment on literature, be it in the academic judgment in the university or in the critical judgment in the press, became a matter of national concern. That dynamic that constantly inflated the importance of literature in both Germanys has come to an end and this will have an impact on both the character of literary culture in the new Germany and the practices of German Studies in Germany and abroad. Perhaps this loss was already announced on November 4, 1989, when the literary leaders of the massive demonstration in East Berlin held back from taking the revolutionary step, another missed revolution in Germany. It was certainly announced in the attacks on Christa Wolf the subsequent year; the conservatives' obvious political agenda in viciously attacking the most prominent writer of the former GDR can hardly hide the more profound issue, the changing status of the intellectual in general especially the literary intellectual in late-twentieth-century Germany. This may be the real death of literature or, at least, traditional literature some twenty years after 1968; although conservative critics may be attempting to reconstruct the desideratum of the nonpolitical author (hence the need to castigate Wolf), it turns out that the activities of the author, political or not, and the autonomous works of literature are undergoing a cultural-historical demotion, just as the symbolic constitution of social practices, material culture, and everyday life increasingly interests the new German Studies.

This connection suggests the substantive connection between the focal points of this volume. Interdisciplinarity and unification are in fact linked through the changing status of literature. Just as neomarxism, arguing against crudely politicizing gestures could appeal to the "relative autonomy of literature," one might speak today of a relative dedifferentiation—literature is less separate and less special than it may have been regarded to be in other cultural periods. Losing the bonus that the Cold War provided especially in Germany—the divided state with two literatures in one language—literature, understood as the linguistic work of art, ceases to overshadow all other objects of national culture. It is important to be precise: the point is not an end of literature or some Hegelian end of art but an ongoing recalibration of the relative resonance of different and competing modes of expression, including both the various types of artistic practice recognized heretofore as significant, that is, the traditional fine arts as well as other symbolic practices such as those of everyday life, the importance of which in the construction of cultural communities becomes increasingly indisputable to a scholarly world influenced by the new ethnography. This implies, if not an end to literature, certainly a deflation of its autonomy and therefore the obsolescence of the paradigm of scholarship organized around literature as the linguistic work of art. For was not "pure literature," the orientation toward the absolutely autonomous and solely formal work of art, also a figment of the imagination of the Cold War and its predecessors? It arose in the conservative fear of mass industrial society, in both the European capitals and the American South, and it was the watchword of Western aesthetics in its cultural war with Communism—which is to say that a new frame for the study of culture is possible, now that it is hardly necessary to demonstrate constant distance from the dogmatic politicization that orthodox Marxism used to represent. Put bluntly, investigations into the symbolic construction of collective identity should no longer have to fear being misconstrued as collectivist.

The reduction in the literary privilege does not ensue solely from the end of the Cold War, of course. Other factors include the emergence of other media, especially film and television, and in general the proliferation of post-auratic forms, that is, art stripped of that sense of sacrality that often characterized earlier cultural reception. There is no a priori reason to applaud or denounce this transformation of cultural sensibility; all the old and familiar doubts still apply, but there is simply no room to avoid recognizing the change. In terms of how we study culture, the impact can best be understood if we refer one more time to the romantic origins of the study of national literature. The assertion of a fundamental identity between literature and people implied that the best way to study literature was as a national literature and that the best way to study a nation was through its literature. Scholarship was, therefore, not interested in literature for its own sake but only because it was understood to be substantively congruent with the nation that, moreover, was configured as a historical teleology. Modernist purists protested against this historicism and began to loosen the connection between literature and nationhood. One result would be the isolation of a pure literature and this has, more or less, been the agenda of comparative literature as a field. It is, however, a program still fully dependent on the privileging of the literary, no matter how divorced it is from its historical context.

There is, however, another possible result when the romantic connections among nation, history, and literature begin to snap. The ability to institutionalize the national literature disciplines derived less from a fascination with literature than with the urgency of exploring the constitution of emergent collective identities. The key challenge is not to master the canon and preserve it nor even, for that matter, to change it (for that still implies maintaining a canon), but rather to understand the processes that elicit and delimit the cultural community. How are traditions bequeathed and transformed? How are symbols deployed and received? What is the role of shared myths, and what about their critics? Who participates in the community and how, who is excluded, and who is included on an unequal basis? To the extent—and it is probably a very large one—that such questions can be raised productively with regard to literary texts, the study of literature is a crucial component of this undertaking, but it is the construction of community and not the production of the text that is the ultimate object of examination. The project therefore must proceed far beyond the realm of literary autonomy and address material previously reserved for other disciplines.

Interdisciplinarity now becomes the designation of inquiries into the articulation of meaning in cultural fields not restricted to the small set of classical literary genre formerly regarded as proper topics of study. This is destined, however, not to remain "interdisciplinary," understood as a site in between several stable and defined units. On the contrary, the new emergent discipline of Cultural Studies has already greatly transformed literary study from within as well as portions of other disciplines too: the new ethnographic self-consciousness in anthropology, post-formalist art history, and the cultural turn in historiography are the most prominent examples of a deep-seated transformation of the structures by which we have begun to examine and understand other cultures and our own. There is certainly a special German or Germanistic perspective on this, which is why German Studies—which is no longer Germanic Languages and Literatures—is not precisely the same as the Cultural Studies envisioned in other fields. Nevertheless the various trajectories of disciplinary transformation appear to be increasingly convergent, no matter how distinct local traditions may remain. The sign of a new discipline cannot be that all participants ask the same questions but that all the different questions that are posed share some, and not all, conceptual orientations. This room for diversity, which characterizes the essays in this volume, is not only a pragmatic eclecticism. It is also indicative of an important difference in the theory of culture implicit in the new Cultural Studies, no matter how much it inherits from prior disciplinary formations. The disciplinary orientation is not a totalizing summation that, encompassing all, leaves no room for outsiders, and it eschews the exclusivity of the nationalism of the erstwhile national literary disciplines; it is on the contrary a methodological orientation toward a more porous interrelatedness—this is what has been meant by "interdisciplinarity"—an opening of borders, a possibility of circulation, difference, and transformation, without an imposed homogenization. An open horizon of questioning that combines an imperative of inquiry with a refusal to declare answers definitive or solutions final is the precondition of this new discipline, Cultural Studies, as it may be of all free scholarship, and this volume is an important step toward an effective institutionalization of the Cultural Studies of Germany.

INTRODUCTION

Ruth A. Starkman

The idea of a smiling German chancellor a decade and half after German
unification seems like a contradiction in terms. Yet there is a photo of
Chancellor Gerhard Schröder from his second term which is particularly
telling. The photo shows Schröder smiling with his arms around two
delighted, if somewhat dazed middle-aged East German women. The
women, Heidelinde Munkewitz and her sister Inge Siegel, are his newly discovered cousins from the eastern state of Thuringia. Having just learned of
their existence a few weeks before, Schröder remarks after their first meeting:
"Considering that we have been reunited after nearly 60 years, this has gone
better than any of us had thought."[1] Such a comment befits a meeting of
citizens from the two former Germanys. No one anticipated the fall of the
Berlin Wall in 1989, or the surprisingly swift German unification of 1990,
and certainly many international observers did not expect things to go well.
In a country that has wrestled with its national self-understanding for the
better part of two centuries, unification of the former Federal Republic
and German Democratic Republic has confounded, rather than solved,
Germany's status both domestically and internationally. Questions concerning the quality of life in the former eastern states, Germany's contemporary economic woes, its changing cultural makeup, its now "doubled"
Stasi and Nazi past, its future in international politics, all remain largely
unresolved. And yet, quoting the now ousted German chancellor, some
things in unified Germany have "gone better than any of us had thought."
Ironically enough, they did not go so well for Schröder, who was narrowly
defeated in October 2005 by CDU leader Angela Merkel, a woman from
the former East Germany. Such a change in government inverts the image
of power represented in the Chancellor's photos with his cousins, but rather
than suggesting a new ascendancy of the East or of women, it merely reflects
the enormous post-unification struggles of the new Germany. What then
has gone well? Is there any cause for optimism in a book where the transformations of the new Germany are nearly all struggles? In the wake of the

peaceful revolution of 1989, democracy remains strong in the new Germany. Half a century after the end of World War II, Germany is beginning to embrace its fundamentally changed society and culture, modernize citizenship laws and participate in a united Europe.

This book provides an interdisciplinary historical study of German culture in the decade and a half since the fall of the Berlin Wall. With essays written by German, Canadian, American, and Australian scholars from such diverse fields as political science, history, sociology, media studies, women's studies, and German language and literature, this book organizes itself not by disciplines, separating questions of the social sciences from the arts and then subdividing by subject (a summative interdisciplinarity, as Berman calls it in his foreword), but rather around three major debates, "intellectuals and German history," "material culture East and West," and "Germany and its minorities." It then looks at each debate in the context of three historical moments after 1989: the *Wende* period, aftermath of unification, and some reflections from the second decade. Such an approach demonstrates at once the continuity in anxieties about the new Germany and its rapid absorption of the German Democratic Republic, and also the distance from many early concerns about an excessively "strong" united Germany in central Europe. Moreover, it shows the greater complexity of events and debates at every stage since the fall of the Berlin Wall: German intellectuals confront historiographical and cultural impasses in 1989 as well as after September 11. The seemingly thorough colonization of the East by the West has had resistances and repercussions on both sides since 1989. The problem of race and culture continue to shape debates on minorities and citizenship.

Making Sense of the *Wende* and Its Aftermath

In reflecting on Germany's recent history, which has run the gamut of receptions from euphoric (both Eastern and Western) to Capitalist triumphalist (in the West) to mutual disappointment, it might help to reflect on the events of unification and their developments since 1989. First and foremost, these events flummoxed scholars and pundits alike. In an article entitled "Blinded by What They Saw," which appeared on November 7, 1999 a couple of days before the ten-year anniversary of the fall of the Berlin Wall, senior correspondent for the *Washington Post* Robert G. Kaiser recalls many of the false prophecies that followed the heady November days of 1989. Kaiser quotes the spectacularly wrong prognostications of his colleague, *New York Times* columnist William Safire:

> Economic crisis will be transferred to Turkey as West Germany absorbs its
> eastern German unskilled workers and sends back the legions of Turkish

workers. . . . Germany, already the world's largest exporter, will dominate the economies of Central Europe and invest heavily in the Soviet Union . . . The phase-out of U.S. troops stationed in Germany will begin soon. . . . Germany, tired of apologetics, will stare down its own Greens and become a nuclear power with Star Wars rocketry making it an Uberpower before the turn of the millennium . . . Other Europeans will work together to "stop the Germans," less out of historic fears of militarism than from the competition of militant industriousness.[2]

If Safire was mistaken about the Turkish workers being expelled from Germany (though there are right-wing elements who would like to do so) or, about "staring down" the Greens (The German Green Party remains the strongest in the world, despite the 2005 ouster from government in Schröder's red/green coalition. It also enjoyed much visibility with the near-rockstar popularity of Joschka Fischer, vice-chancellor and minister of foreign affairs 1998–2005) or, about getting rid of *all* of the U.S. troops (nearly 70,000 remained in 1999 and more arrived after September 11) or, about the Germans' "militant industriousness," surely these cultural, economic, and political issues continue to vex the new Germany. The point is that most observers *were* "blinded by what they saw" at the revolution of 1989. Few would have anticipated the collapse of the Berlin Wall and equally few would have expected such a rapid disappearance of the German Democratic Republic. Even from the GDR perspective within, the events surprised. A decade later, former secretary of the Socialist Unity Party (SED) of Berlin and press spokesman, Günter Schabowski, the very same press spokesman who had read the official brief proclaiming the new travel law that led to the opening of the Berlin Wall on November 9, 1989, remarked: "We hadn't a clue that the opening of the Wall was the beginning of the end of the republic. On the contrary, we expected a stabilization process."[3]

Not until the mid-1990s did scholarship begin to make sense of the fall of the Berlin Wall and the developments since 1989. British historian Mary Fulbrook presents the GDR in her 1995 book, *Anatomy of a Dictatorship: Inside the GDR, 1949–1989*,[4] as a dictatorship, which, in its efforts to create a comprehensively controlled social order, refused reforms and failed to compete with West German capitalism. Fulbrook also discusses at length the history of opposition within East Germany, and shows not simply that the population lost patience and faith in their system, but that "throughout the GDR's history; a lot of people did not like the GDR."[5] Providing a more complex image of a seemingly docile public, Fulbrook asserts that "despite the growth in outward patterns of obedience and compliance, notable particularly from the early 1970s, there was still a degree of rumbling from below the surface. . . ."[6]

In his study *The Rush to German Unity*,[7] German-born American historian, Konrad H. Jarausch reconstructs the historical events that led to unification. Of the essential political factors that precipitated the momentous events of 1989, he identifies Communism's collapse in Eastern Europe, Eastern Europe's subsequent separation from the Soviet Bloc, and the post-Stalinist East German state's fragmentation into largely isolated groups— political elites, intellectuals, and the people.

Harvard historian Charles S. Maier's 1997 study *Dissolution*[8] stresses the dialectic between institutional forces and individual agency of the grassroots movements. Tracing the economic collapse to the 1970s, when the world market began to encroach upon a regime bound to the Soviet Union and COMECON, Maier shows how the GDR fatefully disavowed its swelling debt as it struggled to maintain living conditions and satisfy consumer appetites.[9] Rebellion from the authoritarian police state, with its 85,000 employees and some 180,000 "unofficial collaborators" or Inoffizielle Mitarbeiter (IM) in a population of just 17 million, was long in coming, but ultimately responded to a situation in which "socialism corrupted the public sphere through privilege" while it "corrupted the private sphere through secrecy."[10] Of the popular movement that led to a peaceful revolution, Maier compares the autumn of 1989 to, not the French Revolution as others have, but Germany's spring of 1848. In contrast to the backlash of 1848, however, East Germany in 1989 was suddenly freed of its authoritarian powers when the Soviet sponsor of the once tethered German state was no longer in the position to extinguish a grassroots movement.

Like Maier, Konrad Jarausch also compares the popular East German revolution to 1848.[11] Identifying the "unlikely heroes" of the East German upheaval as the populace itself, Jarausch asks, "where did normal citizens find the courage to revolt?" He answers that the "decision to act was based more on moral feeling than on rational calculation":[12]

> Ultimately, the awakening was a psychological explosion which tried to regain individual self-respect. The tension between private criticism and public conformity had become so unbearable as to drive people into the streets. The solidarity of the like-minded broke through solitude and created a new sense of community.[13]

Jarausch shows how the rise of the civic movement represented a "democratic awakening" for the citizens of the GDR, while it also, "against its own wishes" and through the exhilarated state of public opinion and accelerated official decision-making, ultimately, "undermined the legitimacy of the GDR as a separate state."[14] With the euphoria following the opening of the Berlin Wall in November 1989, the notion of a unified Germany gained widespread popularity.

The naysayers argued against uniting the two Germanys precisely on the grounds of this public euphoria. Many understood the public enthusiasm, which transformed the East German protest slogan of the early demonstration days from "We are the people" to "We are one people" prior to unification, as a slide from a call to reform to an ethnic/nationalist self-declaration. Opponents both in Germany and abroad asserted that the "blood and iron" Bismarckian unification of 1870, which many have identified as part and parcel of the expansionist militarism in the twentieth century, might lead to a resurgent nationalism in 1990. There were those, like social philosopher Jürgen Habermas, who feared for Germany's progress from World War II, which had built the Federal Republic not as a community of fate, but rather as a constitutional democracy.[15] Others, like West German writer and Nobel Laureate Günter Grass, adopted Habermas's notion of "constitutional patriotism" and rejected the idea of unification altogether, arguing that the post-1945 division of Germany arose from the nationalist misdeeds of the past:

> Because there can be no demand for a new version of a unified nation that in the course of barely 75 years, though under several managements, filled the history books, ours and theirs, with suffering, rubble, defeat, millions of refugees, millions of dead, and the burden of crimes that can never be undone.[16]

Meanwhile, Germany's past was by no means stable or universally understood. Rather, it had undergone, according to American historian Jeffrey Herf, "multiple restorations" during the forty-five-year period from the end of the World War II to unification, in which Cold War East Germany suppressed the Nazi past under the rubric of the East's "antifascism," while the West approached it sometimes in a selective and opportunistic fashion.[17]

In this context of incomplete and ideologically driven competing memories, concern about resurgent nationalism and loss of historical memory in Germany elicited calls for a confederation of the two states, or at least, that unification happen more gradually. But by February 1990, Christian Democrats in both East and West Germany argued for rapid unification under Article 23 of the West German constitution or Basic Law. The other possibility would have been to apply Article 146 of the Basic Law, which would have taken much longer to implement in that it provided for a new constitution. Nonetheless, unification ultimately took place under Article 23, the five Eastern states joined the Federal Republic, and the GDR simply disappeared on October 3, 1990. By then, much of the reported euphoria was gone.

The East suffered an economic collapse greater and more burdensome than anticipated when economic and currency union was instituted in the summer of 1990. Unification also ensnared East and West in debates over responsibility for the history of the GDR and its pervasive state security apparatus. Such debates took on a particularly grim look with official Western efforts at *Abwicklung*, the university purges in the East, which instead of creating "a new and better East–West synthesis . . ." went to the point where ". . . 'crisis-beset West German institutions' were introduced into the East."[18]

With the stretches of concrete and barbed wire that once cut through Berlin gone, the "wall in the head," the cultural, social, and economic divisions between East and West persisted.[19] Hans Modrow, who was briefly the prime minister of the GDR from November 1989 to March 1990, assessed the struggles of unification in 1993:

> The frustrated hopes on both sides are leading to indifference, intolerance and a growing apathy . . . Germany has become a disunited rather than a united fatherland.[20]

This "disunity" continues to run through all aspects of culture and society in East and West. Variously described as an "Anschluß" [annexation] a word that recalls the 1938 annexation of Austria to Nazi Germany, a "buy out," "fire sale,"[21] or a "colonization"[22] of the East, Germany unity has been hotly debated in terms of its winners and losers. Some scholars have focused on the West's campaign of globalization and Capitalist incursion,[23] and most observers maintain that in the "transformation" of East Germany the hasty attempt to graft an institutional uniformity from West to the East ignored considerations of what would best develop the former GDR.[24] With the collapse of Communism in the East, many of the old social structures have also disappeared. This has led to a growing nostalgia for the way of life in the past. As one East Berliner put it:

> Of course, we have to admit that there wasn't enough that was good about East Germany. Otherwise it wouldn't have failed. . . . But, nevertheless, I think that quite a few people here believe that in East German times we enjoyed a more peaceful way of life, even a more pleasant way of life. It's difficult to explain this, but it has something to do with human feelings and with values—with the feeling that my neighbor was my friend, and not my competitor.[25]

This statement relates the words of a former East German who has carved out a specialty business capitalizing on the growing nostalgia for the former German Democratic Republic, or "Ostalgie": he packages tours that revisit important places in the socialist world and reproduce the language and ideology of the past. Indeed, although the GDR had rapidly vanished in

October 1990, its culture, memory, and national self-understanding had not. On the contrary, they have developed into a booming business.

Amid the social disintegration that occurred in the newly unified Germany, fears of resurgent nationalism seemed to have been proven right: one year after October 1990, neo-Nazi violence against immigrants and foreigners jumped dramatically. Refugee camps were set on fire in Hoyerswerda in 1991 and in Rostock in 1992. Anti-immigrant violence was not simply confined to the East either. Several immigrants of Turkish origin were killed in arson attacks in Mölln in November 1992 and in Solingen in May 1993.[26] In response to these attacks, especially after Mölln, Germans took to the streets in Berlin, Munich, Hamburg, and many of the other larger cities to protest racist violence. Some praised this public action as a sign of Germany's dedication to democracy. Others saw the demonstrations as largely knee-jerk responses, a rehearsed piety of the "conscience industry" of the old Federal Republic.[27]

Such ambivalence characterizes the German population at large: at once eager to affirm its commitment to democracy, while slow to change its citizenship laws for immigrants and minorities, the new Germany continues its struggles in the Bonn Republic at the same time that it endeavors to acknowledge that it has been a land of immigration for sometime.[28] It is this combination of traditional reticence and cultural ambivalence that prompted German political economist Dietrich Thranhardt to characterize Germany as an "undeclared immigration country."[29]

In the middle of its second decade, however, Germany is slowly moving toward a revision of its citizenship laws. Since January 2000 a new citizenship and nationality law has been in effect. Passed by broad majorities in Germany's Bundestag (lower house) and Bundesrat (upper house) in May 1999, this new law substantially changed the principle of descent (*jus sanguinis*), which has long been the country's traditional basis for granting citizenship. Now, it is also possible to acquire German citizenship as a result of being born in Germany (*jus soli*), as is the case in most other European countries. Thus, the reform marks the belatedly acknowledged fact that more than seven million foreigners live in Germany on a long-term basis. One-third of them have lived there for more than thirty years; half of them have lived in Germany for at least twenty years.

The immigration debate is only the most recent manifestation of the Berlin Republic's growing pains. Still reeling from the costs of unification, Germany's economy, though by far the biggest in Europe, has also become one of the weakest. Unemployment remains nearly 9 percent nationwide, and nearly twice that high in the formerly Communist East. Economic growth is stagnant, and it has been lower than in almost any other European nation since the mid-1990s. Despite this situation, early in 2000, German employers said there were 75,000 vacant jobs for computer programmers and engineers, and asked the government to ease admissions of foreign professionals to fill these jobs. Most of these immigrants would be professionals, including foreign graduates of German universities. The major opposition parties argued against liberalizing law, saying that Germany should not increase immigration at a time of high unemployment. Initially September 11 seemed to play a rather minor role in the national debate over immigration policy reform. Even after September 11, the German government continued its efforts to liberalize immigration laws. More recently, however, with the possibility of an American war in Iraq, Germany appears increasingly divided between those concerned with security and those hoping to retain the focus on liberalizing the laws, such differences often reflect levels of unemployment and other demographic issues.

Interdisciplinary Studies

Intellectuals and German History

Opening the section on intellectuals, Brett R. Wheeler investigates the social and historical significance of the "third way" for the intellectuals during 1989–1990 and argues that because of the intellectual's historic position as a theorist, rather than as an actor in German culture, that the supposed failure of political action 1990 is in fact a canard. The historic role of intellectuals is, Wheeler maintains, a culturally specific identity of the intellectual cosmopolitan German thought. Taking up the "unpopular" position of Jürgen Habermas, Wheeler maintains a critical stance toward populism and underscores the essential function of intellectual debates about formal conceptions of identity and culture in moments of historical rupture.

In his essay on Hans-Jürgen Syberberg and the New Right in Germany, Stephen Brockmann shows how Syberberg, while employing a radical formalism as a filmmaker, appropriates post-unification populist sentiments for the purposes of exercising a conservative cultural critique. Brockmann offers a glimpse into the shift away from a liberal public sphere toward a conservative one, which endeavors to revise German history and reinvent a positive national self-image. His essay speculates on the growing prevalence of conservative intelligentsia as characterized by the writings of Hans-Jürgen-Syberberg and explores the tensions between the generation of the '68ers, to whom Grass and Habermas belong and the '89ers, to whom Botho Strauss belongs.

In her essay, "Are the Towers Still Standing?" The Fall and Rise of the Literary Intellectual," Alison Lewis charts the developments of the last decade in Germany's Left-liberal consensus. She shows a generation struggle between older intellectuals who insist on providing a moral message and the increasingly depoliticized younger generation. The last essay in this section, by Klaus Scherpe, provides an overview of the crisis of Germany's intellectuals after September 11. Scherpe analyzes the discourse of identification with American suffering during September 11 and the subsequent anti-Americanism, which arises in the wake of the "war on terrorism." Scherpe also analyzes German responses to the media event of September 11, showing how these echo the discourse of German modernism and its debates over the "aestheticization of violence."

Material Culture: East and West

Patricia Anne Simpson examines the rock music of the former East Germany and argues that the music and texts provide a counter-history to the fall of the East and the fast-forwarded process of reunification. Examining the texts of songs and their cultural contexts as part of Germany's larger public sphere, she shows how they endeavored to resist the totalizing rhetoric of the West, the compulsion of which is to erase all traces of what was the East. In his essay, "Spies, Shell Games, and Bananas," Gottfried Korff shows how the analysis of material culture contributes to a better understanding of the forces and fears, hopes and efforts in contemporary Germany. Korff maintains that even before unification, expressions of difference and division unmistakably asserted themselves alongside feelings of commonality in the everyday culture and mentalités of Germans. While there has been much discussion of East Germany's growing nostalgia for its former products, few scholars have offered a systematic historical survey of these. Martin Blum examines the fates of East Germany cola, laundry soap, champagne, product design, and consumer practices in the former East Germany.

Germany and Its Minorities

Nora Räthzel provides a historical introduction to Germany's notions of national belonging from the eighteenth century to the present and shows how Germany's views of ethnicity have remained essentially the same since the Third Reich. Elucidating the present debate on German citizenship, Hermann Kurthen describes Germany's current ethnic makeup, elaborating how the changes in citizenship law from a "blood" based ethnic understanding to one of birth in Germany has fared through the recent elections. Approaching a topic discussed more often in private spheres than public, Jonathan Laurence examines the differing treatment accorded to Jews and Turks in unified Germany, arguing that Germany's politics of memory tend to privilege the Jews over the Turks, which creates resentment among both Jews and Turks. Finally, Ruth Starkman looks at the relation between Germans and Jews since unification and shows how the discourse of "normalization" both of Germany's past and its relation to its Jews remain highly unstable, with Germans from both right and left pushing for "normality" and Germany's Jews declaring such efforts as a sign of the impossibility of "normalization."

Together these essays show a mostly tragic and troubled new Germany. Yet, despite the economic burdens and social disjunctions of unified Germany, the events that have followed since the popular revolution of 1989 have demonstrated the manifold positive ways in which Germans have transformed their history. Not only did the Germans bring about a peaceful revolution through popular participation, but they also, several years into the new century, continue to thrive as a European democracy that continues to debate its past beginning to accept its increasingly diverse culture. Given these outcomes, it might indeed be safe to say that a few things in Germany's larger democratic picture have gone better than might have been guessed. The task is to see these among all the current post-unification struggles and conceptualize the future of a European Germany.

Notes

1. Reuters, "Schröder meets new-found cousins," *New York Times* (May 10, 2001): p. A14.
2. Robert G. Kaiser, "Blinded by What they Saw," *Washington Post*, November 7, 1999.
3. John J. Tierney Jr., "Germany: Strides Abroad, Struggles Within," *World and I* v.15, n.10 (October 2000): p. 50.
4. Mary Fulbrook, *Anatomy of a Dictatorship: Inside the GDR, 1949–1989* (Oxford: Oxford University Press, 1985).
5. Ibid., p. 151.
6. Ibid., p. 171. On descent in the GDR see also Roger Woods, *Opposition in the GDR under Honecker, 1971–1985* (Basingstoke: Macmillan, 1986); Jonathon Grix, *The Role of the Masses in the Collapse of the GDR* (New York: Palgrave, 2000), which examines the role of the masses in the collapse of the East German regime and state in 1989 in the northern district of Schwerin. See also John Torpey, *Intellectuals, Socialism, and Dissent: The East German Opposition and its Legacy* (Minneapolis: University of Minnesota Press, 1995). Torpey explores the ambivalence of the status of intellectuals under socialism.
7. Konrad H. Jarausch, *The Rush to German Unity* (New York: Oxford University Press, 1994), see also the more recent Konrad H. Jarausch, Martin Sabrow, *Weg in den Untergang. Der innere Zerfall der DDR* (Göttingen: Vandenhoeck & Ruprecht, 1999).
8. Charles S. Maier, *Dissolution: The Crisis of Communism and the End of East Germany* (Princeton: Princeton University Press, 1999). See also David Child,

The Fall of the GDR (New York: Longman, 2001). *Vorwärts immer, rückwärts nimmer!: interne Dokumente zum Zerfall von SED und DDR 1988/89*, introduction by Gerd-Rudiger Stephan and Daniel Kuchenmeister, eds. (Berlin: Dietz, 1994), *Eine Deutsche Revolution: der Umbruch in der DDR, seine Ursachen und Folgen*, Gert-Joachim Glaessner, ed. (Frankfurt am Main, New York: P. Lang, 1991).

9. Maier, *Dissolution*, p. 70.
10. Ibid., p. 45.
11. See Reinhard Alter's introduction, where he discusses at length the similarities and differences of the revolution of 1989 to the French and German revolutions.
12. Jarausch, *The Rush to German Unity*, p. 50.
13. Jarausch, *The Rush to German Unity*, p. 51.
14. Ibid., p. 200.
15. Jürgen Habermas, "Yet Again: German Identity—A Unified Nation of Angry DM-Burghers," *When The Wall Came Down*, Harold James and Marla Stone, eds. (New York; London: Routledge, 1992), pp. 86–102.
16. Günter Grass, "Don't Reunify Germany," *When The Wall Came Down*, pp. 57–58.
17. Jeffrey Herf, *Divided Memory, the Nazi Past in the Two Germanys* (Cambridge: Harvard University Press, 1997).
18. Maier, *Dissolution*, p. 306.
19. John Dornberg, "Five Years After the Berlin Wall: Are There One or Two Germanys?" *German Life*, January 31, 1995, Erik Kirschbaum, "In Berlin, Some Walls Still Stand," *The Washington Times*, August 8, 1996: p. 20.
20. Hans Modrow, "The Dream of Unity Crashes," Morning Star, October 9, 1993: p. 5. Cited in Jürgen A. K. Thomanecek, "From Euphoria to Reality: Social Problems of Post Unification," Derek Lewis and John R.P. McKenzie, eds. *The New Germany* (Exeter: University of Exeter Press, 1995).
21. Hafner, Katie, "The house we lived in Reclaiming family property in Eastern Europe can be a painful history lesson," *New York Times Magazine* v.141 (November 10, 1991): p. 32.
22. See Günter Grass, "Document 66," *German Unification and its Discontents: Documents from the Peaceful Revolution*, Richard T. Gray and Sabine Wilke, eds. and trans. (Seattle: University of Washington Press, 1996), p. 275. See also Günter Grass's *Too Far Afield*, translated from the German by Krishna Winston, 1st U.S. edition (New York: Harcourt, 2000). Also Wolfgang Dumcke, Fritz Vilmar, *Kolonialisierung der DDR: kritische Analysen und Alternativen des Einigungsprozesses*, 3rd edition (Münster: Agenda, 1996). Peter Christ, *Kolonie im eigenen Land: die Treuhand, Bonn und die Wirtschaftskatastrophe der fünf neuen Länder* (Berlin: Rowohlt, 1991).
23. Stephen Brockmann, "By the way . . . Pious Lies," *German Life*, July 31, 1994.
24. Helmut Wiesenthal, *Die Transformation der DDR—Verfahren und Resultate* (Gütersloh: Verlag Bertelsmann Stiftung, 1999). In his study of post-unification German scholar Jürgen A.K. Thomaneck relates the story of a family from Rostock, which has largely suffered under unification. The fate of family K., as Thomaneck recounts it, encapsulates the spectrum of post-wall ills in the East: The women in the family, once employed in managerial positions at the

Neptun shipyards are out of work and have returned to traditional domestic roles, the men travel to the west for work, and, aside from one sibling who says he has profited from German unification, the family feels largely disappointed and isolated. Jürgen A.K. Thomanek, "From Euphoria to Reality: Social Problems of Post-Unification," pp. 7–10. See also John Borneman, *After the Wall: East Meets West in the New Berlin* (New York: Basic Books, 1991).
25. Mary Williams Walsh, "Ostalgie," *Los Angeles Times*, 1996.
26. Frederick Kempe "Neo-Nazi Menace: Germans Try to Stem Right Wing Attacks Against Foreigners," *The Wall Street Journal*, December 4, 1991. A1. Stephen Kinzer, "The Neo-Nazis: How Quickly They Remember," *The New York Times*, November 17, 1991. E1.
27. Godfrey Carr and Georgina Paul, "Unification and Its Aftermath" *German Cultural Studies* (Oxford: Oxford University Press, 1995), p. 343.
28. Simon Green, "Immigration, asylum and citizenship in Germany: The impact of unification and the Berlin Republic." *West European Politics* v.24, n.4 (October 2001): p. 82.
29. Dietrich Thranhardt, "Die Bundesrepublik Deutschland—ein unerklärtes Einwanderungsland" *Aus Politik und Zeitgeschichte* B24/88 (1988): pp. 3–13.

PART I
INTELLECTUALS AND GERMAN HISTORY

CHAPTER ONE

INTELLECTUALS, THE "THIRD WAY," AND GERMAN UNIFICATION

Brett R. Wheeler

[Immanent critique] takes seriously the principle that it is not ideology in itself, which is untrue but rather its pretension to correspond to reality. Immanent criticism of intellectual and artistic phenomena seeks to grasp, through the analysis of their form and meaning, the contradiction between their objective idea and that pretension.

—Theodor W. Adorno[1]

[Language] can never "pin down" slavery, genocide, war . . . Nor should it yearn for the arrogance to be able to do so. Its force, its felicity is in its reach toward the ineffable.

—Toni Morrison[2]

This chapter begins with the things it cannot do: for here is not the task to analyze, thickly or thinly, the dynamics of popular revolution, the symbols and semiotics of consumerism, or the popular politics of mass demonstrations, but to understand precisely the absence of these things in the words of intellectuals. In Western societies it is unclear whether the word comes from somewhere above or from somewhere on the sidelines of everyday life. Whatever the case, the power wielded by a so-called intellectual either on Alexanderplatz or on the university podium ultimately rests uncomfortably on the morphous word. I am drawn to the relationship of the word from "above" and the deed from "below" not only because of the antithetical locus of my contribution, but because this divergence calls out from all intellectual corners of the unification era. Yet, while foundational for the definition of the German intellectual and accordingly ubiquitous in the unification discussion, throughout most considerations the need to overcome this divergence is regarded as self-evident. While commentators have dutifully situated the intellectual in the dialectic between reality and utopia, they have also impulsively accepted the self-evidence of a possible resolution to this dialectic for the everyday participation of intellectuals in politics. This assumption has, in turn, led to an important oversight regarding the elemental philosophical and historical constitution of "the intellectual." And it is perhaps—so I suggest—this oversight that has forced the profuse discussion of the fate of intellectuals since 1989 into the zone of self-annihilation to which it has almost wittingly digressed.

Intellectuals and "Failure"

In the early winter days of 1989, both immediately before and immediately after the fall of the Wall in Berlin, at meetings, mass demonstrations, and conferences, the words of intellectuals captured the spirit of the hour and likewise drove forward the hopes underlying this spirit to audiences lining the road of revolution in the German Democratic Republic. At the center of the former imperial city of Berlin, five days before the unexpected opening to the West, celebrities from East Germany's literary intelligentsia spoke to a mass demonstration on Alexanderplatz. Christoph Hein, Stefan Heym, and Christa Wolf each spoke different lines, but created together in harmony a utopian image of a future that would never come. Not capitalism, not Stalinism, but a "third way" should be the future of the GDR and its revolution. While in the West images of confederation and the democratic struggles of 1848 offered a momentary historical alternative to annexation or unification,[3] in the East the Paris Commune of 1871 and the 1968 Prague Spring represented moments of obvious heroism established by history to emulate. Alexander Dubcek's faith in the possibility of "socialism with a human face" quickly became the utopian tenet for the followers of the third way between Capitalism and Communism.

So the intellectuals strove to excite the masses with dreams of a democratic socialism. Borrowing from a statement made by fellow East German writer Christoph Hein a few weeks earlier, Christa Wolf recalled to the crowds on November 4 the power of utopian thinking made possible by a newfound freedom of expression: "Yes, language arises from the official and newspaper German in which it was entangled and recalls its more emotional words. One of these is dream. Let's dream with wide-eyed reason: 'Imagine, there's socialism, and no one leaves.' "[4] All of these writers gazed out into the crowd of a million demonstrators that day in November, convinced that the people had, in Stefan Heym's words, "gathered for freedom and democracy, and for a socialism that is worth the name."[5] They believed too quickly that the "reason" of the street had won against tyranny, all in the name of democracy and free expression. Hein, Wolf, and other East German writers felt a sudden relief that their language had perhaps been freed from the obligations of activism and political resistance, and they prepared to turn their attention to a new form of literature, hitherto unknown in the GDR. "Now our literature can become autonomous," contended fellow writer Heiner Müller, "it no longer needs to document. Now the national past can be examined, not through documentary, but, if you will, with mythological exactitude."[6]

Once again, the intellectuals had mistaken their ideals for a real, existing goal; and the path of the third way was never paved. A year later, after unification already had become a surreal historical fact, Jürgen Habermas pointed out a historical delusion at the heart of Wolf's utopian image of a freed language:

> With its political rhetoric this "state of the worker and peasant" has misused progressive ideas for its legitimation; it has scornfully denied them through their inhuman praxis and thereby discredited them. I fear that this dialectic of denigration will be more ruinous for the spiritual hygiene in Germany than the concentrated resentments of five or six generations of anti-enlightenment, anti-Semitic, wrongly romantic, Germanophilic [*deutschtümelnder*] obscurantists. The degrading of our best and weakest intellectual traditions is for me one of the most profane aspects of the inheritance that the GDR brings into the enlarged Federal Republic. This is a destruction of reason that Lukács did not think of.[7]

In the weeks and months after November 9, as East Germans and their Trabis poured over the border into the West, abandoning their purported ideals for the rare and exotic taste of a banana, it became apparent that it was, however, not Christa Wolf's unproblematized misuse of their liberated language and democratic ideals that turned the backs of the masses on the intellectuals. Even in his later patriarchal condescension toward the gullibility of the people of GDR in the face of the vulgar consumerism of the West,[8] many would claim that Stefan Heym continued to misconceive the true motivation for the initial revolution. In general, it is once again proved here, as Helmut Dubiel pointed out, that "from the beginnings of the Frankfurt School, to Gramsci and until the contemporary theory of populism, Marxism has labored with the problem that the masses continually act differently than what is demanded of them in the mandated universalist morality."[9] More decisive than the failure of Marxist doctrine in convincing the masses of its validity may have been the fact that the people's motivation in the revolution never had anything to do with a better utopia, but rather with "the profane goal of a better life," in the words of Monika Maron.[10]

Such resistance to idealistic motivations for the revolution was shared by other East German writers, especially those who, like Maron or Wolf Biermann, lived partially or entirely in West Germany. Yet, unlike other authors, such as Horst Bienek, who were calling for a wholesale departure from utopia,[11] neither of these authors abandoned utopia altogether. Inadvertently recalling the words of Adorno in the epigraph earlier "that it is not ideology in itself which is untrue but rather its pretension to correspond to reality," Maron insisted that "Utopia lives in our heads. When it is coupled with power, it becomes a dictatorship. Utopia is the measure of reality, but it cannot be reality itself."[12] Writers and intellectuals in East Germany were thus confronted first with the abandonment by their former audience in the GDR and then with the knowing gestures of mostly well-meaning former compatriots now living in the West where the pragmatism of civil society and the market had tempered their idealism. In any case, as the winter wore on and the new decade began, the apparent alternatives to the capitalist West and the communist East—both unsatisfactory—withered. Resignation set in; the fundamental counterfactual irreality definitive of utopian ideals had been tragically misunderstood by the proponents of the third way. They saw in the results of their vain efforts more the practical unrealizability of utopia than its fundamentally regulative function. Jürgen Habermas's sober interjection while speaking here as the student of Adorno, rings true. "I do not find it right in this relationship," he said in an interview about unification and the failure of utopia, "to contrast 'practical reason' and 'utopia.' There is not only a pragmatic, but also a normative use of practical reason."[13] Thus far, it was not, therefore, utopia that had not failed, but rather the delusion of its reality.

Thoughts of the third way were found also in the West, though perhaps with a less dreamy overtone. Yet even there, as 1989 drew to a close and the loud voices of euphoria on Alexanderplatz faded away, hopes of utopia dwindled to resignation in the face of consumerism and *Realpolitik*. As early as December 8, Ulrich Greiner wrote in *Die Zeit* of an intellectual "ban on utopia":

> We are now freed for a long time from the unfortunate realization of that craving to want to bring utopia down to earth. But we cannot do without the hope. Whether we call it "Socialism" is just a question of terminology. There are Christian, anarchic, and ecological socialists. They have nothing to do with Lenin, and very little to do with Marx. Meanwhile they all stand guard at lost posts. But that is the proper and upright place for the intellectuals.[14]

Among commentators on intellectuals, Greiner was not so surprisingly isolated in his acceptance of the dysfunctional necessity of utopian thinking. From the nationalist to the postmodernist, unanimity seemed to reign that intellectuals had failed. Not that there was disagreement about Greiner's depiction of the role of the intelligentsia as "guards at lost posts," but rather the opposite: intellectual commentators from Andreas Huyssen to Karl-Heinz Bohrer preferred to further expand Greiner's explication of an underlying intellectual impotence, pointing out not only the end of utopia, but also the explicit elitism that expressed itself in the growing distance between the intellectuals and the masses.[15] There was disagreement, or perhaps lack of comprehension, concerning the essential *necessity* of this gap, which Greiner, for his part, had evaluated so enthusiastically. In addition, the striking fact that Greiner designated the realization of utopia as "unfortunate" went entirely ignored. So the debate on the practical fate of utopia and its intellectuals continued without pause, while the protagonists were apparently unconcerned or unaware that the fundamental relationship between pragmatics and utopia continued to be strained and unattended.

In the West, however, the discussion of the third way had a different history. Embedded in the postwar discussions of the German *Sonderweg* and its problems, mere mention of a utopian third way immediately raised critical eyebrows on the left and the opportunistic hopes of polemicists on the right. For this latter group, any discussion of a third way by the Left offered a window through which a stock of revisionist notions of the German nation could pass under the guise of historical critique. Hearing the echoes from the East of a third way in the pages of West German newspapers, Karl-Heinz Bohrer launched through this window a full-scale condemnation of all left advocates of utopian socialism in the name of the Nation:

> Such intellectuals do not want the heroism of so many Communists who died under Hitler and Stalin to have been in vain. That is understandable. But standing up for this tradition in spite of all obstacles is one thing; intellectual mendacity and blindness are something else. This false hope for a "third path" had already transformed the entirely unpolitical, expressionist dreamer Bloch into a defender of repression.[16]

Here he quite rightly berates the supporters of the socialist third way for overlooking the historical violence of their alternative. Yet, by subsequently rejecting with equal vehemence the "postconventional" solution advocated by others such as Jürgen Habermas, he is willing to risk an analogous violence by restituting instead the irrationalist tradition of conservative modernism:

> But to use constitutional utopia as a substitute for the nation has one disadvantage which is becoming increasingly clear: it cannot avoid repressing entire categories of the psychic and cultural tradition which used to form part of German identity, because these categories supposedly helped prepare the consciousness that ultimately made the Holocaust possible.[17]

Against formal liberal and republican values and their tradition from Kant to Habermas, Bohrer insists on the continuing actuality of an underlying substantivist cultural reality. Instead of a unified Germany, based on socially responsible, democratic traditions of the postwar Federal Republic, Bohrer oddly recommends the reinvigoration of the nation based on a "spiritual-symbolic criterion."[18]

The import of Bohrer's position is twofold. At the same time as he invokes a discussion about the historical problematics of implementing utopian solutions, his comments make us aware of the real concerns the incessant presence of the "irrational heritage" in Germany evokes. For this too easily dismissed substantivist heritage dwelling upon the idea of the "nation," geographically as well as culturally, was itself always an ideology that did not so much sublate as supersede any right/left ideological dichotomies in the German historical self-understanding.[19] While in this way being important in and of themselves, Bohrer's outbursts are interesting in another respect because of the broader discourse regarding the nation and the intellectual atmosphere within which they participated and which they also reinvigorated.[20] It is important to note his role in the unification debates; for, though certainly no one would accuse Bohrer of being on the left, the left seemed to take seriously his concerns.

Of the many intellectuals and commentators on intellectuals concerned with Bohrer's position, Ulrich Greiner made the most extensive response to Bohrer in *Die Zeit*.[21] Insisting that the nation was culturally far larger and geographically far smaller than Bohrer's vision, Greiner cites Max Weber's reflection on the historical construct of nationhood: " 'Nation,' Weber says, 'belongs to a value sphere.' That is to say: It is not a descriptive, not an analytic concept, but rather one, which is laden with emotional and political intentions. Weber says: 'The naked prestige of power is transformed into other specific forms, that is the idea of the nation.' " Greiner derives his vision from what Günter Grass and the other during the entire nineteenth century had called the *Kulturnation*,[22] itself neither geographically real nor merely imagined. During the debate about German unification, Grass's voice most adamantly sounded out against any realization of the problematic "idea" of which Weber spoke. Arguing openly for a conception of nation that he had written about ten years earlier in his fictional narrative *Kopfgeburten oder die Deutschen sterben aus*,[23] Grass produced an outpouring of articles and lectures denouncing the coming unification as historical self-denial and ideologically violent.[24] His much misrepresented argument that because the preconditions for the Holocaust were constituted in a united Germany, the only political solution must then be at most a confederation of the two states was, finally, a corollative reformulation of the culture-nation.[25] For Grass after all, far more important than the political, were the cultural aspects of Germany as a nation. Therefore, for him Germany ultimately dwells in the minds—the "heads"—of its inhabitants, or, more concretely, in their language: "Germany—a literary concept."[26]

Ultimately Grass also was suggesting a third way which, though mediated through forty years of historical reflection, championed a nation neither capitalist nor communist, nor particularly political at all. Like the advocates of the third way in the East, Grass was not satisfied with the irreducible difference of utopia and reality. His utopian "idea of the nation," that is, the ideology of identity, is, he believes, realizable, in fact already realized in a common language and culture. The third way emerges, therefore, from both parts of Germany and through the German left in the year 1989–1990 as neither regulatively utopian nor immediately real, but rather the sublation of both in a realized ideal of humanist socialism or the culture-nation.[27]

Realizing utopia has, however, always been a rather difficult task for intellectuals. It does not, therefore, come as a surprise that 1990 did not hear the joyous founding of either a Cultural Confederation of Germany or a confident socialist state with its western frontier on the Elbe. Instead, while in New York there was an empty seat at the United Nations, in the newspapers and periodicals of the West, editors breathed a sigh of relief that the catchy byword that had sold so many issues in the past had not been rendered obsolete: "failure." The obsolescence of failure in intellectual history would certainly also mean the field's obsolescence. And in this respect, the months and years after November 1989 have certainly posed no threat. Nonetheless, the plethora of intellectuals intellectually decrying the failure of the intellectuals would be striking if it were not so familiar. The discussion of the "failure of the intellectuals" by other intellectuals does not, however, seem to be driven by the insular dynamic of intellectuals' fascination with themselves. Rather, this public controversy should be understood as the necessary aftermath to the intellectuals' ill-conceived attempts at bringing their ideas into fruition. Both the initial "failure" and its ensuing discussion and portrayal are finally guided by an additional failure: the failure to understand the historical constitution of what is called "the intellectual."

In discussion after discussion of the intellectual's failure, the accusations revolve around their inability to either actually realize their utopian models or simply to conceive of models that would be more realistic to begin with. Since the debate was also conducted by intellectuals, the portrayals reflect the intellectual—or anti-intellectual—stance of the critic. Eager to reinstate the notion of nation married to Bohrer's irrational heritage, one analysis by Siegfried Mews defines its own position in a critique of Günter Grass, asserting that Grass's solution was merely a "negative nationalism" that eminently ignores the reality that "nations and national interests continue to be formidable forces and that the age of post-nationalism is not as close at hand as some had thought."[28] The successful intellectual—to Mews, as embodied in the person of Martin Walser—is one who shows "trust in the people" and, more importantly, is "able to discern future developments."[29] In the light of these expectations, the successful intellectual would apparently be a kind of populist prophet.

Though politically not aligned to the problematic national stance of Bohrer and Mews, some of Andreas Huyssen's criticisms unwittingly facilitate their condemnation. He contends that the multifarious positions taken by left intellectuals are unified by the unrealistic character of their political ideals after 1989, a contention that hypostatizes various vague and critical conceptions of the intellectuals' failings into a unified picture, thus creating an easier target for the critics: "Even though the positions differed significantly, it was precisely their joint opposition to the course of events which produces the image of failure."[30] Here intellectuals finally emerge as a group of dreamers unable to cope with reality and equally unable to work within the historical conditions of possibility. Any intellectual expression of dissatisfaction with these conditions is here heedlessly viewed as the requisite for failure. Thus, as utopia becomes predicative of the intellectual in general, the "failure of the intellectuals" is effectively linked metonymically with the existing "ban on utopia" that has served to eliminate any threat to the unlimited affirmation of existing reality, an affirmation at least until recently inimical to the critical left. Speaking about the subsequent *Literaturstreit* in relationship to the plight of the intellectuals in general, Jürgen Habermas attributed the "ban" and the "failure" to neoconservative trends:

> The subtext of the entire debate is of an older style. Finally, it was believed, that the intellectuals from East and West were simultaneously in the position where they can be convicted of utopianism dangerous to the community and exposed as the true enemies of the people.[31]

Certainly the "failure of the intellectuals" as a group trying to implement a specific utopian plan also constituted a defeat of critical alternatives to the reality of the New Germany. However, it does not seem clear yet that the "conviction" of the intellectuals and their failure as a group, which did occur, need to be understood as a failure of the intellectual as a historical category whose very failure is slowly emerging more as constitutive of their definition than as a real problem.

Yet, for the moment, Habermas and Huyssen both seem right from two different perspectives on the political import of the failure, whatever it eventually may have to do historically with intellectuals. For increasingly, as the Frankfurt School had feared, even the Left began to suggest that the alternative, the third way between capitalism and communism, was an unreasonable and even superfluous utopia that did not consider the alleged alternative already in place in the Federal Republic. Helmut Dubiel, in an opinion shared by many pragmatic thinkers, suggests that the proponents of a third way were wrong to think that the "path to a free society is shorter through the ruins of real-existing socialism than through the labyrinth of existing capitalist democracy."[32] Associating the Left with the revision of the socialist rather than the capitalist identity, leftist neo-pragmatists increasingly view the Left intellectual as functionally anachronistic. By understanding the intellectual—especially advocates of a "third" way—as a category that in the modern world has replaced the prophets and mystics as the protagonists of a better future or of "eternal and interest free values,"[33] the category becomes dependent on the desirability of contemporary reality and, moreover, its possibilities. If, therefore, the contemporary capitalist system can offer—as Helmut Dubiel suggests—a better world realizable through its own dynamic mechanisms, then the fate of the intellectual seems imminent or a *fait accompli*.

Accordingly, failure can be measured functionally as a historical problem rather than as a specific "failure" as others had suggested. In an article on the "departure of the Left intellectual," Alexander von Pechmann, in basic agreement with Dubiel, insists that the intellectual's role has simply been eliminated in a pluralist world in which the totalities of utopia and ideals have no place.

> The actual departure of the left intellectual in the sphere of knowledge occurs with the insight that there is no longer a need for the "knowledge of real relationships" . . . "Science" today does not designate an anticipatory future, but rather describes real structures of the present. In the place of the ideal there is now a plurality of scientific conceptions, each of which has to legitimate and negotiate its claim to knowledge vis-à-vis other claims to knowledge.[34]

Under the guise of tolerance, systems theory and neo-pragmatism dominate the West German (now apparently post-intellectual) academy with their new totality of liberal pluralism. Self-guiding and self-producing systems, which also happen to fulfill the necessary tautological criterion that they are able to function according to self-prescribed needs, do not appear to need intellectuals. This seems a truism. In such a universe, there is no need even for a critic where an analyst will do. Precisely the paradoxical universalism of such pluralism demands an alternative that is "outside," however contradictory that may sound to liberalist ideologues seeking an easy answer to the *Unübersichtlichkeit* of the modern world.

The criterion of functionality, advocated by a whole array of what Habermas would probably have to call "neoliberal-conservatives," is by definition in historical opposition to the category of the intellectual; for both utopia and the words that advocate it are historically counter-factual and faced with the dilemma of not so much being anachronistic in a functional worldview, but rather "failing" the tests to which they would be put. Therefore, the category of "failure" returns, like the insistent need for utopia, as Ulrich Greiner asserted, despite—or in spite of—their "antifunctionality."

Thus the perennial question remains: Have the intellectuals failed? Certainly those who tried to implement their utopia or otherwise hoped for its realization failed in their attempts. The third way between utopia (the ideal and the word) and reality (the real and the act) failed. It also failed as a mediator of communism and capitalism. But did the intellectuals fail as a historical category that is defined by the very impossibility of the third way ever succeeding? Understood as such, the mistake would be on the part of those intellectuals who understood their role *as* intellectuals to realize an ideal, to conduct the experiment of socialism on living specimens. It like-wise might be the mistake of their critics to have not differentiated between the words they spoke and the deeds they did.

The ban on utopia has ultimately not been imposed by the intellectuals, but rather by that "real-existing reality" against which, be it socialist or cap-italist, it is their task to rail. The ban would not then be on utopia, but on the sublation of the difference between utopia and reality. It is a sometimes noble and sometimes motley tradition of anti-intellectual intellectuals who, since the 1920s, appeal to the sense of pragmatics, thinking that a desire for something better, a moment of non-affirmation, necessarily represents a recurrence to the grand narrative of intellectual or philosophical totality. Since they apparently think that the possibility of conceiving something in opposition to reality as it "is" must rely on a totality, it may also be the fault of the pragmatists to think, like Alexander von Pechmann, that this totality might be the definition of the intellectual. It is likewise the fault of those who still would speak of a third way, spokespeople of the Left from Grass to Heym, who fail to address the issue with which I began my argument: that the relationship between word and deed—analogous to the tension of thought and politics, praxis, and theory, or utopia and reality—is assumed as one to be overcome, that the regulative ideal is something necessarily his-torically real and teleologically laden. It need not be so. It may be that, as Helmut Dubiel claims, the Left's calling card with the office name of the Frankfurt School, has worn its welcome. Yet, though the instrumentaliza-tion of the name of those critics of instrumental reason should be aban-doned, the value of their arguments and the heirs to their tradition need not be reduced to the names of their fathers and cast aside. Helmut Dubiel is himself an example of this. The historicality of what has emerged as the *category* of intellectuals is also something that is distinctively German. It seems that in their battle between word and deed, German intellectuals—witnessing the unification travesty—are doomed to a unique drive toward self-destruction. For though the category of intellectual is defined by the anti-functional character of their words, it seems caught in a dialectic (might one call it negative?) of autonomy and intervention, the result of which seems properly designated as "failure." Yet it is not only since Nietzsche raised a hammer to his own undertaking that it has been the intellectuals' wont to undermine themselves. The element of incessant self-denigration under the near euphemism of self-critique is partially constitutive of the "intellectual" as an emerging category. Likewise, this dialectic is not, as it was for certain East German intellectuals, only a "dream," but a dialectic of self-destruction which allows for intellectual autonomy. Here, one is again reminded of Adorno's unironic words, that "because philosophy is suitable to nothing, it has not yet become obsolete."[35]

Intellectuals, Modernity, and the Third Way

This dialectical dilemma for the intellectual, which is seemingly also definitive of the intellectual, is one embedded in the history of modernity. And understanding the genealogy of the intellectual seems important to see how the concept of "failure," and the "third way" to which it refers, are not only descriptions of events, but are themselves caught in the dialectical understanding of the German intellectual.

Well before Nietzsche, fourteen years after the first and only four years before the second failed revolution of modern Germany, Heinrich Heine already captured the quandary of the then nascent category of the intellectual. In his 1844 *Deutschland. Ein Wintermärchen*, Heine describes a journey from France across the Rhein on the way to Hamburg. At the first stop in Cologne, the poet-narrator finds himself accompanied by an unknown figure as he sits at his desk and as he walks through the streets, always behind, always silent, never interrupting. One day as he is walking through the streets, the poet finally confronts his shadow, demanding to know his intention. Tersely his companion reports that he is "no friend of rhetoric," but "of practical nature." He will realize in action what the poet thinks. "I am," he finally reports, "the deed of your thoughts."[36]

That night the poet lies in bed and dreams that he is again walking through Cologne. He enters the Cologne cathedral, mark of German nationalism, and debates with the Three Wise Kings who have come to life in their chapel. Instructed by one of the Kings on the reasons why respect must be paid to the king, the poet berates him, bidding him to return to the past to which he belongs, threatening to use force if words were not enough: not an empty threat but without any extra-verbal intention. As he turns to leave, he sees his shadow, the "deep of his thought," approach and with his ax smash to bits the "skeletons of superstition." At that moment cries of horror at the deed ring through the rafters of the cathedral, blood pours from the poet's breast, and he awakens in shock.

This is the birth hour of the intellectual dilemma, an hour of crisis for the German thinkers "after the epoch of art" following the death of Hegel and Goethe. It is an era shared by others' ambivalence about the relationship between thought and action, intellect and politics. Rising from the late eighteenth century, this fundamental problem of modernity and for the emerging individual in the rising industrial revolution was not just a problem, but *the* problem for the thinker no longer at court, but thrust out into the anonymous public sphere where communication was in crisis.[37]

These first children of modernity whose heirs are the "failed intellectuals" of 1989 were also faced with a political reality that was something unique to Germany, very different, for example, from neighboring France. Indeed, it was Heine who had lifted the problem of word versus deed, spirit versus politics, to the level of national problem. While in France the struggle of word versus deed for the intellectual was solved by Zola's words *j'accuse* and the decision for action, in the metropolitan culture of modern Vienna and Berlin the crisis reaching ever new peaks at the *fin-de-siècle*.

It is not surprising that, caught indefinitely between these poles, intellectuals—writers, philosophers, journalists—sought to overcome the trap by seeking a middle way, a third way between writing and acting. In this seemingly logical step toward a "third," more was involved than just a compromise. Few intellectuals were willing to abandon their ideals, their utopia, their attachment to the word to achieve peace. It was precisely this unwillingness that was causing the crisis. This meant that, unlike what Zola said, the mere spontaneity of intervention was entirely inadequate. In this respect, thought won the upper hand; for the relationship between the poles and the consistency of thought and deed with one another was itself guided not by the political reality, but rather the philosophy that constituted this reality for the intellectuals to begin with. Therefore, the intellectuals sought a reality that would either follow from the ideals of their philosophy, would undermine the distinction between reality and their ideals in some sort of organic or decisionist thinking, or, finally, which would separate themselves from the problems of reality altogether.

This last option was already explored by Hermann Bahr in an essay from 1900, "*Die Hauptstadt von Europa. Eine Phantasie in Salzburg.*"[38] While walking together through Salzburg, a friend expresses the surprising desire to purchase the city and transform it into a colony for a particular dispossessed group in Europe that he perceives emerging. Though the irony of the text renders any final political position undecidable, it is clear that a third way is a path taken here only with the greatest degree of scepticism:

> See, haven't you noticed that in Europe a new nation has gradually emerged that simply has not found accommodations? You and I and hundreds or perhaps—I don't know—a thousand, twenty thousand people in Europe have through their entire education gradually detached and disassociated themselves from their populace in such a way that, through language, they are only necessitously connected. . . . These people of the great yearning, strewn throughout the world, who feel the same things and hope for the same things, fear the same things we do, these people are our true fatherland.[39]

It is not, the friend claims here, that one value system and language might be better than another, but rather that the incompatibility of two groups and their inability to understand each other are the only attributes they share. The solution is ultimately a variation of a separatist, intellectual pride movement. Though he never mentions the word, he is speaking clearly of those whom we might call the intellectuals of Europe. Throughout his friend's discourse, the narrator remains bemused. Finally, his friend expresses the concern that if nothing is done their grandchildren will look at their writings and see the hypocrisy of their lives and the fundamental disparity between their words and their actions. There must be a place where that can be realized separate from the broad incomprehending world. To this the narrator responds laconically: " 'The Third Reich. . . . One has to admit that at least you are modern.' "

This surprising reference in 1900 to a Third Reich is perhaps less surprising when we reconsider the polar dilemma of the intellectuals. Indeed, Bahr's ironic and playful dialogue on the issue goes critically well beyond most of the self-righteous existentially burdened discussions of the "third" solution that followed in the 1920s and thereafter. For Bahr's narrator, however, this Third Reich was still certainly an oblique but satirical allusion to mystical and messianic Joachimite prophesies of the High Middle Ages, predicting the second coming and a Third Reich that would conclude with the vanquishing of evil and the restoration of harmony. Yet the satire does not rid the allusion of its political relevance in a Germany looking back to the mystical world of the Middle Ages not only as a practical guide for a new self-understanding,[40] but also for theoretical models of history that would suggest an end to the "real-existing" Second Empire as well as an antithesis to the holism of the premodern that might finally overcome the fragmentation and alienation fundamentally constitutive of the modern world.[41]

Beyond the "separatist movement" Bahr introduces, it is scarcely possible to even begin discussing the two other solutions sought in the form of a third way through the 1920s: either a messianic fulfillment of intellectual ideals and dreams, not unlike the third way model in 1989, or a decisionist destruction of the distinction between reality and intellectual ideals by recurring to some sort of organic or decisionist thinking. Needless to say, the problem of the Third became more than the logical response to the dichotomies of word/deed, thought/politics, and the like, and a harmless allusion to separatist dreams by European intellectuals. In the period after World War I, thoughts of a Third Reich, a third way, a third party, a third force became synonymous with conservative modernists on the right and theorists of neo-Kantian or neo-Hegelian organic universalists on the left.[42]

As has been discussed in so many works on the intellectuals of the period,[43] both sides shared a marked dislike for the reality of modernity, its alienation, and fragmentation. Yet unlike Adorno, few bothered to question the philosophical relationship between their utopia or their ideology and reality at large. For this reason, all too often the distinction of the third became an unreflected medium to realize utopia, rather than to acknowledge reality and its political implications while maintaining the regulative nature of their thinking. Nor did they care to shudder, as did Heine, as the apocalyptic outcome of their words became reality. Instead of the third way being the autonomy of the word, not above politics but besides it, intellectuals made the mistake of conflating the two.

It is important, however, to make the distinction between elite advocates of a Third Reich and the mass movement of national socialism, for certainly not all intellectuals searching for a third way were political supporters of the Nazi rise to power or their regime. Indeed, most were not. According to sociologists of intellectuals, the shared characteristic of these "floating intellectuals"—in the words of Karl Mannheim borrowed from Alfred Weber—can best be defined by their status as writers outside of activist politics, but at the time anticipating an alternative reality in outspoken opposition to the political reality of the Weimar Republic they despised.[44]

The discontinuity of the intellectual trek along the third way since the 1920s makes the occasion for its being revisited in the period 1989–1990 all the more surprising. After 1945, though leftists such as Ernst Bloch continued to advocate in Europe the middle path between East and West, it is difficult to separate such discussions from the raw power interests of the Cold War. In this respect, it was not until after the end of the Cold War, marked by events of 1989, that the allusion could again be politically palatable. Yet, for Germany, as the anti-intellectual opportunists are happy to point out, such a hope too casually overlooks certain legacies of the intellectuals themselves that undermines any project that could have been subsumed under the rubric of the "Third."

In West German intellectual life, especially in the 1960s and thereafter, the open political activism on behalf of free expression and democracy distinguished the intellectual environment from the years before 1933. Resurrecting that "weak tradition" of which Habermas spoke, the intellectuals recalled the pro-republican rhetoric of the converted Thomas Mann stemming from the late 1920s:

> Between aestheticist individuation and the undignified decline of the individual in the general; between mystic and ethic, internalized contemplation and political participation; between the fatal denial of the ethical, the civic, the honorable, and a not so crystal-clear ethical rational philistinism, lies the German middle, the pleasantly human quality from which our best dream. And we pay homage to our legal form in whose purpose and aim we have comprehended the unity of political and national life by prompting our yet awkward tongues to the cry: "Long live the Republic!"[45]

The resurrection of this "German middle" has been the project of such thinkers as Jürgen Habermas and writers such as Günter Grass and Heinrich Böll who have not shied away from open political involvement both in writings and, in Grass's case, in political campaigns. Against what Habermas calls the neoconservative spokesmen of the cultural right, such as Karl-Heinz Bohrer in Germany or Daniel Bell in the United States,[46] the democratic institutions of which Mann spoke are not utopian solutions or replacements for utopian solutions, but a political space within which "the individual and the general" are not conflated. As is well known, Habermas advocates the institutional preservation of a legally grounded "public sphere" where individuals can negotiate political responses in communication with each other as individual members of a larger community, both political and cultural.

In this democratic solution, the relationship between theoretical ruminations and political decisions should not occur in the mystical space of a third, but in the democratic institutions of modern society. This solution, most ardently introduced into the unification debate by Jürgen Habermas, is greatly in accord with Adorno. Yet it does not so much yield to the extreme negativity of the relationship of the individual to society or philosophical thought to politics, as offer limits to both, denying the claims to totality that the priority of decision and politics over philosophy would make, as well as the analogous claims of philosophy to be the warden for the conditions to all truth.[47] Against the liberals who condemn the putative totalities of utopia, Habermas at the same time insists on the necessity of plural utopias as integrating visions of totality in everyday life for which critical theory has no answer.[48] It is here that, against the advocates of political unity based on a national soul, Günter Grass or his 1920s counterpart, Hugo von Hofmannsthal,[49] can champion the utopian visions of a "literary concept" of a nation that has no empirical derivative or result. Utopia is thus reinforced as a regulative totality in whose empire intellectuals write without sublating the difference utopia demands by definition between itself and reality. While the warnings of Heine, not to mention the imperatives of history, bar the way back to a third way or a Third Reich, the theoretical legitimacy of intellectuals and their relationship to utopia can be reinstated.

The question to be finally asked of the critics once again is whether intellectuals *can* fail. Certainly those whom we call intellectuals can be wrong, their ideologies and utopias necessarily unfulfillable. They can even be guilty of not recognizing "that a radical rethinking has become necessary as a result of the sheer force of historical events," as Huyssen claims.[50] But when understood as a historical category, can they actually fail? Can the very quintessence of modern ambivalence, locked between work and deed, ideal and reality, fail? Or does the designation of failure not merely reinforce intellectuals' constitutive role in modernity? For reading their failure with an eye to Adorno, the collapse of their value for everyday life does call into question their views. The discrepancy between their views and reality propells them, however, into the dialectical confusion of their negative function in late-capitalism, only reinforcing for the moment the autonomy of the word against the realm of political and social instruments. This dialectical autonomy leaves the intellectuals and their words alive with at least a minimum of freedom, a freedom to verbally surpass but not supplant democratic institutions that protect the political freedoms of the individual. Finally the truth is revealed in Toni Morrison's warning that the very power of the word's appeal to the ineffable excludes it from the "arrogance" to "pin down" political categories or make any claims to any correspondence between utopia and reality.

Notes

1. Theodor W. Adorno, "Cultural Criticism and Society," in Samuel and Shierry Weber, trans., *Prisms* (Cambridge, MA: MIT Press, 1981), p. 32.
2. Address upon receiving the 1993 Nobel Prize for literature; cited here from John Darnton, "Accepting Nobel, Morrison Proves Power of Words," *New York Times*, December 8, 1993.
3. This position was represented most prominently by Günter Grass; see "Kurze Rede eines vaterlandslosen Gesellen," *Die Zeit*, February 9, 1990, as well as "Schreiben nach Auschwitz. Nachdenken über Deutschland: ein Schriftsteller zieht Bilanz aus 35. Jahren. Die Frankfurter Poetik-Vorlesung," *Die Zeit*,

February 23, 1990. A selection of Grass's essays on the German Question have been collected in *Two States—One Nation?* Krishna Winston with A.S. Wensinger, trans. (San Diego: Harcourt, Brace and Jovanovich, 1990), pp. 94–123.

4. Christa Wolf, "Christa Wolfs Rede auf dem Alexanderplatz, Berlin, 4.11.1989," in Benno Zanetti, ed., *Der Weg zur deutschen Einheit* (Munich: Goldmann, 1991), pp. 205–206. The original statement by Christoph Hein was made on October 24 in a talk entitled "Ein Berliner Traum im Oktober 1989, der bereits im August 1968 von deutschen Panzern auf dem Wenzelplatz überrollte wurde. Zur Podiumsdiskussion 'DDR—wie ich sie träume.' " This and other contributions to the unification discussion are collected in *Die fünfte Grundrechensart* (Frankfurt am Main: Luchterhand, 1990). When not otherwise noted, translations are mine.

5. Stefan Heym, "Rede auf der Demonstration am 4. November, Berlin, Alexanderplatz," in *Einmischungen* (Aalen: Bertelsmann, 1990), p. 271.

6. Heiner Müller, "Dem Terrorismus die Utopie entreißen. Alternative DDR," in *"Zur Lage der Nation." Heiner Müller im Interview mit Fritz Raddatz* (Berlin: Rotbuch, 1990), pp. 9–24. Appeared first in *Transatlantik* v.1, n.90 (1990). This sentiment was echoed by Christoph Hein in "Weder das Gebot noch die Genehmigung als Geschenk," *Berliner Zeitung*, November 4–5, 1989, reprinted in *Die fünfte Grundrechensart*, pp. 189–193: "Kunst strickt ungern mit heißer Nadel. In der Vergangenheit hatten Kunst und Literatur von einem Bonus gelebt, der sich auf einem Mißverhältnis gründete. Statt der Zeitung kauften sich die Leute ein Buch. Jetzt sehe ich Anzeichen dafür, daß sich die Zeitungen mit Politik befassen und die Kunst dadurch entlastet wird. Damit wird Kunst wieder auf ihre eigentlichen Aufgaben zurückgeführt. Langfristig wird eine Entlastung von Literatur stattfinden. Ich finde gut, daß wir wieder Shakespeare spielen, statt aktuelle Bösartigkeiten zu verhandeln, deren Ventil-Strickmuster schnell zu durchschauen ist. Es ist für Literatur völlig unwichtig, Neuigkeiten zu reportieren." (193)

7. Jürgen Habermas, *Vergangenheit als Zukunft*, Michael Haller, ed. (Zurich: Pendo-Verlag, 1990), p. 51f.

8. See Stefan Heym, "Aschermittwoch," *Der Spiegel* December 4, 1989, reprinted in *Einmischungen* (Aalen: Bertelsmann, 1990), pp. 265–270; trans. Stephen Brockmann as "Ash Wednesday in the GDR," *New German Critique* v.52 (1991): pp. 31–35.

9. Helmut Dubiel, "Linke Traurigkeit," *Merkur* v.49, n.6 (1990): p. 488.

10. Monika Maron, "Writers and the People," *New German Critique* v.52 (1991): p. 40.

11. See Horst Bienek, "Bitte keine Utopie," response to survey of intellectuals published as "Ist der Sozialismus am Ende," *Die Zeit*, November 24, 1989.

12. Maron, "Writers and the People," p. 41.

13. Habermas, *Vergangenheit als Zukunft*, p. 62.

14. Ulrich Greiner, "Utopie-Verbot. Die deutschen Intellektuellen und das deutsche Volk," *Die Zeit*, December 8, 1989.

15. Andreas Huyssen accused especially the eastern intellectuals of "a fatal aloofness from reality and a desperate clinging to projections, and, when under fire, melancholic self-pity and unrepentant self-righteousness." Andreas Huyssen,

"After the Wall: The Failure of German Intellectuals," *New German Critique* v.52 (1991): pp. 109–143.

16. Karl-Heinz Bohrer, "Why We Are Not a Nation—And Why We Should Become One," trans. Stephen Brockmann, *New German Critique* v.51 (1991): p. 73. Originally appeared in *Frankfurter Allgemeine Zeitung*, January 13, 1990.

17. Ibid., p. 82.

18. Ibid., p. 83. Based on this substantivist assertion, many on the right argued that denying Germans their national unity would only serve to foment irrationalist desires. See Ulrich Oevermann, "Zeit Staaten oder Einheit?" *Merkur* v.49, n.2 (1992): pp. 91–106. Significantly, this was also used opportunistically to legitimize the callous *Realpolitik* of Helmut Kohl.

19. See George G. Iggers, *The German Conception of History; the National Tradition of Historical Thought from Herder to the Present* (Middletown, CT: Wesleyan University Press, 1968). For further discussion of this see Ruth Starkman's article in this volume.

20. Many of the arguments for and against unification in 1989–1990 were mobilized from the general discourse in the West around "nation" since 1945. Most immediately this discussion recalled the 1986–1987 *Historikerstreit* revolving around efforts to relativize the historical singularity of the Holocaust within German historiography. Although in this earlier controversy substantivist culture had not been explicitly addressed, revisionist historians had been accused of instrumentalizing the possibility of such historical relativization in order to free the notion of "German Nation" from the grips of the discredited irrationalist tradition. Documentation of this debate in English can be found in *New German Critique* v.44 (1988), special issue on the *Historikerstreit* as well as in *Forever in the shadow of Hitler?: Original Documents of the Historikerstreit, the Controversy Concerning the Singularity of the Holocaust*, trans. James Knowlton and Truett Cates (Atlantic Highlands, NJ: Humanities Press, 1993).

21. Ulrich Greiner, "Das Phantom der Nation. Warum wir keine Nation sind und warum wir keine werden müssen-ein vergeblicher Zwischenruf im Intellektuellen-Streit um die deutsche Einheit," *Die Zeit*, March 16, 1990. See also Jürgen Habermas, "Zur Identität der Deutschen. Ein einig Volk von aufgebrachten Wirtschaftsbürgern?" in *Die nachholende Revolution* (Frankfurt am Main: Suhrkamp, 1990); an abridged version appeared as "Der DM-Nationalismus," *Die Zeit*, March 30, 1990; the unabridged version appeared in English as "Yet Again: German Identity—A United Nation of Angry DM-Burghers?" trans. Stephen Brockmann, *New German Critique* v.52 (1991): pp. 205–225.

22. See Hinrich C. Seeba, "Nationalliteratur," in Franz Norbert Mennemeier and Conrad Wiedemann, eds., *Deutsche Literatur in der Weltliteratur—Kulturnation statt politischer Nation?* (Tübingen: Niemeyer, 1985), pp. 197–207.

23. Günter Grass, *Kopfgeburten oder die Deutschen sterben aus* (Frankfurt am Main: Suhrkamp, 1980), pp. 8ff.

24. Some of these are available in English in Günter Grass, *Two States—One Nation?*

25. See Günter Grass, "Kurze Rede eines vaterlandslosen Gesellen."

26. Grass, *Kopfgeburten*, p. 9.

27. This argument of utopian historical responsibility was turned on its head and used for the opposite ends by others; see Oevermann, "Zeit Staaten oder Einheit?"
28. Siegfried Mews, "After the Fall of the Berlin Wall: German Writers and Unification," *South Atlantic Review* v.58, n.2 (1993): pp. 1–19.
29. Ibid., p. 10. For Walser's recent contribution to the "German Question" see Martin Walser, *Über Deutschland reden* (Frankfurt am Main: Suhrkamp, 1989).
30. Huyssen, "After the Wall," p. 117.
31. Habermas, *Vergangenheit als Zukunft*, p. 87.
32. Dubiel, "Linke Traurigkeit," p. 485.
33. Alexander von Pechmann, "Abschied des Linksintellektuellen," *Widerspruch* v.22 (1992): p. 28.
34. Pechmann, "Abschied des Linksintellektuellen," p. 35.
35. Theodor W. Adorno, "Wozu noch Philosophie," in *Eingriffe. Neun kritische Modelle* (Frankfurt am Main: Suhrkamp, 1963), p. 26. The beginning of *Negative Dialektik* echoes this sentiment: "Philosophy, which at first seemed obsolete, keeps itself alive because the moment of its realization was missed," *Negative Dialektik* (Frankfurt am Main: Suhrkamp, 1976), p. 15.
36. Heinrich Heine, "Deutschland. Ein Wintermärchen" (1844), in *Sämtliche Werke* v.2, Ernst Elster, ed. (Leipzig and Vienna: Bibliographisches Institut, 1890), p. 444f.
37. See Jürgen Habermas, *Structural Transformation of the Public Sphere*, trans. Thomas Burger with Frederick Lawrence (Cambridge, MA: MIT Press, 1989); for a more extensive explication of modernity applicable here, see Habermas, *The Philosophical Discourse of Modernity*, trans. Frederick Lawrence (Cambridge, MA: MIT Press, 1987).
38. In Hermann Bahr, *Essays* (Leipzig: Insel, 1921), pp. 235–241.
39. Bahr, "Die Hauptstadt Europas," p. 238.
40. For a discussion of the important mythico-political ramifications in Germany of prophesies by Joachimite de Fiore, especially as a reaction to the death of Frederick II and the possibility of the last Hohenstaufen to return, vanquish the pope, and restore the imperial piece see Thomas Ketron, "The Myth of Identity: Frederick II as a Legendary Figure," unpublished manuscript.
41. For a thorough and broad discussion of the academic intellectual response to these problems from the end of the Second Empire to the end of the Weimar Republic, see Fritz Ringer, *Decline of the German Mandarins. The German Academic Community, 1890–1933* (Hanover and London: Wesleyan University Press, 1990).
42. Certainly Arthur Moeller van den Bruck's *Das Dritte Reich* (Hamburg: Hanseatische Verlagsanstalt, 1931), first published in 1923, is the most outstanding example. The greater discourse of the third in general, however, should not be underestimated. See George Mosse, *Germans and Jews. The Right, the Left, and the Search for a 'Third Force' in Pre-Nazi Germany* (Detroit: Wayne Press, 1970), pp. 181–225, esp. pp. 3–33.
43. The extensive literature on intellectuals and the 1920s is an intellectual historical phenomenon itself, primarily in the 1960s, but also extending to the present. See, e.g., in order of their original publication: Helmut Plessner, *Die verspätete*

34 / BRETT R. WHEELER

Nation (Frankfurt am Main: Suhrkamp, 1974), esp. pp. 17–40; Fritz Stern, *The Politics of Cultural Despair* (Berkeley: University of California Press, 1961); Georg Lukács, *Die Zerstörung der Vernunft* (Frankfurt am Main: Luchterhand, 1962); Kurt Sontheimer, *Antidemokratisches Denken in der Weimarer Republik* (Munich: Deutscher Taschenbuch Verlag, 1992); George Mosse, *The Crisis of German Ideology: The Intellectual Origin of the Third Reich* (New York: Grosset & Dunlap, 1964); Fritz Ringer, *Decline of the German Mandarins*; George Mosse, *Germans and Jews*; Jeffrey Herf, *Reactionary Modernism. Technology, Culture and Politics in Weimar and the Third Reich* (Cambridge: Cambridge University Press, 1984). Throughout this literature, the discussion of the right intelligentsia outstrips that of the left. The connection between the two in relationship to the common search for a third way is discussed partially by Mosse (1970), but needs more exploration.

44. See Josef Schumpeter, "The Sociology of the Intellectuals," in *The Intellectuals*, George B. de Huszar, ed. (Glencoe, IL: Free Press, 1960), p. 79; Karl Mannheim, *Ideologie und Utopie* (Frankfurt am Main: G. Schulte-Bulmke, 1965), p. 135.

45. Thomas Mann, "Von deutscher Republik," in *Gesammelte Werke* v. XI (Frankfurt am Main: Fischer, 1960), cited here from Sontheimer, *Antidemokratisches Denken*, p. 312.

46. See Jürgen Habermas, *Die neue Unübersichtlichkeit* (Frankfurt am Main: Suhrkamp, 1985), pp. 30–117; in addition to the neoconservative move he identifies in the late 1970s in the Federal Republic, he also refers to the neoconservative movement in the United States is rightly identified with Daniel Bell, *The Cultural Contradictions of Capitalism* (New York: Basic Books, 1976).

47. See Jürgen Habermas, *Moral Consciousness and Communicative Action*, trans. Christian Lenhardt and Shierry Weber Nicholson (Cambridge, MA: MIT Press, 1990), esp. pp. 1–20.

48. Habermas, *Die neue Unübersichtlichkeit*, p. 75f.

49. Hugo von Hofmannsthal, "Das Schrifttum als geistiger Raum der Nation," in *Gesammelte Werke. Reden und Aufsätze III* (Frankfurt am Main: Fischer, 1980), pp. 24–41; originally published in 1920. The similarity of utopian vision between Grass and Hofmannsthal should not, of course, collapse their political differences.

50. Huyssen, "After the Wall," p. 143.

CHAPTER TWO

THE REBIRTH OF TRAGEDY: SYBERBERG, STRAUß, AND GERMAN IDENTITY

Stephen Brockmann

Intellectually, one of the major results of World War II in Europe was the virtual elimination of the Right-wing anticapitalism that had flourished in Europe up through the end of the Weimar Republic and which has been so well documented in such famous scholarly studies as Fritz Stern's 1961 *The Politics of Cultural Despair*[1] and Armin Mohler's *Die konservative Revolution.*[2] As Stefan Breuer has rightly noted in his recent well-received contribution to the ongoing debate on the concept of a "conservative revolution," it is very difficult to sift through the various strands of this Right-wing anticapitalism, from Ernst Rohm to Arthur Moeller van den Bruck in Germany alone—not to mention the various related strands of thought in other European countries—and find a common thread.[3] Hence it is probably wrong to speak of *a* conservative revolution; rather, it would be more correct to use the plural and speak of a multiplicity of conservative revolutions. In general, however, it would probably be correct to assert that most conservative revolutionaries in pre-1933 Europe shared both a distrust of finance capitalism and a glorification of the nation state, which they perceived as an organic unit. Such conservative revolutionary sentiment did not, for the most part, survive World War II in Western Europe, even if, as Breuer and others have suggested, it did migrate to various Third World nationalist regimes in the postwar period. In Western Europe, however, postwar conservatism made its peace with the capitalist system of production. In Germany this peace is represented most forcefully by the creation and success of the Christian Democratic Party, which has dominated most of postwar German politics, and which drove all revolutionary or anticapitalist strands of conservatism into political marginality. As a result of the widespread disappearance of conservative anticapitalism in Europe after the end of World War II and the lengthy Cold War between the Soviet Union and the capitalist democracies of the West, anticapitalism in the postwar era came to be associated almost exclusively with leftism, not with conservative or reactionary ideologies.

The domino-like collapse of the East Bloc which started in the late summer of 1989 with the implosion of the German Democratic Republic (as keystone of Soviet domination in Eastern Europe) has not yet significantly altered this state of affairs. However, there has been a noticeable growth in anticapitalist sentiment on the European Right, as evidenced, for instance, by the 1989 founding and subsequent success of the newspaper *Junge Freiheit*, a young right-wing weekly resembling the left-wing *Tageszeitung* and giving ample space to right-wing anticapitalist sentiments. The relative rise in visibility of right-wing anticapitalism has, of course, been helped by the decline in visibility of left-wing anticapitalism. With the disappearance of Communism from Europe, even the anticommunist left suffered a significant loss of credibility and confidence from which it is yet to recover. This has left the field of anticapitalism largely to the European Right. Most prominent in this development has been the philosopher of the French Nouvelle Droite, Alain de Benoist, whose influence has been felt strongly among young right-wingers in Germany.[4] Captivated by ideas of a German "Third Path," which steered clear of the Scylla of materialist Communism and the Charybdis of materialist capitalism, young German right-wingers interviewed de Benoist after the collapse of the Soviet Bloc about his idea of a "Third Path." De Benoist declared, in spite of his sympathy with the proponents of a Third Path, that such a Third Path did not exist:

> Of course I have a great deal of sympathy with the idea of a "Third Path"—neither Moscow nor Washington, neither liberalism nor Marxism. This idea, by the way, has a geographical incarnation: Europe is the continent in the "middle," and Germany is in the center of even this "middle." But from the perspective of the history of ideas, one can ask oneself whether this expression does not have its limits. If one admits that liberalism and Marxism are heirs to one and the same ideological matrix, specifically the philosophy of the Enlightenment and its main strands (utilitarianism, rationalism, internationalism, etc.), one could assert with just as much justification that in reality there are only two "paths." The collapse of the Soviet system can only underline this way of looking at things. The real challenge is to find an *alternative* to the dominant ideology (axiom of interests, terrorism of consumerism, political spectacle, etc.).[5]

Such a philosophy upholds the essence of the "Third Path"—a rejection of both capitalism and Communism—while denying its tertiary nature. In this view, both capitalism and Communism are incarnations of the same spirit—rationalist materialism—and hence constitute one and the same path. As the traditional geographical, intellectual, and spiritual center of Europe, Germany has, in de Benoist's view, an important role to play in constituting a genuine opposition to this "one path." Referring to the Germany as a Central European "idea" whose time has come again with German unification, de Benoist relates the spiritual to the political by suggesting that "the rebirth of the German nation . . . can create the necessary conditions for the appearance of this idea in the future."[6] With respect to a German identity which de Benoist sees as having been lost in West Germany through many decades of consumerism and mindless slavery to the United States, de Benoist declares,

> The only thing that one can say is that the rebirth of the German nation will by its very logic *force* the Germans to assert their identity, even though they are far removed from actually desiring this.[7]

The most consistent and prominent defender of conservative anticapitalism as a necessary part of any authentic German identity within Germany over the last thirty years has been the filmmaker Hans Jürgen Syberberg. In addition to his many films, the most important of which concern the problem of German identity and aesthetics from Karl May and the mad king Ludwig of Bavaria to Adolf Hitler, Syberberg has produced a series of books which address similar themes. Syberberg's greatest claims to fame were his films *Hitler, a Film from Germany* (1977) and *Parsifal* (1982), each of which treated irrationalism, music, and Romanticism as the core of German identity and intellect. In Syberberg's view, this basic core of German identity had been lost after World War II, leaving Germany largely without a fixed identity and reliant upon foreign and particularly American culture to fill in the void. Syberberg has consistently met with more praise outside Germany than at home. This is partly because he deals with uncomfortable aspects of the German past more readily accepted abroad than at home; and partly because Syberberg's Germanic essentialism tends to prescribe to Germans what is authentic in their identity and what is not. One of the most remarkable aspects of Syberberg's talent is his ability to synthesize, crystallize, and focus major and sometimes complex and contradictory strands of thought about modern German identity and culture into a consistent and relatively coherent whole. This is true of both his magnum opus, the film, *Hitler* that crystallized thinking about German identity in the late 1970s, and of his 1990 book *Vom Unglück und Glück der Kunst in Deutschland nach dem letzten Kriege* ["On the Misfortune and Fortune of Art in Germany after the Last War"], which focused such thinking around the time of the collapse of the German Democratic Republic and German reunification, expanding at great length some of the themes that Alain de

Benoist had also laid out. Although Syberberg's thinking itself has remained relatively consistent over the last few decades, his work serves quite different functions in the different social and political contexts in which it has appeared. In the late 1970s, for instance, when the film *Hitler* was released, it became part of a widespread critique of materialism and commercialism still largely associated with the Left, not the Right. With the publication of Syberberg's 1990 *Vom Unglück und Glück der Kunst in Deutschland nach dem letzten Kriege*, the critique of contemporary German represented by Syberberg was much more readily associated with the Right than the Left. It is quite likely that the new context created by German reunification and the rise of an anticapitalist right in Europe will force a rereading and reinterpretation of Syberberg's major films as well.

When Syberberg published *Vom Unglück und Glück der Kunst in Deutschland nach dem letzten Kriege* in the summer of 1990, he thrust himself into the center of the debate on the meaning of German reunification. In that strange twilight period between the East German election victory of the conservative Alliance for Germany in March 1990 and Germany's reunification at midnight on October 3, 1990, Syberberg, himself originally from East Germany, published a book that sought to examine the core of German identity and aesthetics in the light of the revolution inside the German Democratic Republic and German reunification. With its stinging indictment of West German postwar culture, the book was strangely at odds with the political situation in Germany in the summer of 1990 and an East German populace that seemed to want nothing more than immediate and full participation in the West German economic miracle.[8]

In the March, 1990 parliamentary election the voters of the German Democratic Republic had given a massive and unexpected victory to an electoral coalition whose mandate was to dismantle as quickly as possible the nominally sovereign state it now found itself governing. That election marked the end of the dreams of a "Third Path" between Communism and capitalism for the German Democratic Republic that had so fascinated East German intellectuals in the revolutionary autumn of 1989. After all, one of the most effective election slogans of the Alliance for Germany had been: "No Experiments!" The March elections were crudely but relatively accurately understood as a vote for the West and against the East. Hans Jürgen Syberberg's musings appeared on the German book market at about the same time as Christa Wolf's *Was bleibt*, which caused the biggest literary debate of the year and quite overshadowed the relatively minor stir caused by some of Syberberg's more outlandish sentences.[9] Almost simultaneous, the events were—the currency union between East and West Germany, which occurred on July 1, 1990; Helmut Kohl's trip to the Caucasus mountains with Michael Gorbachev later in July 1990, during which

Gorbachev allowed the future reunified Germany to become a part of the North Atlantic Treaty Organization (NATO); the final working out of the state treaty on reunification between the Federal Republic of Germany and the German Democratic Republic, largely organized by Chancellor Helmut Kohl's lieutenant Wolfgang Schäuble; and the first major debates on coming to terms with the Stasi past in the wake of GDR interior minister Peter-Michael Diestel's attempts to restrict or even end access to Stasi files, including a hunger strike by writer-activist Wolf Biermann and others at the former Stasi headquarters in Berlin's Normanenstraße. When asked by an American journalist what it all meant, what the ultimate goal of all these confusing and rapid events was, the West German Chancellor Helmut Kohl replied: "That things will normalize. That's the most important thing for us, that we become a wholly normal country, not 'singularized' in any question . . . that we simply don't stick out. That's the important thing."[10]

From the "Gnade der späten Geburt" ("the grace of late birth") through Bitburg and the *Historikerstreit* (Historians' Debate) to German Reunification itself, along with the Gulf War, German out-of-area, non-NATO military actions, *Bundeswehr* troops on Paris's Champs-Elysées in the summer of 1994, and the fiftieth anniversary of the end of World War II in May 1995, the "normalization" of Germany has been, perhaps, Helmut Kohl's leitmotif. The summer of 1990 was the high point of Kohl's triumphs, a period when almost everyone from the left to the right acknowledged his persuasiveness and effectiveness in handling German reunification. At this time of triumph for a vision of German normality, Syberberg's awkward and strange book, which proclaimed a completely different vision of German alterity, was doubly out of place. As Russell Berman has accurately suggested, "precisely as a reactionary he [Syberberg] is perhaps the most consistent thinker of alterity, i.e., Germany as different from the West."[11] Syberberg's 1990 book continued many of the themes and motifs of his epochal *Hitler*, a film taken so seriously, albeit sometimes critically, both at home and abroad in the late 1970s; that it became one of the crucial texts in a reemergence of pessimistic German conservatism after a long hiatus. Just as the film caught the spirit of its times with remarkable precision, so too did Syberberg's book shedding light on post-unification Germany. It might even be dubbed the bible of a renewed anticapitalist conservatism still too weak politically to deserve the title "conservative revolution."

Syberberg's thinking itself has changed very little between the film and the book. In both the film and the book the question of German cultural identity plays a central role. But while Syberberg's critique of Americanization and pop culture in 1977, in the context of a seemingly permanent German division and almost a decade of social-liberal government under Willy Brandt and Helmut Schmidt, appeared at least to sympathetic foreign critics as a positive reclaiming of German national tradition, by 1990, after almost a decade of conservative government under Helmut Kohl and the sudden collapse of the Cold War system in Europe, the same positions meant something entirely different. This time Syberberg's ideas were condemned at home as cryptofascist and largely ignored abroad.

One of the reasons for the relative obscurity of Syberberg's book is no doubt his prose style, which sometimes reads like a Mark Twain caricature of Germanic ponderousness and impenetrability. As German intellectual Thorsten Hinz observed of Syberberg's style, "In Syberberg's prose, the aporias of modernity all too frequently disappear behind the foggy curtain of pompous syntax."[12] Syberberg's German prose style is an unfortunate cross between Julius Langbehn, the eccentric self-proclaimed visionary of late-nineteenth-century German nationalism, and the early Friedrich Nietzsche, with Langbehn, whose prose is notoriously murky, mostly winning out over Nietzsche. And yet the book's prose style is also a function of its philosophy, which consciously refers back to an earlier German tradition of pessimistic anticapitalism. In his 1990 book Syberberg presents important arguments that need to be considered seriously. The book has three major sections and an introduction "On the Aesthetics of German Postwar History." Within these larger sections the argument is organized epigrammatically, in segments as short as one paragraph to those several pages long. These divisions and markers, however, are more or less arbitrary. They do not result from the logic of any particular argument; rather, they appear to result from the process of writing itself. Hence the book resembles a kind of stream-of-consciousness monologue in which significant themes recur again and again, but without the visual creativity and formal rigor of Syberberg's films.

In spite of its stream-of-consciousness format, Syberberg's book has a distinct philosophy, much of which will be familiar to those who know his *Hitler, a Film from Germany*. At the core of Syberberg's philosophy is the belief that art or aesthetics is the most important or primary sphere of human existence, and that all other spheres are secondary. In contrast to the Marxist or materialist understanding of art, which views art as a superstructure resting on and reflecting relations of power in the base of material economic relations, Syberberg reverses the picture and views the material world as a superstructure resting on and reflecting the aesthetic relations of power in the base of culture and art. With Syberberg we are not far from the early Friedrich Nietzsche's famous dictum that

> The entire comedy of art is neither performed for our betterment or education nor are we the true authors of this art world. On the contrary, we may assume that we are merely images and artistic projections for the true author, and that we have our highest dignity in our significance as works of art—for

it is only as an *aesthetic phenomenon* that existence and the world are eternally *justified*.[13]

Such a philosophy may have been (and was) decried as absurd reactionary idealism by German critics of Syberberg in the 1970s, but in a postmodern intellectual world where the concepts of semiotics and simulation have become so important, it can no longer be discarded of hand. As Syberberg writes, "It is not true that art is what it is because the world is what it is; rather, the world is what it is because art is what it is."[14] For Syberberg, as for Marshall McLuhan, "the medium is the message."[15] Hence, for Syberberg *Hitler* is precisely a work of art, a film, not a historical figure, and the German question is primarily aesthetic, not political: "The German question is art" (154). In contrast to, say, a Jürgen Habermas, who would suggest that the primary postwar West German cultural achievement was the assimilation of Western democratic constitutional values,[16] Syberberg suggests that "the real cultural event after the end of the last war was the victory of meanness in art" (29). In history, as Syberberg writes, the "most tragic victim" of the twelve years of Nazi rule was not German democracy or millions of Jews, Poles, Russians, and Ukrainians; not even millions of Germans; rather, it was art itself, which, Syberberg writes, "was destroyed after the reeducation in 1945." Such a view, however shocking, is entirely consistent with Syberberg's ideas about the primacy of the aesthetic. Syberberg's use of the passive voice makes it unclear whether he believes art was destroyed by the twelve years of Nazi rule or by the postwar reeducation; but the distinction itself might well be meaningless to him, since Syberberg stresses that he believes Hitler himself to have been the unwitting tool of a world spirit bent on destroying German culture. If Syberberg's celluloid Hitler had literally been a sometimes ridiculous puppet or marionette manipulated by others, so too in Syberberg's book Hitler is a useful tool "who is only being used to beat people down with Auschwitz" (127). In other words, Hitler had to come and Auschwitz had to happen so that postwar Germans could be intimidated, terrorized, and kept in check morally. The historical phenomena of 1933–1945 become important not in and of themselves but as discursive markers.

In viewing Hitler himself as a function of modernization, Syberberg is not far from recent historiographic approaches to Hitler as a modernizer.[17] "I believe him [Hitler] to be the brilliant medium of world history in the demonic self-interest of this technological century of mass movements," writes Syberberg (18). Syberberg's language is nineteenth century, but his thinking resonates with contemporary historiography. The director agrees with Hitler himself in seeing Hitler as the tool of fate but differs in that he, unlike Hitler, sees Hitler as a tool for the destruction, not the resurrection of German culture. As Syberberg writes, "Hitler's profiteers were Stalin's Russia, which expanded into the middle of Europe, the United States, which inherited Europe's West, and Israel, which founded itself" (119). Syberberg's argument that the two post–World War II superpowers profited from Hitler's defeat is obviously true; and that the foundation of Israel was directly related to the Holocaust and Hitler's defeat can hardly be denied, even if Syberberg's argumentation seems to fly in the face of logic by implying that the "profiteers" actually wanted to be attacked by Hitler. That victors benefit from their victories is hardly a new or surprising observation. Syberberg adds, "It is difficult to believe in ingratitude on the part of the victors toward their Hitler, against this agent of their secret desires; and not to believe in the secret desire that he [Hitler] should do it, that it should become, called to service by the world spirit up to the destruction of everyone, through us" (120). Syberberg's conception of agency here is significant: it is the "world spirit" that is the agent of destruction, cheered on by the United States and its allies; while "we" Germans are simply tools being used by a foreign power. Hitler, in other words, is a secret and highly successful puppet of the Allies in their plan to destroy German culture. While the conspiratorial elements of Syberberg's thinking may seem absurd here, the central problem continues to be Hitler as an agent of modernization and the dark side of modernity and Enlightenment, in which, Syberberg insists, the Germans alone are not complicit. Such an argument is not as easy to dismiss.

Syberberg does not believe in either human agency or coincidence as a factor in history; he is a historical structuralist. Hitler is not really even a person in Syberberg's scheme; he is simply an embodiment or a vessel of powerful currents in world history, which is always primarily aesthetic history. Here again Syberberg's thinking is consistent with recent trends in historiography, which focus on large-scale structures rather than individual intentions. For Syberberg the primary agents in history are a "Weltgeist" leading with seeming inexorability to a completely degraded and bastardized materialist consumerist culture and an aesthetic fundamentalism that arises out of resistance to that "Weltgeist." Hitler and the Holocaust were, for Syberberg, incarnations of precisely such a resistance that backfired: noble but failed warriors of the resistance (80). Germany, in Syberberg's view, is or at least ought to be the land of aesthetic resistance to a brutalizing, degrading modernity.

With regard to art itself, Syberberg writes, "Since the devil's aesthetic was called Hitler, and since the European culture of beauty which is not out for profits and whose heroes are unpaid led to Auschwitz, the revenge now is art as the business of the ugly, mocking cripple" (48). If Hitler and the Germans had tried to eliminate what the National Socialists called "degenerate art" and install a regime based on pure aesthetic beauty, then revenge against Hitler and the Germans meant the triumph of the ugly and degenerate—again and again Syberberg uses the term "cripple," even going so far as to posit a postwar "world of spiritual crippling" (124) with its own degenerate aesthetics—and the banishment of the beautiful. Syberberg's thinking is extremely fuzzy here. He does not explain why "the European culture of beauty . . . led to Auschwitz"—was the primary purpose of the death camps really the destruction of ugliness and the creation of beauty? He instead believes that the "culture of beauty" had to lead to Auschwitz and leaves no doubt in stating it. "The goal, however, was life, to realize art, beauty as the highest freedom down to the collapse of 1945" (58). That aesthetics was of utmost importance to the National Socialists is doubtlessly true; and that the Nazis did indeed seek to eliminate people and races they believed to be ugly is also true; but Syberberg seems to conflate all phenomena as part of a monocausal and highly implausible quest for beauty. Moreover, Syberberg leaves it unclear as to why it was precisely the Germans who became the willing tools of the world spirit in the destruction of their own culture. Syberberg suggests that in resisting the onslaught of modernization Germans ironically became the servants of modernization:

And whoever asks why it was that Germany, the *Volk* of culture in the middle of Europe, was capable of such things as in its most recent past, then one has to answer that it had to be precisely this country, the most neglected of the peoples of the world, men and women who have sacrificed their lives for the eternity of art [again we have here the idea of Auschwitz as an aesthetic program], always the most foolish and comical between pathos and gnome-like awkwardness, especially when it came to the inventions of the senses, to food, incapable of love and untalented. They were needed and used for the uncanniness of the historical deed, because the world spirit walks over corpses and art consumes the world. (142)

This is powerful rhetoric but not very strong as an explanation for an admittedly problematic and complex historical phenomenon. In contrast to insist on the fundamental nature of Hitler's anti-Semitism his personal agency seems much more convincing.

Syberberg refers to Germany and/or its parts variously as Europe's "backbone" (77), the "center of Europe" (18), "the central country of Europe" (56), "the middle of the world" (185), "just yesterday the most boring country of Europe and now the most exciting point and the center of the world" (144). He writes that "the decision about Europe will be made not in Warsaw and not in Budapest, but here; therefore the annoyance and the fear of Berlin" (139). Berlin is for him the "center of the world, the last stand of hope" (145). Syberberg writes that "since the opening of the wall in the middle of the continent this old structure of culture has found a new symbolic middle" (152). The director is thus torn between a view of Germany as victim to the capitalist-materialist world spirit and Germany as the most powerful locus of aesthetic resistance to the world spirit. While the two views appear mutually contradictory, they nevertheless form a dialectical unity in Syberberg's thinking. More problematic is Syberberg's assessment of the relative strength of the German alternative in the late 1980s and early 1990s. Occasionally Syberberg writes that the world of German art and authenticity that he sees as having existed up until 1945 is lost forever; occasionally he seems to think that it can be resurrected. This tension in the book is due at least in part to the circumstances of its writing: shortly before, during, and after the autumn 1989 revolution in the German Democratic Republic. In the parts written before the revolution Syberberg tends toward a heroic pessimism, writing at one point somewhat confusingly about the space–time continuum of his Western Pomeranian home, "I can not go back there, not because no childhood can ever be reentered, but because something else is there. The land is gone, no other is in its place, because the place of that time is gone . . . I cannot go back to this land of a Tolstoy, because that world no longer exists . . ." (95). At another point Syberberg writes that pre-1945 art is lost forever: "No one can save it for the future. It is like life condemned to death, without immortality" (127).

Yet the autumn 1989 revolution in the German Democratic Republic gives Syberberg hope for a resurrection and reunification of German art. While Syberberg dislikes the official GDR as much as any other anti communist, his hatred for the West is, if anything, stronger. In Syberberg's view, both American capitalism and Soviet communism were occupying armies and ideologies aimed at the heart of German culture. Moreover, significantly, both are agents of an instrumental rationality that is fundamentally ugly and inhumane. But American capitalism was more effective and harmful and insidious, while Soviet communism, precisely because it left less of a mark on the East German people, failed to completely expunge German culture as a culture of resistance to modernization. Syberberg uses the fact of tens of thousands of rapes of German women during the last year of the war as a metaphor for the situation of postwar German culture itself: "The Russians raped the Germans, the Americans gave them chocolate and they opened their legs willingly. Now the two peoples are coming together, the victims of rape and the victims of seduction"[18] (157). Better raped than seduced, at least according to Syberberg, because a rape at least allows the preservation of a sense of identity, however violated. For Syberberg the German Democratic Republic preserved an intact core of German culture which could not fail to have an impact on the degenerate West. In the German Democratic Republic Syberberg recognized traces of his lost and tragic Prussia. He refers to the GDR as "this shrunken Prussia from Kleve to Western Pomerania with Berlin and Brandenburg in the middle" (153). And it is here, in this shrunken Prussia that the basic elements of German historical and cultural memory have, according to Syberberg, been preserved. Syberberg has an unusual twist on the popular (or unpopular) 1990 question as to "What Remains" ("Was bleibt") of the German Democratic Republic. According to Syberberg, what will remain are not any socialist achievements but rather an essential German core that the Communists in the East, unlike the capitalists in the West, were unable to destroy. "The wealth of Eastern Europe is not what it became through socialist achievements, but rather what it remained, what Marxism left out through refusal or incapacity" (91). The challenge for the future will be to preserve and expand this German memory, to move from the aesthetics of ugliness and degeneracy to a new musical, tragic beauty, from the "Bonn democracy of money" (192) to a Berlin Reich of art. Here we are not far from the end of Wagner's *Meistersinger*, in which holy German art outlives the destruction of emperors and empires:

> Everything will depend upon the extent to which the Eastern part of Europe will have the strength to stand up against Western dangers, to resist many temptations at the root, if it can free itself from its deadly ossification. Already many Western attacks have pounded in vain upon the originality of Eastern spirit. The Western danger of self-destructive tendencies is deceptively strong, but in spite of many self-made obstacles in the East and lack of freedom of the political system, after the removal of these problems this reunification of Eastern and Western Europe can be one last chance. For after the erasure of Prussia Western temptation and Eastern powers of still unfathomed depths of thought and feeling stand face to face. Perhaps the East will awake to new reflection on an intelligent symbiosis. (90–91)

For Syberberg Germany is "the province Germany on the map of a European authenticity, which means the home of a new depth that has to be rediscovered" (181). In 1990, when East German intellectuals were criticizing their fellow countrymen for rushing into Western capitalist materialism, Syberberg was, of course, on the losing side of the argument. But this fact does not negate the power of the fundamental critique of Western materialism that is shared by many in both East and West.[19]

It is too easy to dismiss Syberberg's ideas as the ramblings of an eccentric, self-obsessed, and confused curmudgeon unheeded in his own country, whose political education ended in boyhood somewhere toward the end of the Third Reich and who, in spite of the idiosyncratic modernism/postmodernism of his own films, remains fundamentally mired in a National Socialist critique of modernism and a glorification of physical strength and beauty. Syberberg is, after all, the man whose *Hitler* was a major triumph one and a half decades ago in France and the United States. His film was understood, like the work of the painter Anselm Kiefer, as an authentic expression of a German attempt to come to terms with themes, motifs, and myths from the unhappy German past. Syberberg addresses fundamental problems of modernity, postmodernity, and German identity in a way that is all the more powerful precisely because it seems so naive. In this sense Syberberg clearly perceives himself as something of a modern German reincarnation of Richard Wagner's *Parsifal*, the "pure fool" who, precisely because of his lack of sophistication, achieves salvation in Wagner's last music drama, upon which Syberberg based his most successful film, and from which he took much of the music for *Hitler*. The similarities between Syberberg's description of the German people as "foolish and comical" but nevertheless sacrificing themselves for "the eternity of art," cited above, and his own view of himself and his project cannot be ignored. Even after the publication of Syberberg's 1990 book, Thomas Elsaesser declared that "because Syberberg raises questions about the utopias both promised and betrayed by popular culture and populist politics, his thesis deserves to be heard,"[20] while historian Rudy Koshar reaffirmed *Hitler*'s status as an "extraordinary work," demanding that it "deserves more sympathetic and thorough consideration by historians than it has had so far."[21] It is, of course, true that Syberberg continues to be largely marginal in political discourse within Germany itself, and that his thinking is widely criticized. But this fact alone does not indicate either that Syberberg is fundamentally wrong or that his thinking does not reflect important currents in contemporary Germany. On the contrary, the fact of Syberberg's marginalization and the allergic reactions to his thinking inside Germany may well indicate that he has touched a raw and very much live nerve. In his very successful portrayal and positioning of himself as an outsider in contemporary German life Syberberg continues a tradition that dates back to Friedrich Nietzsche's *Untimely Meditations* and Thomas Mann's *Reflections of a Non-Political Man*, as well as to the spirit of the conservative revolutionaries, all of whom also portrayed themselves as nonconformists in a world of cultural regimentation and homogenization. Whether we like it or not, Syberberg matters, in spite of—indeed even because of—the fact that he continues so successfully to portray himself as an outsider in German intellectual life. Even if Syberberg's book is now sold primarily through right-wing mail-order catalogues and cannot be found in most bookstores, it resonates, like his film, with the spirit of its times.

The fact of this resonance and of a resurgence in conservative anticapitalism was clearly demonstrated by the 1993 publication, first in *Der Spiegel* and then in *Der Pfahl*, of playwright Botho Strauß's controversial essay

"Anschwellender Bocksgesang" ("Goat Song, Swelling Up"), which picked up on many of the themes Syberberg had raised in his book.[22] In the wake of the general conservative realignment of Germany after unification, several broad political and cultural debates emerged by the middle of the 1990s. Critics like Frank Schirrmacher declared "the end of the literature of the Federal Republic"; pedagogues called for a new strictness and discipline in German schools, particularly as a result of growing youthful right-wing violence against foreigners, the disabled, and homosexuals; military strategists suggested that it was now important for Germany to take part, along with its NATO and United Nations allies, in military actions like the 1991 Gulf War or in humanitarian relief actions such as the 1992–1993 efforts in Somalia; philosophers and writers asked how it was possible to develop a sense of values in a society devoted entirely to the pursuit of money; and political scientists and historians asked whether, given the changing situation in Central and Eastern Europe, Germany's integration into the West needed to continue or rather, ought to be a thing of the past. Botho Strauß's essay was one of the most important contributions to the ongoing conservative reorientation. Strauß's plays, books, and essays had frequently and critically depicted the empty sterility of West German life. In the 1991 *Final Chorus*, whose title referred to the final chorus of Beethoven's Ninth Symphony, played during the 1990 Berlin festivities celebrating German unification, Strauß had portrayed a self-absorbed, trivial West Germany completely unprepared to deal with the arrival of the national in the form of a St. John the Baptist-like crier who repeatedly shouted the word "Germany!" into the quotidian boredom of postindustrial life. In the final passage of the play, one of the characters symbolically defeathers and devours a German eagle.[23] In his 1993 play *Equilibrium*, Strauß portrayed a Germany beginning to lose its equilibrium in the face of deep emotional currents and longing. *Equilibrium* was the story of the relationships between a materialist German businessman, who declares that "the world will be totally liberal, or it won't exist at all!", a fundamentalist son, who calls West German materialism a "spiritual bully, a liberal moloch that has transformed our life into a stinking trash heap. Europe is sick. Much sicker than we think . . .,"[24] and the businessman's more emotional, mysterious wife, who declares that beneath the facade of placid liberal materialism deeper mythic forces are seething:

> Somewhere behind all the silly words, behind our painful nervousness something of the tragic life must be hidden, something for which we don't have the right expression. Do you understand? It doesn't show itself to us. We make faces, we rush past one another, and yet we feel it, somewhere behind us something big, strong is moving, something for which we're not providing the right face, the right hands, the right container.[25]

Strauß's essay seemed to sum up much of the post-unification ferment in German intellectual life. "The song of the goat" was a literal translation of the Greek word, tragedy, which means "goat song." In giving his essay this title, Strauß rather vaguely alluded back to Friedrich Nietzsche's *Birth of Tragedy*, in which the figure of the goat-man or satyr, "the offspring of a longing for the primitive and the natural" as well as "the archetype of man, the embodiment of his highest and most intense emotions," is the choral singer whose song gives birth to tragedy itself.[26] Nietzsche's influential essay of 1872, itself a summing up of Nietzsche's youthful thinking and a launching pad for Nietzsche's subsequent spectacular career as a philosopher, had been an invocation of the power of art and culture, particularly tragedy, in the face of a sterile Socratic rationalist culture which Nietzsche believed to have run its course. Strauß's essay was also an invocation of the power of tragedy which lurked inexorably and inevitably behind the shallow accomplishments of West German consumerism. If Nietzsche, with Schopenhauer, had argued that the root of human life was suffering, and that in its Greek origins tragedy had been a sacred musical-religious ritual that enabled human beings to bear an otherwise unbearable existence, Strauß declared that the materialist West had reached its limits and was facing catastrophe without the hope of cultural traditions that would help it survive:

> The rumblings we are now hearing, the negative sensibility of competing reactions that immediately transform themselves into outbreaks of hatred, are seismic premonitions, anticipations of a greater danger that announces itself through those who will feel it at its worst.[27]

The young right-wing hooligans in East and West Germany beating up on and killing foreigners, the disabled, and homosexuals, Strauß argued, were in fact the unfortunate messengers of even greater tragedies and catastrophes to come. The increasing volatility and unpleasantness of German public life, Strauß suggested, came from the feeling that an entire way of life had reached its unnatural limit, and that it was impossible to go on with the thoughtless, smug, wasteful materialism of the West German past. Strauß referred to the general feeling of fear as "the terror of premonition" ("der Terror des Vorgefühls").[28] Like Hans Jürgen Syberberg, Strauß mourned the loss of what he saw as the most valuable part of Germany's cultural heritage: its irrationalism as a critique of economic utilitarianism and materialism. An economic philosophy that saw money as the only value that offered no protection at a time of declining standards of living, whereas spiritual and cultural values remained unaffected by economic shrinkage. But Germany's cultural heritage was dead, Strauß suggested, and those who had helped kill it—German liberals—were the ones who would need it most in the coming crises:

> It is too bad, quite simply too bad that our traditions have been ruined. Yes, our culture is rotting outside in front of the gates like a cargo of valuable nourishment which the population has to go without because of some tariff disputes. Our culture is wasting away in front of the limits of an arrogant overestimation of contemporary life, it is dying in the face of the politicized ignorance of educational and youth institutions that have been constipated for one or two generations, epicenters of the darkest Enlightenment, which find themselves in an endlessly ambivalent battle of temptation and rejection against the spirits of a repetition of history: "Beware the beginnings!" . . . Oh! Make a useful beginning yourselves![29]

In the face of growing cultural sterility, Strauß suggested, tragedy was inevitable, even if one knew nothing of the form it would ultimately take:

> We know nothing about the face of the future tragedy. All we can hear is the sound of the mysteries growing stronger, the song of the goat in the depths of our actions. The sacrificial hymns swelling at the very center of what we have created.[30]

While Strauß referred implicitly back to Friedrich Nietzsche in his analysis of the contemporary German situation, his concept of tragedy was nevertheless different from Nietzsche's. For Nietzsche, tragedy had been an art form that helped people deal with inevitable suffering. For Strauß, tragedy was the suffering itself, and there seemed no hope of an art form that would help human beings deal with it. Nietzsche's essay on the origins of tragedy had also been a lament on what he saw as the death of tragedy, the dying out of all that was natural, honest, and real in human culture—culminating in the cry that nature itself was gone: "Great Pan is dead!"—a lament that antedated and foreshadowed the subsequent lament that God Himself was dead. Strauß's essay, on the contrary, was a reminder that in spite of magical appearances, irrational forces were at work in society and in nature that would bring about the end of Western sterility and materialism. Nietzsche's essay had been a call for the rebirth of tragedy as a saving art form; Strauß's essay was a call for the rebirth of tragedy as a beautiful catastrophe, as a kind of cleansing, purifying flood or Armageddon, of the sort that some ecological fundamentalists had dreamed of in the early 1980s.[31] Like so many other cultural conservatives, Strauß had been strongly influenced by German ecological philosophy of those years:

> It was the ecologists who first cried out that things can't go on in this way, driving it into our consciousness with some success. The dictum that there

are limits could be translated into politics, morality, and social economy. The limits of freedom and permissiveness show themselves quite clearly in what we have created.[32]

And like other cultural conservatives, including Alain de Benoist, Botho Strauß declared that there was no such thing as a Third Path between social-ism and capitalism, since both socialism and capitalism were different man-ifestations of economic materialism. On the contrary, there were only two paths, according to Botho Strauß: acceptance of the materialist, economic status quo or forceful opposition to it. Echoing de Benoist, Botho Strauß also suggested that there was only one significant conflict in modern West German society: between (decadent Western) materialism and (healthy German) idealism. All other conflicts and forces were merely paper tigers:

> Irreconcilable conflict exists today only between the realm that is striving for political and social hegemony over spirit, morality, science, and faith; and, on the other hand, decisive opposition to such claims of hegemony. There is in a certain sense a political correlate to resistance to and denial of the claims to total power of the political. A spiritual reserve which does battle against polit-ical relativizations in the name of the wisdom of the peoples, in the name of Shakespeare, in the name of demoting worldliness, in the name of improving the human strength to suffer.[33]

In suggesting such an opposition, Botho Strauß was aligning himself with a long German tradition of dichotomies: culture versus civilization, art versus money, spirit versus politics, personality versus mass, community versus society, quality versus quantity, in which the first term in the dichotomy always represents the "healthy" wisdom of Germanic tradition and the sec-ond the decadent rationalism of Western materialism. The spirit of the German *Kulturnation* was raising its head after a long period of sleep.

Strauß's essay caused a massive intellectual controversy in Germany after its publication in February of 1993. This controversy continued for the next several years and was still raging at the middle of the decade. Strauß was attacked by many as a cryptofascist, but praised by others as the brave res-cuer of an important and sadly neglected German tradition. Even one year later, in the spring of 1994, Ignatz Bubis, the President of the Central Council of Jews in Germany, accused Strauß of being one of the "spiritual pathbreakers" for the brutal neo-Nazi hooligans burning Turkish women and children alive and preying on foreigners, the disabled, and homosexuals. Moreover, Strauß's intervention in the national debate led to renewed dis-cussion of the place of traditional conservatism in contemporary German life, and to a renewed conservative questioning of Germany's materialism and relationship with the West, particularly the United States of America.

Increasingly it became clear that with reunification it was not just the old German Democratic Republic that had disappeared. With it had disappeared an entire framework of international, intellectual, and political antagonisms and structures which served to provide the Federal Republic with a political and military focus. The "change from the Federal Republic into Germany," as Dan Diner, a historian at the University of Tel Aviv, called it,[34] had meant more than simply the expansion of the old Federal Republic. It had meant a qualitative change in social and political culture. Diner suggested that the change affected "basic concepts of political speech and semantics, it is affecting institutions and, evidently, undermining the system of political parties." Not only that, but the Federal Republic's very westernness was seriously and massively being called into questions by conservatives for the first time. Arnulf Baring wrote that sixteen million East Germans were perfectly capable of pulling sixty million West Germans substantially to the East,[35] and East German satirist Mathias Wedel wrote that East Germans were changing the face of the Federal Republic: "The Easternization of the Federal Republic has begun."[36] There was growing fear that West Germany's commitment to western values and democracy had been nothing but an epiphenomenon of the larger East–West struggle, destined to disappear with the struggle itself. With the growing internationalization of the world economy, further progress on European integration and union, and further "normalization" of Germany itself, this debate promised to be one of the most significant aspects of post-unification German culture and politics. Reunification had opened a blocked path to an almost forgotten cultural past.

Notes

1. Fritz Stern, *The Politics of Cultural Despair* (Berkeley: University of California Press, 1961).
2. Armin Mohler, *Die konservative Revolution in Deutschland 1918–1932: Ein Handbuch* (Darmstadt: Wissenschaftliche Buchgesellschaft, 1972).
3. Stefan Breuer, *Anatomie der konservativen Revolution* (Darmstadt: Wissenschaftliche Buchgesellschaft, 1993), p. 180.
4. On Alain de Benoist and his development as an intellectual, see Pierre-Andre Taguieff, *Sur la Nouvelle Droite: Jalons d'une analyse critique* (Paris: Descartes & Cie, 1994).
5. Alain de Benoist, "Zwang zur deutschen Geburt," interview in Stefan Ulbrich, ed., *Gedanken zu Großdeutschland* (Vilsbiburg: Arun, 1990), p. 219.
6. Ibid., p. 205.
7. Ibid., p. 207. Emphasis in original.
8. Little has yet appeared in English on Syberberg's 1990 book. The most extensive analysis to date has been Ian Buruma, "There's No Place Like Heimat," *The New York Review of Books* v.37, n.20 (December 20, 1990): pp. 34–43. See also

Marilyn Berlin Snell's related interview with Syberberg, "Germany's Heart: The Modern Taboo," *New Perspectives Quarterly* v.10, n.1 (Winter 1993): pp. 20–25, which deals with similar topics but does not mention the book explicitly; and John Rockwell, "The Re-Emergence of an Elusive Director," *The New York Times*, September 2, 1992, C13, 15.

9. On that debate, see my "The Politics of German Literature," *Monatshefte* v.84, n.1 (Spring 1992): pp. 46–58.

10. Serge Schmemann, "Kohl, the Man for the German Moment," *The New York Times*, July 1, 1990, pp. 1, 4.

11. Russell A. Berman, *Cultural Studies of Modern Germany: History, Representation, and Nationhood* (Madison: University of Wisconsin Press, 1993), p. 7.

12. Thorsten Hinz, "Großes Theater, schwächer die Theorie," *Junge Freiheit*, November 21, 1994, p. 12.

13. Friedrich Nietzsche, *The Birth of Tragedy and The Case of Wagner*, trans. Walter Kaufmann (New York: Vintage, 1967), p. 52.

14. Hans Jürgen Syberberg, *Vom Unglück und Glück der Kunst in Deutschland nach dem letzten Kriege* (Munich: Matthes & Seitz, 1990), p. 30. All future references to this book contain page numbers in parentheses.

15. Marshall McLuhan, *Understanding Media: The Extensions of Man* (New York: McGraw-Hill, 1964), p. 7.

16. Jürgen Habermas, *Eine Art Schadensabwicklung* (Frankfurt: Suhrkamp, 1987), p. 75.

17. See, e.g., Martin Broszat, ed., *Bayern in der NS-Zeit*, six volumes (Munich: Oldenbourg, 1977–1983); Rainer Zitelmann, *Hitler: Selbstverständnis eines Revolutionärs* (Hamburg: Berg, 1991) and Rainer Zitelmann and Eckhard Jesse, eds., *Nationalsozialismus und Modernisierung* (Darmstadt: Wissenschaftliche Buchgesellschaft, 1991). In English, see David Schoenbaum, *Hitler's Social Revolution: Class and Status in Nazi Germany, 1933–1939* (Garden City: Doubleday, 1966) and Jeffrey Herf, *Reactionary Modernism* (Cambridge: Cambridge University Press, 1984).

18. This is not the place for an exploration of the sexual imagery of German "liberation." However, Syberberg is not completely outside the bounds of contemporary German discussion in his musings. While Syberberg was writing these lines Helke Sander was working on her controversial film *BeFreier und Befreite* ("Liberators and the Liberated," a title that plays with the German word "Freier" that also means "suitor"; David Jonathan Levin has suggested the translation "Liberators Take Liberties"), about the problem of rapes, particularly by Soviet soldiers, in Germany during the last year of the war. Christoph Hein's short story "Die Vergewaltigung" ("The Rape") deals with the same issue. Christoph Hein, *Exekution eines Kalbes* (Berlin: Aufbau, 1994), pp. 131–138. Much earlier, in 1970, Christa Wolf's short story "Liberation Day" had already presented American soldiers as gum-chewing seducers. See Christa Wolf, "Liberation Day," trans. Heike Schwarzbauer and Rick Takvorian in *Granta* 42 (Winter 1992), pp. 55–64, esp. pp. 63–64.

19. By 1994 Syberberg had admitted that his hopes for German reunification had been dashed, and that the process of cultural erosion had continued. See Hans Jürgen Syberberg, *Der verlorene Auftrag* (Vienna: Karolinger, 1994).

20. Thomas Elsaesser, "Hitler, ein Film aus Deutschland," *Sight and Sound* v.2, n.5 (September 1992): pp. 49–50; here, p. 50.
21. Rudy Koshar, "Hitler: A Film from Germany," *American Historical Review* v.96, n.4 (October 1991): pp. 1122–1124; here, p. 1124. On Syberberg's *Hitler*, see also Koshar, "*Hitler: A Film from Germany*: Cinema, History, and Structures of Feeling," in Robert A. Rosenstone, ed., *Revisioning History: Film and the Construction of a New Past* (Princeton: Princeton University Press, 1994), pp. 155–173.
22. For a useful analysis of Strauß's recent writing, see Arthur Williams, "Botho Strauß: The Janus-Head above the Parapet—Final Choruses and Goat Songs without Beginnings," in Arthur Williams and Stuart Parkes, eds., *The Individual, Identity and Innovation: Signals from Contemporary Literature and the New Germany* (Bern: Peter Lang, 1994), pp. 315–344.
23. Botho Strauß, *Schlußchor* (Munich: Hanser, 1991).
24. Botho Strauß, *Das Gleichgewicht* (Munich: Hanser, 1993), p. 53.
25. Ibid., p. 27.
26. Nietzsche, *The Birth of Tragedy*, p. 61.
27. Botho Strauß, "Anschwellender Bocksgesang," *Der Spiegel* v.6 (1993): p. 204.
28. Ibid., p. 204.
29. Ibid., p. 207.
30. Ibid., p. 205.
31. See Stephen Brockmann, Julia Hell, Reinhilde Wiegmann, "The Greens: Images of Survival in the Early 1980s," in *From the Greeks to the Greens: Images of the Simple Life* (Madison: University of Wisconsin Press, 1989), pp. 127–144.
32. Strauß, "Anschwellender Bocksgesang," p. 205.
33. Ibid.
34. Dan Diner, "Feinde des Westens," *Frankfurter Allgemeine Zeitung*, May 11, 1994, p. 33.
35. Arnulf Baring, *Deutschland, was nun?* (Berlin: Siedler bei Goldmann, 1991).
36. Mathias Wedel, *Einheitsfrust* (Berlin: Rowohlt, 1994); cited in Henryk M. Broder, " 'Zu kurze Banane,' " *Der Spiegel* v.12 (March 21, 1994): p. 210. Wedel used the neologism "Ossifizierung," which translates literally as "easternization" and is a play on the word "Ossi," i.e., a resident of the former German Democratic Republic. The word also suggests a relationship to "ossification."

CHAPTER THREE

FEAR AND LOATHING AFTER 9/11: GERMAN INTELLECTUALS AND THE AMERICA-DEBATE

Klaus R. Scherpe

I will try to keep out emotions in order to make clear some of the German reactions to the September 11 suicide attacks in New York and Washington. By "make clear" I mean observe *attitudes* (the *German* word "Haltung" is important), not to only report *opinions*. Sometimes odd for the German intellectuals—writers, artists, journalists, editors, and researchers in the field of social sciences and the humanities—to not only direct the attention at reality as such but also at the reality of *symbolic* speech, the rhetoric of politics. And, of course, refer to the background of German history, the collective memory: the past being a reservoir for the very present. "Ground zero" for a person of my generation in Germany, refers to what has been called the *zero degree* in our history, the *Zero Hour* of 1945 (die *Stunde Null*), not as in America where *Ground Zero* has been connected to Los Alamos.

I will argue that anti-Americanism and pro-Americanism as experienced after September 11 together belong as a result to the past German American relationship. Moreover, the immediate solidarity felt with the United States as well as the recent criticism can be understood in a pattern of *kairos* (action) and *chronos* (evolution) used by historians to explain the different experiences of time. I would also like to suggest that what we normally call *war* and *violence* must be redefined. This, however, is more a task for the military historian or the political scientist. I will only follow some of the intellectuals' responses in an attempt to spell out what *cultural* violence in particular and *cultural politics* in general mean in the year after the event. Referring to cultural politics we are, of course, on the side of the "soft categories," the "opinion machine" and the "fear market," moral issues and aesthetic devices, challengers to the notions of the human.

When I read an article written by the critic Michael Rutschky on "Anti-Americanism" recently,[1] it became clear to me why the United States has become a kind of symbolic fatherland to many Germans, including myself, in a very special way. In postwar West Germany the United States was the *paternal nation* when Germans felt that there was no German nation any longer. America represented the helping hand, the GI who gave away bars of chocolate and Camel cigarettes, the Marshall Plan, American reeducation as reported by German writers like Alfred Andersch and Hans Werner Richter, who were prisoners of war in a West Virginia camp in 1946. We first learned, Andersch wrote, the definition of democracy. "Democracy is the art of compromising." We learned what it meant to have equal rights, "freedom of speech"; then, twenty-five years later the welcome of American troops in Berlin a few days after the erection of the wall in 1961, and John F. Kennedy's "Ich bin ein Berliner." In short: The United States were the "parents' imago" in all these matters of democracy. But then came the rebellious sons: "We shall overcome," the Vietnam war, intervention politics, race riots: that is "arrogance of power" which has been a German leitmotif of intellectual criticism since the Kaiserreich. Thus, one can argue, philo-Americanism and anti-Americanism somehow belong together, they can be symbolized in the generation pattern, in the pattern of a family relationship, and, of course, generally true, in patterns of otherness; the other is admired and demonized at the same time.

In the days after September 11 in Berlin all clichés, it seemed, became true: "We are all Americans," "Your house is my house"; phantom-pains, it was called later. "Berlin was hit in its unconscious," the *Frankfurter Allgemeine Zeitung* wrote on September 18, and referred to the switch of images: from the Berlin (or rather West Berlin)–New York identification of the nineteen seventies and eighties, the rhetoric of sprawling metropolitan life, back to visions of Berlin's postwar bomb sites, displaced persons, people wandering in the ruins, women clearing away the rubble, scenes of neighborhood friendship. I think the emergence of pictures like these was more than media spectacle. The most horrifying as well as the most joyful event is experienced as "the real thing." As in November 1989, when the Berlin wall was opened, "the medium was not message enough," to put it in terms of Marshall McLuhan. At that time people traveled to Berlin to see it all with "their own eyes," to touch the wall, to have it cut into small pieces. What happened then? Something like authenticity was restored, or rather a desire for authenticity, the magic of the "real thing."

In other words: In spite of all our electronic devices and permanent networking and recycling of pictures there still is this *difference in times*: the time of action and the time of reflection, *kairos* and *chronos*—the moment of strike and "blitz" on the one hand, the zero point of destruction, a kind of "timeout" in the flow of time, and, on the other hand, there is *continuity*, contemplation, the rebuilding of connections and the processing of what has happened. The "opinion machine" starts immediately afterward, as Susan Sontag said in her talk at the American Academy in Berlin on September 15; as a critic of the media circulation she confessed that she hesitated one whole afternoon, to join it, but then succumbed to it, unfortunately. At the same time the "fear market" was put into operation: the broad spectrum of good and evil, the threat and trauma of such horrific events and the shock of the unforeseen, the unbelievable, even the sublime.

If we take all this seriously in terms of culture and cultural politics (opinions, habits, mentalities) we have to define violence, focus on this horrific act, and also define *terrorism*, as the political scientist Herfried Münkler from Humboldt University did (to whom I will refer later). Cultural theorists since Walter Benjamin's *Kritik der Gewalt* started out with a definition of violence as *pure* violence, that is, as an action of absolute presence, unconditioned, unexpected, and, therefore, of high intensity: immediate action, *without*—and this is the point—any form or shape, regardless of any circumstances and consequences. Of course an "immediate" definition like this, does not provide the whole truth: it says nothing about so-called *structural* violence, about strategy, psychology, and relationships maintained by power, nothing about politics and warfare. But still, when we take this radical definition of the radical moment, the outburst of violence, we get a *feeling* and regain an *idea* about the tremendous effort to come to terms with this event beyond all events: the extreme challenge to politics, science, law, the media, art, and literature. There is no political party, organization, or cultural institution in Germany, which denies this tremendous challenge, nobody who would deny this *zero-fact*, so to speak, the scar, the crater, this zero point of attitudes and strategies.

The sentence "Nothing will be as it used to be" is right and wrong at the same time. There is this a point of no return, the *Wendepunkt* that will last in our collective memory, especially, I am sure, in Germany. But since September 11 this sentence has to be qualified according to different activities. In politics German American friendship, cooperation, and competition will certainly be what they used to be, but at the same time the issue will be *dramatized* according to economic and military demands and challenges, different cultural standards, and the language being used. Chancellor Schröder's "challenge to civilization" ("Herausforderung an die Zivilisation") brings to the minds of some people in Germany the term "Zivilisationsbruch," a term closely connected with *Auschwitz*, the corruption of Western civilization by Nazi barbarism. To reduce complexity in such a sentence can probably not be avoided in the rhetoric of political speech. Such is the tenacity of symbolic formulas referring to traditions, covering actual events with quotations from past leaders such as Hitler, Stalin and others. But politicians are *actors*, not *reflectors*, philosophers, poets, or the like. A German politician will avoid, using the word "axes," so closely connected with the fascist politics of the Führer, the Duce, and the Tenno. No German politician, right or left, I am sure, would voluntarily speak of a "crusade" as President Bush did (the German word "Kreuzzug" being heavier), or talk about a "fight between good and evil." Our collective memory would remind us that such a catchword was common in August/September 1914 at the outbreak of World War I, when it was used to denounce the enemy. German politicians of our day, of course, have other formulas to reduce the complexity of political facts than simple binary opposites, and, as in America, this is part of the political exercise of power.

I come back to my first point: the need to speak about the unspeakable, to represent in words and images the horror that actually could not be represented, even though it was repeated again and again on the television screen. Media experts said that the pictures of the September 11 did a lot in fulfilling the terrorists' psychological strategy to stamp the *imaginary* into the real, imprint the wound. The metaphors we read in the German newspapers as well: "America is deeply hurt," the "strike right into the heart"— did not originate in the microelectronic systems. They stem from the archives of the "human condition." Identification with what had happened was represented in the well-known language of body and soul. In the initial few days a sense of mourning for the victims, passed on from person to person, was felt in the neighborhoods. We had eyewitnesses, personal experiences summed up in community spirit and solidarity. And this—*only* this, as it turned out—was what people could share across the Atlantic in phonecalls and reports back and forth. Alexander Osang, a journalist who writes for *Der Spiegel, Die Zeit,* and *Berliner Zeitung,* sent eyewitness reports of survival in Manhattan, striving for ultimate concreteness when he wrote: "On the floor of our apartment lies the yellow helmet of a construction worker they gave to me at ground zero. I keep it as a trophy, and it will show me for a while how close I was."[2] Is not this, one might ask, a certain kind of *fetishism*: fetishizing the concrete (the yellow helmet) because the whole cannot be conceived? Quite a natural reaction, though. But then suspicion rises: perhaps the faraway experience of solidarity, as in Germany ("We are all Americans"), rests only on this kind of fetishizing of the terrible experience? In that case we would have *sympathy* according to *kairos,* the actual experience; *solidarity* in contrast would depend, and it did indeed, on *chronos*: the German American experience of a shared history, continuously developed since the end of World War II.

The journalist Jane Kramer, reporting back to New York from Berlin and writing down her notes on German reactions for the *New Yorker,* does not mention details like these.[3] Kramer observed that as far as everyday life is concerned, one notices "Betroffenheit"—a typical German word expressing deep concern—a feeling that a terrorist might "sleep" comfortably next door, just as Atta, the terrorist leader, who steered one of the aircraft, "slept" in his apartment in the Hamburg-Harburg neighborhood. Jane Kramer's point here is that the feeling of solidarity ("We are all Americans") in Germany was soon transformed into a discussion of how to balance "transparency"—the "most revered word in West Germany since World War II," a fundamental democratic achievement, she writes, also referring to the Stasi practices in East Germany—with *security*? The problem lies, as Kramer sees it, in the word "balance." Otto Schily, the German minister of the interior, meanwhile managed to get his two packages of new security laws through the legislative. In Germany the US government was admired by some but mostly scorned for its rigid process of legislature: how strong they are, these Americans, but how far they have drifted from their own principles of democracy. There are two problems with German "cooperation," Kramer suggests. One is, of course, the assumed professional and financial inefficiency of the European allies, a frequent complaint on the American side, which offends the Germans in particular. The other is, as Otto Schily said while having a drink with his visitor from New York, the "problem of *political culture*." Individual rights of the citizen and human rights issues in general were significant imports from the United States to build up this democratic "political culture" that we now have in Germany. The intellectual and cultural elite in Germany, to sum up Jane Kramer's report, has its own "identity crisis." I would like to support this argument by my own thesis that the events of the September 11 were used to clarify and modify or simply to confirm long-held positions as the following examples will show.

Not much attention has been paid to East German attitudes. So I will briefly take up the case of the young poet laureate Durs Grünbein. In his Berlin diary published in the *FAZ* issue dated September 19, 2001, Grünbein is full of concern on the level of the *private* experience. He refers back to literary history, quoting from Joseph Conrad's *Heart of Darkness* ("the horror, the horror"), William Blake and T.S. Eliot's *The Waste Land* ("Ash Tuesday"), and he confesses (German poets are still going strong with confessions) that he feels—having lost the shelter of what he had thought to be the "Pax Americana" and remembering stories of bombed German cities in World War II—like a motherless child. Now he feels frightened by this "empty space" in the center where, to fill the gap, American flag waving patriotism takes command. It could be that Grünbein, the former GDR citizen, remembers another center, the communist central committee, which also occupied an empty space, the wasteland of civil society. I would hesitate to comment on what is more "irrational": American patriotism or this German angst of American patriotism, this fearful self-concern. In occupied Germany after the end of the war, American reeducation officers observed a typical German self-centeredness. In Grünbein it is not a lack of courage ("Why turn ourselves into a target"). It is more, I am afraid, this deeply rooted attitude of "leave me alone," more effective, to be sure, than any public confession of pacifism which could be dated back to communist politics in the GDR, as some columnists suggested.

Let me present another example of the German intellectual mind, which, I guess, must appear as being very strange to an American. Karlheinz Stockhausen, one of the best known present day German composers next to Hans Werner Henze and Wolfgang Rihm, declared in a press conference in Hamburg on September 16 that now we all would have to switch our thoughts. Commenting on the events of September 11 he said: "What happened is, of course, the greatest possible work of art which ever existed, that such minds in just one action can accomplish something that we could never dream of in music, that for ten years people practice incessantly and absolutely fanatically for one concert and then they die. That is the greatest work of art one can imagine in the whole cosmos. Just imagine what has happened. These are people who are so intent on that one and only performance, and then 5000 people are sent into resurrection in one moment. I could not do that."[4] A storm of protest broke loose in the German public and a long discussion followed: politicians, artists, and writers as well as institutions expressed their disgust, tried to explain, condemned, and sent numerous letters to the editors. In Hamburg, Stockhausen's concerts, in which two of his new works were to have been presented for the first time, were immediately cancelled by the officials. György Ligeti, the famous composer of Hungarian origin, reacted strongly when interviewed by *Financial Times Germany*. He felt that Stockhausen had taken the side of the terrorists and should be confined to an insane asylum.[5] György Konrad, the president of the Berlin Academy of Arts, said, more cautiously, that Stockhausen had not been elected a member of the academy for his political wisdom but for his art.

Looking back into the tradition of avant garde art, one finds exactly this kind of imagination, for instance, in Marinetti's futuristic dream to destroy Venice in order to rebuild it as a cathedral of the modern. Or in André Breton's famous surrealistic saying that one should fire a shot into the crowd to arouse protest. Incorporated in such provocations is the revolutionary impulse of breaking through the limits of autonomous art and draw attention to this very act of crossing and violating the border. Christoph Schlingensief, an author and performer from Berlin famous for his artistic intrusions into daily life in order to extract political consciousness, commented on Stockhausen in terms of the avant-garde.[6] Schlingensief found that

Stockhausen's offense showed how limited we are with our outright human concerns and moral consensus. Stockhausen's remarks might have been, he suggested, the strongest protest possible, intended to break the bounds of public opinion, stronger than those easy-going and well-meant protests and appeals which cost nothing. But art can also, according to Schlingensief, commit a crime, for example, a crime of aestheticism, like in Leni Riefenstahl's Nazi films which by virtue of their aesthetic aura justify the death of thousands and millions. On the other hand, art cannot be entitled simply to ensure the moral or political conventions. Apart from these inter-pretations of the event that take us back to cultural traditions, it is a fact that public opinion in Germany as well as in America was extremely sensi-tive toward any *incorrectness* of speech when it came to the events of September 11. "The bomb is the message," Florian Rötzer, a media expert, wrote to indicate that all kinds of speech, hate or hope, could and still can be directly connected to the mega event of communication which the suicide attacks on the WTC have become.[7]

Stockhausen's fruitless and fatal effort to express the unbelievable and unspeakable of the event in terms of avant-garde art ends up having metaphysical and religious dimensions: "Descent to Hell," "Devil's Work." This imaginary symbolism, closely connected with religious fundamentalism, has to be taken seriously as Jürgen Habermas said when he received the "Friedenspreis," awarded by the German publishers, in Paulskirche in Frankfurt am Main on October 14, 2001: "Religious fundamentalism is a modern phenomenon," according to the dialectics of modernism."[8] We cannot attribute it to the "others," the "barbarians"; fundamentalism unfolds its violence in the midst of our societies that Habermas argued, which we see as completely secularized, thus neglecting to take into account the other side, the dark side of enlightenment, as it is often called. Habermas took the opportunity to plead for more attention and a perma-nent deconstruction of essential and dogmatic beliefs. Religion, when it only follows such strict rules, is dangerous to civilization, and we should have been in a state of alert before the attacks. Beyond Habermas' argu-ment, the problem is, however, that religious beliefs are not only *substantial* but *proliferate*, dispersing elements of fundamental convictions here and everywhere, so that they cannot be grasped as such and at once.

This brings me to another point closely connected to religious funda-mentalism. The resonance of the traditional pattern of *apocalypse* can be found in a great number of the readings and writings on September 11, in America and Europe as well as in the Islamic world. According to Christian belief (*The Book of Revelation of St. John*), the end of the world comes as punishment to a world of sin (Sodom and Gomorrah), as catharsis and purification to clear the way to Heavenly Jerusalem. When German intellectuals read such newspaper headlines, highly symbolical, as "Angriff auf das Neue Babylon"[9] ("Attack on the New Babylon"), they took heed, of course. And again one can hear, in this context and remembering the cultural traditions of Germany, the sounds of anti-Americanism. For more than a hundred years America has been the epistemy of capitalism, the symbol of reckless modernization. In German literary history there are many fictions of a cataclysmic America, and of New York being destroyed as a symbol of modernization (in the novels of Max Dauthendey, Bernhard Kellermann, Gerhart Hauptmann). Apocalyptic thinking has always been part of utopian thinking, in Ernst Bloch's *Das Prinzip Hoffnung*, for example, "New life will spring from the ruins" is a slogan of the German socialist movement at the end of the nineteenth century. In our days, in countermovements, the attacks on globalization—the networks of multinational capitalism— again are understood as a *substantial* evil, which, when defeated will give way to a more human and authentic life. Apocalypse, of course, was also the basic idea in Oswald Spengler's German epic of cultural pessimism *Der Untergang des Abendlandes* (*The Ending of Western Civilisation*), written after the end of World War I (1918–1922). Spengler saw the "the money at the end of its successful career," something to get rid off like worn out clothes. Translations to the present are too obvious and don't have to be explained although capitalism's clothing has come up with more fantastic styles—In the Muslim world, as David Cook has spelt out[10] we find the apocalyptic belief that the modern world is a repetition of that sinful state of the world (according to *The Protocols* of the *Elders of Zion*), which prophet Mohammed had to clear away on the road to heaven, and, clearly enough, as Cook explains, America again is the "Great Babylon," Antichrist in person, the central symbol to be destroyed by an elite of men to repeat and fulfill the sacred prophecy.

When we read these pseudo-religious texts, be they historical or contemporary, as ideological and political outpourings, we can observe very clearly the disastrous effects of substantial and fundamental convictions. And again it becomes clear why critical European intellectuals like Paul Virilio, Giorgio Agamben or Umberto Eco feel something like a holy tremor when fundamental opposites like those of Heaven and Hell, of Good and Evil show up again in political rhetoric, now being used in reverse, in defense against the terrorism of Islamic fundamentalists. In Germany the intellectual elite, after the "apocalyptic disaster" of the 1000 Year Reich, cannot, by any means, "cooperate" linguistically or ideologically, in terms of a "holy war," "crusade," or "axis of evil." This rhetoric is extremely incriminating in Germany. And it can be, I am afraid, a new source of anti-Americanism when this kind of hate speech is used by official sources. The enemy, of course, must always be invented to build up a political strategy in times of war.

It would be naive to neglect this basic fact of political acting. And as Europeans know quite well—at least since the publications of the February 2002 manifesto by the 60 intellectuals in Washington D.C.[11]—the rhetoric of war on the part of the US government is, of course, "substantial" in preparing the way of American interests and influence. Among intellectuals naïve pacifism has become less prevalent, and this implies their preparedness to stop incipient civil wars, by military means if need be. The logic of destruction must be interrupted, not illustrated, Paul Virilio said in an article against the apocalypse as the ultimate reason of terrorism[12]; consequently he advocated political action by the Europeans, and not indifference and relaxation under the umbrella of US patronage. And public elites, of course, know about the catastrophic nonsense to compare anything with everything: New York to Babylon, Saddam Hussein to Adolf Hitler, Bin Laden to George W. Bush, or as one German did recently comparing Bin Laden's worldview to Ernst Jünger's fundamental scorn of a dying bourgeois world.[13] This delirium of reasoning also fits into the pattern of apocalyptic thought, Virilio claims. What is really needed are certain standards of a political culture across the borders.

Since September 11 some rearranging of the well-known arguments concerning Germany's culture and history could be observed, for the moment perhaps causing even more ideological problems and recalling again the so-called German identity crisis (as a nation, as a state and a society after World War II). Karl Heinz Bohrer in the editorial of the November 2001 issue of his journal *Merkur*, took the opportunity of rehashing certain national and cultural standards of reasoning. For many years, notably in the East–West debates after the fall of the Wall, Bohrer was a prominent spokesman for a renewed German "nationstate" ("Staatsnation"), seen also as a revival of the traditional standard of a German "cultural nation" ("Kulturnation"). He stressed that the nation should no longer feel burdened and confined by the shame and guilt of Auschwitz. Bohrer's demand (or rather command) for greater self-confidence instead of endless self-criticism to some people sounds convincing in terms of a radical cultural critique. After September 11 Bohrer was extremely successful in stirring up the German feuilletons from *Die Zeit* to the *FAZ*. But if one takes a closer look and at the same time looks back into German cultural history, one can see that this effect was achieved by well-known formulae of the past, Carl Schmitt's political philosophy of decision ("Philosophie der Entscheidung"), for example, advocates the "state of emergency" versus the principles of democracy, parliamentarianism, division of power etc. Bohrer shares the elite conservativism of Carl Schmitt and Ernst Jünger, to whom he devoted his dissertation. I feel that it is impossible that this kind of a nation-elitism, this heroic attitude on demand, which Bohrer assumed after September 11, could ever conform to America's new born popular heroism which is observed so somberly on the other side of the Atlantic.

"The murderous energies of today cannot be traced back to any tradition," Hans Magnus Enzensberger wrote in an article in the *FAZ* of September 18, 2001, thus accentuating the tremendous challenge of understanding the New York and Washington attacks on Western civilizations as a whole. But a closer look at Enzensberger's 1993 essay *Aussichten auf den Bürgerkrieg* shows that, like Bohrer, Enzensberger, after September 11 only renewed his conviction that global violence would follow global modernization after the collapse of the communist regime and the Cold War balance of power. A strong reaction against Enzensberger's book had come from Francis Fukuyama, who reviewed the English translation of his essay (published as *Civil Wars: From L.A. to Bosnia*) in the *New York Review of Books*. This is not surprising since Enzensberger turned Fukuyama's concept of the end of history as a success story of Western civilization upside down. With the notion that any terrorist leadership could equip itself with Western know-how and acquire an intimate understanding of the Western mentality and psychology, Enzensberger now fosters a more or less nihilistic prospect of "the end": the end of the universal concepts of human rights, of democracy, of what we used to call enlightenment—an apocalypse without catharsis. To highlight these speculations of an ultimate "state of emergency" Enzensberger goes back to a Nietzschean concept of self-destructiveness of reason, also to Freudian ideas of an irresistible pleasure in one's own demise: "What we are witnessing now," he proclaims, "is the globalization of another species' ancient custom: the human sacrifice."[14]

When you hear this you might ask yourself, as the New York author Walter Abish did in the title of his book *How German is it?* even though the frenchman Jean Baudrillard came up with the same nihilistic vision of self-destruction. Quoting Nietzsche's "only barbarians can defend themselves," Enzensberger obviously takes pleasure in presenting himself as a barbarian, elite style. This, I assume, might be part of his own *aesthetic* experience in reaction not only to September 11. To cut short my rationalistic criticism of such post-rational reasoning: Firstly, this is a well-known expression of the intellectual anxiety, German "angst," also concerning the intellectual's position itself, the outdated king's role of the *Dichter und Denker* leading public opinion. Secondly, it is the intellectuals' contribution to the "fear market," taking advantage of what Enzensberger himself calls the "gray area" where, as a result of a traumatic experience, certainties are lost and all manner of conspiracy theories fill the empty space.

In searching out among German intellectuals a more serious political analysis of what has happened on September 11 and what is to follow, being confronted as we are with a new kind of warfare, I would recommend the books and recent articles of Herfried Münkler, who like the war-historians John Keegan in Britain and Martin van Creveld in Israel, tries to spell out what "terrorism" means as a political-military strategy.[15] "Asymmetric warfare"—war between unequal opponents as we know it from guerrilla fighting and partisan activities—has risen to new heights. We must revise, Münkler suggests, our concept of "crossing borders" with which we only negotiated the economic, political, and cultural conflict in *times of peace*, as far as the Western world is concerned. This concept needs to be revised in the direction of "violating borders" as a civilian *and* military strategy, which operates destructively on a global scale and also within the homelands of civilization. *Global violence*, not taken at first glance, like Enzensberger's cataclysmic imagination as an unseen and unknown "murderous energy," but taken instead as a powerful strategy which combines civil and war economies, must lead us to certain redefinitions of the terminology so familiar to us. Consequently the word "der Feind" (the enemy as the symbolic "evil") has to be understood within a realistic concept of networking and information warfare, also words such as "state" and "nation" (all in contrast to Bohrer's resurrection of a "nationstate") must be rethought. Münkler uses the term "Entstaatlichung des Krieges" (denationalization of the war) consequently redefining "cooperation" (the alliance against terrorism) not only as a concept of agreement between governments but also as a concept of *cultural politics* dealing with *cultural violence*, so far an unknown contamination of structural, physical, and military violence. "The more developed the societies against which terrorist attacks are directed," Münkler writes, "the larger and more consequential their psychological effects will be."[16] With a high degree of urbanization, complex interconnections, and a strong commitment to cultural and political values Western societies are extremely vulnerable to terrorist networks, which infiltrate and use these structures as a weapon. For Münkler the "privatization of war" is *the* new condition for all future strategies against terrorism.

But what is meant by *cultural violence* in particular, on the level of attitudes, habits, and symbolic action? It can be executed by acts of humiliation, for instance by dishonoring central values of "the other" at significant points, by destroying symbols such as monuments, statues, and culturally significant constructions or, to provide further examples, one might also count as *cultural violence* the showing of icons, pictures, or significant videos, as well as the symbolic action of kidnapping or detaining of a prominent person, and, of course, burning a flag, or doing nothing more than showing a flag at a special moment, at a certain event. All this must be included in what we call *cultural violence* to indicate its overall potential that would need to be specified and differentiated according to terrorism and antiterrorist action.

The event itself—and this is my last example—can attract symbolic meaning even though it is meant as nothing more than a *discussion* of cultural violence. In Berlin the culturally interested public was recently shocked (at least some people were) when Richard Rorty—a member of a Trotzkian family, presently a professor at Stanford University, and well known for his philosophy of open-minded pragmatism—appeared at the *Schaubühne* that was once the stronghold of the Left and a seat of cultural revolution, Berlin style. It is significant that the debate with the guest speaker from California took place on Germany's Memorial Day, November 14. Rorty spoke out, as he had done before, against the reactionary Bush administration and its politics of unilateralism. But this time he too was harshly critical of multiculturalism. Inclusion and intrusion into other cultures, he argued, have always been part of the project of "secular humanism," and, if Western culture could pacify the world, he would go so far as to accept "MacDonaldization." Rorty, as we know, is a master of irony, and in Berlin he felt that he should say something at this point and at this place against a hypocritical anti-Americanism, as he put it, especially of the left in order to enjoy the comforts of American protectionism and, at the same time, refusing to accept the consequences of war against terrorism on the other. In the discussion following his statement it came up again: the *image of the father* and the disobedient son, America taking the lead and the Europeans following. Multiculturalism, one of the last gifts imported from America, helped in building up a culture of variety against centralism in postwar Germany, an unfinished project, as we know. Rorty spoke out against the naïve multiculturalism: a "culture of dialogue" does not work when "the other" goes by the name of Taliban and Bin Laden. Rorty accused the German intellectuals of idleness of thinking, being unwilling to negotiate their long-held positions in this extreme situation post-September 11 (which in a way is also true of Bohrer and Enzensberger, as we have seen). As was to be expected, there was open protest in Berlin's *Schaubühne* against this accusation, and in the ensuing discussion Rorty withdrew his reproach of anti-Americanism as a name for the German phenomenon he had just described. From my own observations I would not say that pro- or anti-Americanism was at stake here. As an American, Rorty reacted to the shock and fear of the absolute and unbelievable experience of the terrorist attack on his country, and he obviously felt that this absolute und unique event somehow lost focus in the discussion with the German audience by relating it to other issues and problems, namely those, at this point and at this place, of German history and culture, typical German fears and threats which were revived after September 11.

What was and still is at stake in these debates became evident in a commentary Wolf Lepenies, the former director of Berlin's Institute of

Advanced Studies (the Wissenschaftskolleg), delivered in the *Süddeutsche Zeitung* on February 5, 2002. The topic was once again *cultural politics* related to September 11. As Rorty had done, Lepenies stressed that something akin to a "cultural noninterference agreement" (intrusion into other cultures) does not exist ("eine Art kultureller Nichtverbreitungspakt"). What does exist, however, is on the one hand a desperate "UNESCO-Cosmopolitanism" of tolerance, as an anthropologist whom Lepenies quoted put it; while on the other hand there is Samuel P. Huntington's *Clash of Civilizations* which after September 11 could be reread as a "war of evil against good." Lepenies' point in the light of September 11 is that we have to rethink our use of the word "culture" or "civilization" so that we may learn something new not only about its meaning but also about its *function*: the strategies of cultural discourse. I agree with Lepenies when he states that the "dialogue of cultures" is too simplistic an expression not only in leftist discussions but also in the globalization discourse of economic liberalism if it is not accompanied by *cultural politics* of the so-called other, and if it does not take into consideration the mechanism of cultural *violence*. The promise of "equal rights" must be something more than "Sunday speeches" if it is not to become just another word for humilation. To quote Lepenies: "It is as if you were to pat somebody's shoulder whose hands and feet are tied up."

Germany—represented by its intellectual elite which is giving shape to cultural discourse—has indeed, as one can hear very often these days, lost its "innocence" after the heinous attacks of September 11. The diagnosis would somehow go like this: in Germany after two World Wars and the Holocaust we still have this so called *crisis of identity* as a nation, a state, and a culture, a state of affairs which has become more and more evident since reunification. If "innocence" means noninterference, a lack of authority and sovereignty, combined with a typical attitude of indulging in doubts, postwar self-centeredness, self accusation, and also self pity, then one comes close to understanding that these features are not exactly what one would desire from a reliable partner in times of international crisis and warfare. Otto Schily, the government official from Berlin, put it similarly in his talk with Jane Kramer, the journalist from New York. If simplification is allowed and if it is needed at this point, one could say: The Germans may have to learn two lessons in terms of *cultural politics*—the older lesson from their own history and memory of the twentieth century, a German century of catastrophe, and a new lesson on how to adjust to a worldwide historical situation so greatly changed at the beginning of the twenty-first century. So far 1989 and 2001 have provided the evidence and cleared the way. But who would like to be taught in this manner? We are no longer in school. Reeducation is not needed, nor is American paternalism. Cooperation cannot simply be offered or demanded, it cannot be the result of a patronizing attitude. In terms of cultural politics: Solidarity, coming from, but not limited to the emotional experience of terror must be a concept to strengthen long-time cooperation, particularly in terms of cultural similarity and difference. Cooperation should be limited in the best way possible. It should be limiting in the sense that it gives form and contour, but it should also be competent to criticize the other in order to make one's own position more remarkable and noteworthy to the other, as we say in German: "merkwürdig," worthy to attract attention.

Lecture given at the *American Institute for Contemporary German Studies*, Washington D.C., March 25, 2002. Hanne Hence from Washington University in St. Louis has patiently corrected the English text.

Notes

1. *Merkur* v.56 (January 2002): pp. 64–68.
2. Berliner Zeitung, October 6/7, 2001, magazine, p. 2.
3. I refer to her report of February 11, 2002.
4. Quote from the tape recording of the press-conference http://www.swin.de/kammer-chorstockhausen, my own English translation.
5. *Frankfurter Allgemeine Zeitung*, September 20, 2001.
6. Karl Schlingensief, *Intensivstation, Frankfurter Allgemeine Zeitung*, September 27, 2001.
7. *Frankfurter Allgemeine Zeitung*, September 27, 2001.
8. *Frankfurter Allgemeine Zeitung*, October 15, 2001.
9. Richard Herzinger, *Dienstag* September 11, 2001, p. 87ff.
10. *Die Propheten des Weltuntergangs, Die Zeit*, n. 39, 2001.
11. *What we are Fighting for*, <http://www.propositionsonline.com/Fighting>.
12. *Lettres International*, 54, 2001.
13. Götz Aly: *Den Tod nicht fürchten, Berliner Zeitung*, November 21, 2001.
14. Enzensberger: *Human Sacrifice Is a Thoroughly Modern Phenomenon, Frankfurter Allgemeine Zeitung*, English edition, September 18, 2001.
15. Münkler, "Asymmetrische Gewalt. Terrorismus als militärisch-politische Strategie," *Merkur* v.56 (January 22, 2002): pp. 1–12.
16. Münkler in *Constellations* v.9, n.1, 2002.

CHAPTER FOUR

"ARE THE TOWERS STILL STANDING?" SEPTEMBER 11 AND THE RESURRECTION OF THE LITERARY INTELLECTUAL

Alison Lewis

Four weeks after the terrorist attacks on the World Trade Center on September 11, 2001 the German weekly magazine *Der Spiegel* ran a feature that was designed to coincide with the opening of the annual Frankfurt Book Fair. Titled "Literature: Early Tremors of Fear," the article opens with the question that was on every literary editor's lips in the wake of the terrorist attacks: what immediate impact will the acts of terrorism on the United States have on German publishing? The editors of *Der Spiegel* settled on a face-saving solution to the problem they faced of running with the scheduled promotional piece on new releases in the book industry in a dramatically changed international climate. In acknowledgment of the gravity of the situation, the editors decided to interweave publicity for the season's new books with spontaneous outbursts from fiction writers in response to the catastrophe. What is especially interesting about the article is the justification given for the relevance of literature post–September 11. The magazine makes a forceful case for the continued relevance of works of fiction in an appeal to the role of the writer as interpreter of history and world events. As the magazine argues: "Writers are always seismoscopes of 'Zeitgeist', observers of intellectual tremors, chroniclers of historical ground shifts, some of them—such as Franz Kafka and George Orwell—have the gift of prophesy."[1]

Six weeks later, *Der Spiegel* proved to be far less enamored of the doomsday prophets of terror and global chaos it had celebrated only a few weeks earlier. In its feature essay by Cordt Schnibben the disaffection with the nation's writers and intellectuals was striking. "Are the towers still standing?" the article asks, not of the twin towers of the World Trade Center but of those fallen pillars of German society—the nation's writers and intellectuals.[2] The article is appropriately subtitled: "Why *Weltanschauung* has become a difficult business for intellectuals after September 11." The attack on the World Trade Center was an attack on our "thinking," Schnibben observes, "what we knew before is not worth anything any more." Those most to blame are not, as Hans Magnus Enzensberger once prophesized, the shop assistants and the taxi drivers but instead the country's intellectuals: "We have read Günter Grass in the *FAZ*, Peter Schneider in the *Woche*, Botho Strauß in the *Spiegel*, Diedrich Diederichsen in *der taz*, Alexander Kluge in the *SZ* (*Süddeutsche*) and were amazed that they were as baffled (*ahnungslos*) as we were." As the "advisors of the powerful" and advocates for all manner of things, for "*Ostpolitik* and Vietnam, for the emergency laws and Chile, abortion and Biafra, nuclear energy, Nicaragua and rearmament, always to hand whenever the world's conscience was called for," Germany's intellectuals had, it seemed, after a fleeting renaissance, proved to be a disappointment yet again.

The so-called failure of intellectuals has been a recurrent theme in the self-posturings of German intellectuals for longer than the last ten years, as frequent and regular as similarly pessimistic pronouncements about the death of literature, the death of the author, the death of history and the death of the public intellectual. The lament about the failings of Germany's poets and philosophers stands out much like a major chord in the postwar (West) German nation's theme song, running like an insistent trope through the story the German nation habitually tells about itself. It is this recurrent refrain of failure and insufficiency that has effectively supplanted older, more positive, and self-congratulatory foundational narratives of the German nation. One myth of origin that has been drowned out in the current rhetoric of crisis, which has its roots in German Romanticism and the Enlightenment, in particular in Herder's notion of the *Kulturnation*, is the belief that Germany is a nation of *Dichter und Denker*, of writers and thinkers, poets and philosophers. In modern times, Germany has drawn much of its sense of identity and self-worth from its rich intellectual traditions and this foundational narrative. Almost from the time of its birth, however, this story has been accompanied by a counter-narrative that construes writers and intellectuals as a potential danger to national stability and accordingly places a high premium on conformity and complicity. Periods of censorship and repression in German history, such as during the Metternich era in the nineteenth century (1815–1948) and the Weimar Republic, forged a new role for the public intellectual, at least on the left, in the figure of the oppositional writer that represents a challenge to power. This faith in the intellectual and his/her duty to resist state interference and to engage in politics was dealt a severe blow with Hitler's assumption of power in 1933, World War II, and the radical caesura of the Holocaust. Since that time unadulterated national pride in Germany's intellectual traditions and its past achievements in the fields of culture and the arts, philosophy and music, poetry and opera has been replaced by a partly healthy, partly obsessive skepticism with respect to the role of intellectuals. The moral failure of the intellectuals during the Third Reich has left an enduring legacy, which, for better or worse, has been to raise the moral stakes for intellectuals. Since Germany's writers had failed so spectacularly to serve the nation during the Third Reich, any failure on their part to steer the nation safely through troubled waters in the postwar era and to warn of historical dangers ahead is reported in tones redolent of a national disaster. In few other countries do intellectuals have such a large and thankless burden to bear in the services of the national good as they do in postwar Germany. As prophets and soothsayers, clairvoyants and crystal-ball-gazers they are welcomed but only insofar as they manage to maintain a neat separation of powers between *Geist* and *Macht*, intellect and power. Where intellectuals have used their moral authority to prop up or appease authoritarian or nondemocratic regimes, as during the Third Reich and subsequently in the GDR, there has been a high price to pay.

To provide a historical context for the pronouncements in the *Spiegel*, and to make sense of the most recent warnings of yet another "crisis of intellectuals," it is necessary to return briefly to the events at the end of the Cold War and the response of German intellectuals to the end of the GDR as a sovereign state and to the unification of the two Germanies. The collapse of Eastern European communism and the abrupt end of the Cold War—experienced in Germany with the fall of the Berlin Wall and the velvet revolution of the East German populace in 1989—marked a singular turning point in the life of the German nation and the thinking among the intellectuals in both states. At the time, the dissolution of the GDR and the pending accession of East Germany to West Germany were described in terms of a crisis for Germany's *Dichter und Denker*. In the fraught debates on the role that intellectuals had played in toppling the SED, writers and intellectuals from both countries faced the first sustained challenge to their moral authority since the War. This effectively brought to a close the forty-year-old alliance between *Geist* and *Macht* on the left side of politics that had held sway—albeit to different degrees—in both Germanies since 1948. The result of the severe battering that a significant number of German intellectuals were subjected to in the early 1990s was, it seemed at least until the middle of the decade, a retreat from public concerns and social engagement and a realignment of the relationship of literature to politics in accordance with international and European trends.

The immediate question that the September 11 terrorist attacks pose for intellectuals is whether September 11 marks a turning point of any significance in the fortunes of Germany's *Dichter* and *Denker*? It is unclear whether the shift signaled in the *Spiegel* was precipitated by developments in the international stage of politics or whether it marks the turn to the "special path" (*Sonderweg*) that German intellectual life has taken since 1945. In order to offer some tentative answers to these questions I will outline the main shifts in public perception that affected the status of the intellectual in Germany after the end of the GDR. Thereafter some key debates in the first decade since unification will surveyed.

If September 11 is to be considered a turning point in Germany it may be useful to place German intellectual life in the broader context of the remarks by Zygmunt Bauman, Richard Rorty, and a host of others who have reflected at length on the global crisis of the intellectual. Bauman sees the end of the twentieth century as a time of massive "disengagement of the knowledge classes" from social issues. In a collection of recent essays, Bauman asks whether the current "gospel of the 'end of ideology' " or the 'demise of grand narratives' (and overarching them all, of the 'end of history') as an act of surrender on the part of the knowledge class and of withdrawal of the collective bid or whether it can be seen as another updated version of the 'self-organic' strategy and, accordingly, of that ideology which supplies its justification and *raison d'être*."[3] The overriding concern of this chapter is to offer some observations on whether German intellectuals have become, like their American and European counterparts, increasingly self-referential and introspective, as Bauman observes, or whether they have become simply less compulsively political and more autonomous in their social functioning. A final consideration is to ascertain whether the discernible lack of engagement of literature in the 1990s was merely an aberration and, hence, a detour off the well-trodden path of Germany's *Sonderweg* or whether it was the beginnings of a more "normal" attitude to the relationship between politics and art.

In the postwar reconstruction period, both German states looked to their writers for guidance on moral and ethical issues and, increasingly, on questions of day-to-day politics and current affairs. The collapse of communist regimes across Europe and the disintegration of the Soviet Union brought the undisputed reign of the literary intellectual on both sides of the Cold War divide to an abrupt and unexpected end. By contrast, with critical intellectuals such as Vaclav Havel and Mircea Dinescu in Eastern Europe, Germany's intellectuals played anything but a noteworthy role during the "velvet revolution" of the autumn of 1989. Intellectuals from both sides distinguished themselves in 1989 and 1990 through a series of embarrassing misjudgments and misguided attempts to give the revolution direction and focus. The end of the Cold War marked a paradigm shift in which, in the words of Andreas Huyssen, "important building blocks of a long-standing, broadly based consensus have been dismantled or have disintegrated."[4] It was one that was to irrevocably change the high esteem that Germany had previously held its literary intellectuals in.

In 1991 Andreas Huyssen identified three "cumulative" phases in what he considered to be a "crisis of intellectuals." The first was a series of rolling debates about domestic politics that revolved around the fate of the imploding remains of the socialist state. The second focused on issues of culture and literature and the third he saw erupting in response to the Gulf War.[5] But of all these crises, it was predominantly the lukewarm response from many intellectuals from East and West Germany to what they saw as the "annexation" of East Germany and to the inevitable abandonment of the project of socialism that led observers to declare 1989 a watershed in the intellectual life of the nation. Not only had intellectuals failed to predict the course of events that was to change Germany's political landscape in a lasting way; they had also been unable to offer any viable alternatives or a vision for the future.

The second, partially overlapping phase of the debates of the time pertained to cultural matters, the role of the literary intellectual, the relationship between art and politics, and the link between culture and the nation. It appeared as if the marriage of leftist politics and literature on both halves of the divided country had come full circle. Wolfgang Emmerich speaks of 1989–1990 in terms of a "stock market crash" in which the value of the writer plummeted to undreamed of depths.[6] As the share price on intellectual goods dropped so too did the share price of other goods on the market—the "whole of West German literature of non-conformism of four decades and even more than that: *littérature engagée* in general" collapsed in the bargain.[7]

From its relatively localized beginnings in June 1990, the debates on the failure of the intellectuals gained momentum throughout the following two years as Germany moved from the Literature Debate of the summer of 1990 through to the various Stasi Debates of 1991–1993. At issue in both controversies was the question of the limits of "repressive tolerance," or how far intellectuals (*Geist*) should go toward accommodating power (*Macht*) without loss of integrity and face. By the conclusion of the Stasi Debates in 1993 it had become obvious who were the main stakeholders in these heavily politicized public disputes. For East Germans the debates about the moral reprehensibility of the East German intelligentsia, which had been the focus of both debates, had another agenda. East Germans saw them as a poorly disguised attempt to discredit GDR writers and their reputations and to devalue the entire cultural legacy of forty years of East German culture. For them the rhetoric of morality masked at base the desire of the West German literary establishment to set a different agenda for the future of a unified Germany by calling into question the postwar marriage of aesthetics and politics. While there was some truth to this, public concern about the conformism and complicity of the writer, as expressed by the West German intelligentsia, did involve a degree of self-reflection and criticism. The debates were partly motivated by the guilt-ridden desire to face up to the fact that political and emotional investments in the "other" Germany were fundamentally misguided. While the debates had a cathartic element, the invective used revealed a bad conscience on the part of West German left-liberal intellectuals because of the "dissident bonus" that they had bestowed on East German writers such as Christa Wolf. What was really at stake was the future direction of German culture, which is best encapsulated in the words of Ulrich Greiner: "The interpretation of the literary past is no academic question. Who determines what was also determines what will be. The dispute about the past is a dispute about the future."[8]

Two cultural critics from the nation's most influential newspapers, Ulrich Greiner from the left-liberal *Die Zeit* and Frank Schirrmacher from the more conservative *Frankfurter Allgemeine Zeitung*, both issued an appeal for a literature unencumbered with political and moral concerns. They unilaterally called for a literature freed of "Gesinnungsästhetik," literally "an aesthetics driven by opinion or political conviction." According to Greiner the paradigm of "Gesinnungsästhetik" that had dominated the literature industry after the war, elevating moral and political concerns over matters of style, form, and aesthetics, was now passé. Karl Heinz Bohrer, the editor of *Merkur*, a journal known for its nonaligned eclectic mix of political and aesthetic views, went even further in his condemnation of East German literature, much of which was little more than "Gesinnungskitsch," he contended, in obvious reference to Christa Wolf.[9] The old guard of those responsible for meaning production, whether on the left or the right of politics, had always been "religious devotees" who wanted to see in their art "metaphysics instead of aesthetics."[10] As a secularized society, Germany had no need for quasi-religious high priests of culture; literature was "not a drug for the oppressed" and ought not to be "a quietistic balm."[11]

By October 1990 the accusations of literature's irrelevance had spread to implicate West German literature and its authors. Both Schirrmacher and Greiner called for a "farewell to the literature of the Federal Republic," naming writers such as Günter Grass, Heinrich Böll, and Siegfried Lenz as part of a postwar "conscience industry" that had outgrown its purpose. Like their counterparts in the East, they too were guilty of lending their support to a morally bankrupt political system. Bohrer concurred with Greiner and Schirrmacher and observed that by clinging to the chimera of GDR culture as a more utopian version of their own, West German writers like Grass had sought to turn the GDR into a type of wildlife park for endangered cultural species, a "nature reserve for culture" (*Kulturschutzgebiet*). In this, West Germany's "cultural pastors" had merely demonstrated their narrowness of vision. "Who are Günter Grass and Walter Jens today?," Bohrer asked and answered, "Two important public figures to be sure, constantly 'committed' and deserving, but politically and intellectually long since stretched to their limits."[12] Bohrer called for several articles penned at the time for a "coming-of-age of the aesthetic process," a dawning of a new aesthetic age and a separation of powers in which literature could be literature and politics was allowed to be politics.[13] As Klaus Scherpe summarized, "the role of the literary intellectual that is predicated on that peculiar relationship between the good, true and beautiful [the role] as soothsayer, someone who says no and who speaks for others, as professional utopianist, as a nonconformist and representative of the whole now seems to have finally exhausted itself."[14]

Despite the predictions of the demise of intellectuals at the time, writers from both Germanies continued to engage in public debate about issues that went far beyond the narrow confines of the literary academy. The more insistent the cries of irrelevance were, the more vocal many members of Bohrer's "conscience industry" became. Grass in particular was persistent in his opposition to unification, invoking the specter of fascist Germany and Auschwitz in relation to the question of unification. In particular, they mourned publicly the passing of really existing socialism, or as Helmut Dubiel points out, they mourned without engaging with the real business of "mourning work" (*Trauerarbeit*). Instead, they indulged in what some commentators have seen as melancholic self-pitying stemming from a profound "narcissistic injury" when confronted with the loss of those very ideals that made up the core of their self-image and understanding.[15] The real failure of intellectuals lay, according to Dubiel, in their refusal to come to terms with the loss of leftist utopias and the loss of the GDR as the concrete realization of this utopia.[16] In the view of Bathrick, "many leftist never overcame a strangely libidinal attachment to these societies as potential purveyors of a postcapitalist alternative, as a preservation reserve for the idea of a noncapitalist utopia."[17] Dubiel explains that both sides of German politics had suffered from a form of paralysis which left them caught between a conservative anticommunism on the one hand and a largely impotent "anti-anticommunism" on the other.[18] The left had been more preoccupied with discrediting anticommunist distortions of GDR socialism than it had been in confronting head-on the really existing deficiencies of the SED regime and exposing the evils of Stalinism.

The question to be answered more than a decade on is what remains of the socialist project and what is the legacy of the forty-year long experiment with a better and more just Germany. More importantly, what remains of the "committed" and concerned literary intellectual? Has life been breathed back into the old paradigm of the writer as the conscience of the nation or has the model been finally laid to rest? Have we seen the postwar generation of left-wing intellectuals (born between 1927 and 1945) replaced by a cohort of "renegades," as one critic suggested not entirely tongue-in-cheek in 1999, and indeed, by a new generation of writers whose primary concerns are literary and not political? Are there signs that writers in Germany are now undergoing a rehabilitation that has seen them returned to the center of moral and political debate?

In his reckoning with the literary intellectual in East and West Germany, Huyssen points to the significance of the Gulf War as the last stage of the debates at the end of the Cold War that formulated the crisis of intellectual discourse in terms of a crisis of intellectuals. From the vantage-point of 2003, however, the conflicts during the Gulf War can be seen more as the beginning a new sequence of public debates with similar players, that unfolded throughout the 1990s. While quite disparate in motive and topic, these disputes over literature and culture can be loosely characterized as "renegades" debates, in which the left and the right attempted to reposition themselves in the face of the rapidly changing landscape of European and global politics.

The Gulf War was the first of the full-blown renegade debates in that it provided an occasion for testing the limits of leftist tolerance in a post-communist order. It also provided East and West intellectuals, still uneasy about sharing the same intellectual space, an opportunity for forming a united front in opposition to the UN's actions against Iraq. Leftist intellectuals such as Hans Magnus Enzensberger, Wolf Biermann, and Jürgen Habermas who defied the left-liberal consensus by defending the UN's war on Saddam Hussein were branded renegades for their pro-American stance. Enzensberger, in particular, was singled out for criticism because of his comparison of Hussein to Adolf Hitler. In many ways the Gulf War served as a convenient distraction from the more urgent issues facing the unified nation and offered a type of different security in the "firming up of shop-worn convictions about what is good and bad in this world."[19]

Of course, the figure of the postwar renegade is much older in origin than the 1990s; accusations of betrayal of leftist ideals have been habitually leveled at those involved in the 1968 student movement as well as at writers once affiliated with the Communist Party of Germany. In an article in *Die Zeit* in 1999 Jörg Lau announced, "Never were the renegades so influential as they are today," and goes on to ask, "Is their inconsequentiality smartness or opportunism?" Times have changed according to Lau and it is the renegade who has drawn the most appropriate consequences from the loss of leftist utopias. The clearest indication of a shift in leftist politics was the NATO intervention in Kosovo. Leftist radicals and left-liberal intellectuals previously affiliated with the SDS, KPD, and diverse Maoist groups all ranked among the most ardent advocates of the NATO intervention, Lau argues. Among them were "Hans Magnus Enzensberger, Hans Christoph Buch, Richard Herzinger, Peter Schneider and Andre Glucksmann as well as Alain Finkielkraut and Bernard-Henri Levy."[20] The common denominator is a commitment to universalist principles and human rights obligations and a disavowal of early pacifist positions.

Allegations of revisionism are nothing new in the postwar period. Members of the older generation of postwar writers born between 1920 and 1930 have periodically been accused of running with the wolves, most notably Martin Walser, who after Günter Grass must rate among the better known writers of his generation. He broke ranks with left orthodoxy in the seventies and in the eighties over the "German question," raising eyebrows over his laments of feeling "a phantom pain" where the other Germany had been amputated. He spoke provocatively and irritatingly of his "Leipzig-Stuttgart feeling," as if there was still an invisible bond between the two Germanies.[21]

But the most recent incidence of betrayal among Germany's literary intelligentsia was committed, Lau argues, by Hans Magnus Enzensberger. Enzensberger, who had demonized the Americans as Nazis during his days as a student revolutionary, left the "phalanx of anti-Americanism" in 1991 in spectacular fashion. In a much publicized article for the *Spiegel* he accused the Germans of failing to rally behind Operation Desert Storm in the Gulf War because they secretly identified with the Iraqis. This was, he suggested, possibly because they were reminded of themselves in 1938 and 1945 and their equally thwarted attempts to invade neighboring countries.[22]

In 1994, Enzensberger published a long essay on the subject of violence and the new world order with the title *Prospects of a Civil War* in which he contended that the end of communism had lead to a proliferation of localized, often random outbursts of violence among pre-political groups. At the time he was roundly criticized for his pessimism and for overstating the dangers of sectarian violence and the threat of Islam. Interestingly, in the light of the events of September 11 the work now seems remarkably prophetic in its prediction of terrorism and new sources of violence, and especially in the context of September 11 it seems worthy of revisiting.

Another writer who has long since passed through the renegade encampment and entrenched himself in the ranks of conservative cultural critics is Botho Strauss. Strauss's dramatic works decry in insistent and poignant fashion the loss of community values in Western societies and its cities and bewail the permanent state of alienation into which modern Germany has fallen. In 1993 he stirred up controversy with his swan song to the Western world in a provocative essay published in the *Spiegel* with the title

Anschwellender Bocksgesang (Rising Tragedy or Ram's Song). In the essay he warned of complacency among democratic nations in the West and predicted an escalation in the conflict between the West and Islam. Lambasted at the time for being a mouthpiece for the New Right, Strauss's cultural pessimism and indeed his full-blown pathos, judged grossly inappropriate at the time, has in the interim found a good deal more converts to the cause. "Between the forces of tradition and those that permanently do away with, get rid of and extinguish there will be war," he predicted ominously. "Modernity will not come to a gentle postmodern stop but will break off with a culture shock. The culture shock will not affect primitive cultures but those devastatingly forgetful ones." "What capacity does what we call ours have to transform and to solve this mess? Apparently none. What we are witnessing is the durability of the self-correcting system. Whether that is democracy or already democratism: a cybernetic model, a scientific discourse or a political technological surveillance association, remains to be seen."[23]

Perhaps the most important of the renegade debates of the 1990s was the Walser-Bubis Debate of 1998, which was incited by the speech delivered by Martin Walser on the occasion of receiving the *Friedenspreis des deutschen Buchhandels* (Peace Prize of German Booksellers). The debate that ensued between Walser and Ignaz Bubis, Head of the Association of the Jews living in Germany, has been described as the "most painful" of the disputes of the 1990s. It was to leave, as Schirrmacher put it, "only injured behind but no victors or vanquished."[24] Walser's acceptance speech delivered in the somber surroundings of the Paul's Church in Frankfurt on the instrumentalization of Auschwitz as a "moral cudgel" sent waves of indignation around the nation, the media, and the Jewish community. It is not entirely clear what Walser's intentions were, other than to provoke discussion (see Starkman, chapter 11) about Germany's memorial practices, the role of the Holocaust in public and private memory in the context of Germany's desire for "normality." What Walser appears to have had in his view, beyond the issue of the instrumentalization of the Holocaust, was the issue of taboos and political correctness and the right of the intellectual to challenge prevailing norms on the basis of personal experience.

In Walser's view it is the media and Germany's intellectuals who are at fault in the perpetuation of the memory of Auschwitz in Germany, which he links to the perpetuation of "Germany's shame." Especially to blame are intellectuals who delude themselves that they have more affinities with the victims of the Holocaust than with the perpetrators—an allegation that is puzzling given Walser's own attempts to cast himself as a victim of the media. He attacks those who see everything as having the potential to lead to Auschwitz because they run the risk of trivializing the Holocaust.[25] He calls these individuals the nation's "opinion soldiers," who have sacrificed their integrity to the services of morality. Moreover, he chastises the Left for silencing the narrative of Germany as a nation of perpetrators by overly identifying with the victim's story. He reminds his listeners that to identify too strongly with the division of Germany as a necessary punishment for World War II is ultimately counterproductive and self-defeating.

Walser's speech and the following debate were not without a degree of deliberate theatricality.[26] While it was a bold move to broach the sensitive topic of the Holocaust and to challenge the boundaries of left-liberal consensus, he appears to have overstepped the mark in his choice of polemics. He frequently strikes the wrong tone, particularly through his use of the powerful symbolic gesture of "looking away" or "looking the other way."

In the view of Frank Schirrmacher, who held the congratulatory speech at the ceremony, Walser's most significant contribution to his country lies in his ability to silence the catchwords of his time: the end of history, the end of the nation, the division of Germany as a just punishment. Schirrmacher praises Walser's works dedicated to the task of "cleaning up": cleaning up "catch phrases, the rubble of public opinion, speech of others, unfree speech."[27] The key to Walser's moral commitment to Germany and his own personal politics of remembrance lies according to Schirrmacher in his desire to confront the contradictions of his generation.[28] A major cornerstone in this is Walser's call for recognition of the formative experiences of the generation of Germans that was socialized during the War. The "trauma" of this generation was the shocking awakening in 1945 to the atrocities perpetuated by the German nation that effectively turned Germany overnight into a nation of perpetrators.[29] In a rather contentious rereading of Franz Kafka's *Metamorphosis*, Schirrmacher claims that Walser had dedicated his works to the existential plight of the German nation, a plight which he likens to the dilemma faced by Kafka's traveling salesman Gregor Samsa. Like Gregor Samsa, Walser had awakened from the nightmare of World War II to find himself part of a nation that metamorphosed overnight into a nation of perpetrators. Only Walser's heroes can know what it feels like to literally lose your identity overnight and awaken as vermin.[30]

Of interest in this speech on the role of intellectuals is Walser's revival of the rhetoric of the writer as the "conscience of the nation" and a leader in morality. Walser dedicates his talk deliberately to what he calls, rather ambiguously, a "matter of conscience." He speaks moreover openly of his apparent "moral-political weakness" in a clever rhetorical gesture that flags his own morally flawed speaking position. He feels it is his duty to speak up against those who detect signs of "moral-political decrepitude" in the German population today. For him it has become a "matter of conscience" to defend Germany's "normality" against its skeptics. Not only does he refuse to believe in the decline of values in modern Germany, he wishes to also impute to proponents of these theories the explicit intention to hurt "all Germans" because "we have deserved it."[31]

Schirrmacher's opening words are designed to reinforce Walser's message about the public duty of intellectuals to speak out in defense of national pride and personalized forms of memory of the Holocaust. The writer now has a responsibility in Schirrmacher's view, not any more as a morally and politically correct rewriter of the past or as a chronicler of injustice, but as a "chronicler of unpredictability and innocence."[32] Walser's achievements are seen to lie in the way he divests the reader and literature from the burden of history and of "knowing what comes tomorrow." Walser insists that we cannot impose the superior knowledge of today onto biographies. That is, according to Schirrmacher, what defines the "innocence of memory."[33]

For all the damage the debate did to German Jewish relations, distracting attention as it did away from the problems of the present, from the "normal" problems, and indeed responsibilities of a Western democracy,[34] it was helpful, if only because it opened up possibilities for new narratives of the nation to be written and heard. The most recent example of a ground-shift in the self-understanding of the nation is the latest publication by Walser's traditional rival and critic, Günter Grass. Early in 2002 Grass published a novel about the sinking of a passenger liner carrying ethnic German refugees and soldiers by a Russian submarine in January 1945. In an astonishing about-face, Grass appeared to have joined the ranks of unpredictable "taboo-breakers" such as Walser in pointing out blind spots in German memory and history. In his latest work *Im Krebsgang* or "Crab-wise"[35] Grass ostensibly champions one of the traditional causes of the far-right in the concerns of the expellees from the lost territories to the South and East of Germany such as the Sudetenland, now in the Czech Republic. Simply to broach the topic was previously thought to be making a political statement about the right to return of the expellees, or the right to return of property abandoned by the refugees or, even worse, about the right of Germany to re-annex areas lost after the War. Given the history of the debates on these issues, it is surprising that Grass's book was so well-received by critics on the left and right. It has thus far been widely understood as a courageous attempt to reclaim the forgotten story of the refugees from Germany's lost homelands and to legitimize the grief of the survivors and the victims' relatives.[36]

Grass and the generation of writers who were part of the "Group 47" have, it seems, much unfinished business in the minefield that is twentieth-century German history. It would appear that Grass has finally responded in the way that Walser did in the seventies to the demands for a greater diversity and richness in the nation's story. It took perhaps the prompting of exiled Jewish writer W.G. Sebald to encourage Grass to tell the untold stories of his generation. In 1999 Sebald raised the topic of the absent or missing themes from German literature, remarking on the lack of narratives on the sufferings of the German population, such as the emotional devastation wreaked by the bombing of German cities and the Allies' air raids. According to Grass, the Left has much to answer for, even holding his generation responsible for the rise of right-wing extremism. As Thomas Schmidt remarked in *Die Zeit*, paraphrasing Grass, "The right is allowed to help themselves in the unploughed field of German collective traumata because no-one else wants to harvest the potatoes."[37]

Grass's recent interventions in his literary works as well as in political, historical, and moral debates may well be a belated attempt at putting the finishing touches on his biography while he still has the chance. In his mid-seventies, he and his compatriots such as Walser had most probably most of their masterpieces behind them; as Thomas E. Schmidt observes in *Die Zeit*: "Something is coming to an end." As we witness a changing of the literary guard, the role of the public writer as public intellectual that the "Group 47" arrogated to itself will become increasingly hard to sustain, as the succession of public debates throughout the nineties has shown. Looking back over the first decade since unification it would appear that the more pessimistic predictions of a "stock market crash" in the value of literature and the intellectual did come true for a number of years, at least for one section of the literary market. The end of the Cold War and communism clearly saw the demise of the East German public intellectual and his or her dangerous liaison with state socialism. The disengagement with politics that Bauman speaks about, and the detachment from discredited socialist utopias was for most of East Germany's intellectuals a painful but necessary process. Neither the ideal of socialism, whose purity had to be upheld and protected from the impurities of lived experience, nor the practice of really existing socialism held out any realistic promise of redemption. The "ego-ideal" of a socialist alternative to the capitalist West that had underpinned what I have called elsewhere a "hopelessly depressive-paranoid sense of national identity" among socialist intellectuals in the East, was recognized for what it was, largely an illusion and a fata morgana.[38] The discrediting of the ideal of socialism represented the loss of the possibility of transcendence for East German intellectuals as well as for their West German sympathizers and brothers-in-arms whose anti-anticommunist stance only contributed to the problem.

The first decade of unification represented for many previously "engaged," "critical-loyal," and dissident East German writers such as Christa Wolf, Christoph Hein, Volker Braun, and Stefan Heym a difficult period of readjustment during which they were forced to return to being mere writers of literature. With few exceptions, the exponents of dissidence and reform who were vocal during 1989 and 1990 were pushed to the margins of the media and the literature industry. Even Monika Maron, who had disassociated herself from those "critical-loyal" writers at the beginning of the decade, and acted as a spokeswoman for the more pro-Western of East German intellectuals, was unable to defend her public position as an anticommunist critical intellectual for long. She too was to experience her own Literature Debate *en miniature* when it was revealed in 1996 that she had had a brief flirtation with the Stasi in the 1970s.[39] Only Wolf Biermann, as the most stubbornly persistent of East Germany's intellectuals, is still granted a hearing in the media when the authentic voice of the dissident is called for.

West Germany's public writers were granted the sort of graceful exit from the public arena that East Germany's authors were not. It is thus noteworthy, but not altogether inappropriate, that Grass himself should raise the question of the failings of his own generation and, somewhat surprisingly, not be censured for it. Because the recent turnaround is so entirely unexpected, Grass's critics have been full of admiration for the "old man and his sea" and his courage in articulating German victim myths in a sensitive manner. The real significance of *Im Krebsgang* can be seen to lie in the way it points out both the limits of the postwar left-liberal consensus and the limits of "discourse pedagogy and literary politics of history."[40] But Grass is far from wishing to berate himself or any others, on the contrary, he has assumed the demeanor of the grand old man who is strong enough to provide leadership in matters of national myths and self-perceptions. Grass's latest literary contribution must therefore be seen as marking the "apotheosis of the leftist intellectual."[41]

There are good reasons to believe that with September 11 the German media has finally made its peace with Walser's and Grass' generation of committed and concerned intellectuals and allowed them to come in from the cold. The best illustration of the current climate of reconciliation between politics and art are the cosy fireside chats and photo shoots between the Chancellor Gerhard Schröder and intellectuals like Günter Grass and Christa Wolf throughout the 2002 election campaign and again as war against Iraq looked imminent. Despite these almost anachronistic attempts on the part of Schröder to rub shoulders with Germany's icons of morality and integrity, which are more due to his populist strategies than to any real willingness to listen to writers, the time when Germans looked to their writers rather than their politicians for political and moral guidance on matters of conscience as well as day-to-day politics would appear to have long gone. The moral imperative to engage with politics is not shared by subsequent generations of writers who have different concerns. The literary landscape in Germany today displays a far greater diversity in keeping with the multiple functions that fiction has in a democratic society. What the

Spiegel article quoted at the outset demonstrates is that Germans still want to listen to their writers, to read their fiction, and to use fiction as a template through which to view and interpret the world. It remains uncertain, however, how far the will of the German public tolerate direct political interventions from its writers of prose and drama. The case of Grass—and the benevolent reception of his ideological *volte-face* and breaking of all established principles of political correctness—is too much of an exception to constitute the rule.

The *Spiegel* article clearly illustrates a general reluctance to put too much store by the Cassandra cries of writers. When the *Spiegel* published the first responses from writers to the attacks on the World Trade Centre, contributions from seasoned West German civilization critics such as Botho Strauß were not received favorably. Strauß's fantasies of global war and the "end of civilization as we know it" were seen to indulge in the same obfuscatory myth-making and the mystification of evil that characterized many of his earlier works. His invocation of a "struggle of the evil against evil" reveals too little distance between the language of power and the rhetoric of the Bush administration for German comfort.[42] As prophesy, literature of the sort written by Strauß is most problematic when it crosses the line between enlightened critique and modern myth-making. Where literature, be it in the form of diaries or works of fiction, does appear to have come into its own in the last few months of 2001 is in its capacity simply to give expression to extreme human emotions and shocks and to tell stories: stories of pain and suffering.

In the first decade after unification literature witnessed a revival of sorts in the emergence of a younger generation of writers who have made their mark in unexpected places: in the international arena (such as Ingo Schulze) and in traditionally underselling genres such as the short story with Judith Hermann's *Sommerhaus, später*.[43] The media phenomenon of the "Fräuleinwunder" and its concomitant sensation of the "boy wonder" may have been a canny marketing ploy devised to stimulate a tired book market, but both have been instrumental in raising the profile of a younger, less politized generation of German writers who just want to write stories, mostly about themselves.[44] Among this group of debutant writers, authors from the former GDR are well-represented. While these writers are still too young to be considered to have acquired the stature of a public intellectual, there are signs that some of East Germany's younger intellectual offspring may well be taking the place of Germany's older "consciences of the nation." Interestingly, some of the most moving pieces of literature that manage to capture the *Zeitgeist* in Germany and in Europe as well as some of the more intelligent essays to be published in recent years come from younger East German writers such as Durs Grünbein.

There are moreover indications that the younger generation of West German-born writers aged between twenty and forty who in the 1990s experimented with pop styles and themes to the point of narcissistic self-absorption, may be capable of engaging with themes of wider political and social relevance. An example of what might be a new trend in literary publishing is the latest book by Christian Kracht (born in 1966) *1979* in which Kracht has dropped his overly cool attitude of disengagement and has written a book that engages even in its extreme pessimism with the issue of Islam, violence, and the alienation of the Western intellectual. It would thus appear that into the second decade of German unity the knowledge classes, and the creative classes along with them, may well have rediscovered their long-standing interest in ideology and matters of global concern and won back some of their socio-political relevance in public life.

However, it seems unlikely for the time being that literature will revert to the overt moral and political function that it assumed in the postwar era. Germany's writers have become too accustomed to being mere writers and too used to delegating responsibility on political issues to politicians and elder literary statesmen like Enzensberger, Walser, and Grass to be unduly perturbed by the events of September 11. In the meantime, it seems that the Germans have rediscovered Günter Grass and come to appreciate his writing and his value as a concerned public intellectual. As Ursula März wrote in 2002 in the *Frankfurter Rundschau*, Germans have at last disbanded the ever-popular anti-Grass club. There has always been a section of the population who consider Grass "nothing more than an irritating phenomenon" ("eine nur noch nervtötende Erscheinung"), an "active anachronism," and "a museum piece from the postwar era." This group has patently no respect for his political warnings and petitions, finds little of interest in his non-literary utterances, and habitually decries the deteriorating quality of his works. As März remarks, "To be annoyed by Grass is has become a popular habit; to find Grass interesting would be to break the habit" ("Von Grass genervt zu sein, ist vereinbarter Stil, Grass interessant zu finden, wäre Stilbruch").[45] It is ironic, she observes, that it has now become politically correct to desist from traducing Grass and to admit, albeit reluctantly, that he has become a writer of international stature who is granted the *Narrenfreiheit* of being the occasional moral conscience of the nation.

Notes

1. "Literatur: Vorbeben der Angst," *Der Spiegel* v.41 (2001): p. 224.
2. Cordt Schnibben, "Stehen die Türme noch? Warum Weltanschauung nach dem 11. September für Intellektuelle ein schwieriges Geschäft geworden ist," *Der Spiegel* v.47 (2001): pp. 223–224.

3. Zygmunt Bauman, "Private Morality, Immoral World," *The Individualized Society* (Cambridge: Polity, 2001), pp. 197–198.
4. Andreas Huyssen, "After the Wall: The Failure of the Intellectuals," *New German Critique* v.52 (1991): p. 109.
5. Andreas Huyssen, "After the Wall" p. 110.
6. Wolfgang Emmerich, "Affirmation—Utopie—Melancholie: Versuch einer Bilanz von vierzig Jahren DDR-Literatur," *German Studies Review* (1991): p. 325.
7. Ibid.
8. Ulrich Greiner, "Die deutsche Gesinnungsästhetik," *Die Zeit*, November 1, 1990.
9. Karl Heinz Bohrer, "Kulturschutzgebiet DDR?" *Merkur* v.44, n.10, 11 (1990): p. 1016.
10. Ibid.
11. Ibid., p. 1017.
12. Karl Heinz Bohrer, "Kulturschutzgebiet DDR?" p. 1015.
13. Karl Heinz Bohrer, "Die Ästhetik am Ausgang ihrer Unmündigkeit," *Merkur* v.44, n.10 (1990): pp. 851–865; see also Karl Heinz Bohrer, "Und die Erinnerungen der beiden Halbnationen?" *Merkur* v.44, n.3 (1990): pp. 183–188.
14. Klaus R. Scherpe, "Moral im Ästhetischen: Andersch, Weiss, Enzensberger," *Weimarer Beiträge* v.42, n.1 (1996): p. 109.
15. See Scherpe, 110 and Huyssen and Lewis.
16. Helmut Dubiel, "Linke Trauerarbeit," *Merkur* (1990): pp. 482–491.
17. Bathrick, "The End of the Wall, Before the End of the Wall," *German Studies Review* v.14, n.2 (1991): p. 299.
18. Helmut Dubiel, "Linke Trauerarbeit," p. 484.
19. Andreas Huyssen, "After the Wall: The Failure of German Intellectuals," p. 112.
20. Jörg Lau, "Die Verräter sind unter uns," *Die Zeit* v.17 (1999).
21. Martin Walser, "Ich hab' so ein Stuttgart-Leipzig-Gefühl: *Stern*-Gespräch mit Martin Walser," in Klaus Siblewski, ed. *Martin Walser: Auskunft: 22 Gespräche aus 28 Jahren* (Frankfurt: Suhrkamp, 1991), p. 249.
22. Jörg Lau, "Die Verräter sind unter uns," *Die Zeit* v.17 (1999).
23. Botho Strauss, "Anschhwellender Bocksgesang," *Der Spiegel* v.6 (1993): pp. 203–204.
24. Frank Schirrmacher, ed., "Nachwort," *Die Walser-Bubis-Debatte: Eine Dokumentation* (Frankfurt am Main: Suhrkamp, 1999), p. 681.
25. Martin Walser, *Erfahrungen beim Verfassen einer Sonntagsrede*, p. 19.
26. Frank Schirrmacher, ed., "Nachwort," *Die Walser-Bubis-Debatte*, p. 681.
27. Frank Schirrmacher, "Sein Anteil: Laudatio," in Martin Walser, *Erfahrungen beim Verfassen einer Sonntagsrede*, p. 38.
28. Ibid, p. 40.
29. Ibid, pp. 36–38.
30. Ibid.
31. Martin Walser, *Erfahrungen beim Verfassen einer Sonntagsrede*, pp. 16–17.
32. Frank Schirrmacher, "Sein Anteil: Laudatio," in Martin Walser, *Erfahrungen beim Verfassen einer Sonntagsrede*, p. 47.
33. Ibid, p. 48.
34. Richard Herzinger "Die Keulenschwinger" *Tagespiegel*, December 6, 1998.

35. Günter Grass, *Im Krebsgang* (Göttingen: Steidl Verlag, 2002).
36. John Hopper, "Günter Grass breaks taboo on refugees," *The Guardian*, February 8, 2002; Volker Hage, "Das Tausendmalige Sterben," *Der Spiegel* v.6 (2002): pp. 184–190; see Günter Franzen, "Der alte Mann und sein Meer," *Die Zeit*, February 15, 2002; Thomas E. Schmidt, "Ostpreußischer Totentanz," *Die Zeit*, February 15, 2002.
37. Thomas E. Schmidt, "Ostpreußischer Totentanz."
38. See Alison Lewis, "The Writers, Their Socialism, The People and their Bad Table Manners," p. 260.
39. She had been enlisted as IM "Mitsu" before falling foul of the regime and becoming the object of an operative operation with the code name OV "Wildsau." As a result of the harsh public dressing down to which she was subjected, most vehemently from the likes of fellow countryman and Stasi-victim Jürgen Fuchs, she no longer appears in the culture pages of the major weeklies with such regularity as before.
40. Thomas E. Schmidt, "Ostpreußischer Totentanz."
41. Ibid.
42. "Literatur: Vorbeben der Angst," *Der Spiegel* v.41 (2001): p. 225.
43. Judith Hermann, *Sommerhaus, spatter* (Frankfurt: Fischer, 1998).
44. "Die Enkel kommen" *Der Spiegel*, March 22, 1999.
45. Ursula März, "Abschied vom Phantom: Vor der Novelle: Grass und der Anti-Grass-Verein," *Frankfurter Rundschau*, February 2, 2002.

PART II

MATERIAL CULTURE EAST AND WEST

CHAPTER FIVE

BORN IN THE "BAKSCHISCHREPUBLIK": ANTHEMS OF THE LATE GDR

Patricia Anne Simpson

Since the fall of the Berlin Wall, that eruption of History accompanied the collapse of a theoretical socialist utopia, the German Democratic Republic (GDR). The changed political climate influenced the production of litera- ture and popular culture in the vanquished and vanishing GDR; but it also brought tensions that had existed within GDR culture of the 1980s to a boil. Throughout that decade, a rupture between officially sanctioned and alternative culture emerged, even within the hegemony of state-controlled media.[1] In the realm of "popular" culture—a term made problematic by the totalizing and occasionally didactic function assigned to cultural produc- tion in socialism—the generation "born into socialism"[2] seemed willing to indict the pedagogical and political imperatives of the ruling Socialist Unity Party (SED). In other words, alternative artists, usually, though not exclusively, unofficial, filled the absence of critical thought and attitude left vacant by the much official culture of the GDR. The emergence of alternative "amateur" bands played a crucial role in this critical "filling in"; they were often criminalized along with their fans.[3] One thing is clear: the politicization[4] of popular culture played a part in the decline and demise of the SED; the utopian myth of "real existing socialism" and the propaganda that sustained it contributed significantly to the collapse of the state that had produced the vision in the first place.

Several GDR bands took advantage of the gap between cultural theory and praxis; they thematized aesthetically and politically the real existing problems of state socialism. Through an almost hit-and-run performance strategy and "passing" for in certain official venues, these bands established a close bond with their audience: concerts became a forum for the expression of any and every instance of discontent. Even if a band was not consciously or intentionally critical, the music it produced and performed, given the conditions of this production and performance, was received by the fans as an encoded explicit and potentially explosive critique. On an official level, the production of GDR rock music in the 1980s involved an elaborate balancing act. While the party line was officially liberal in the mid-1980s, concurrent compensatory action was taken by the Stasi to keep a close watch on that "liberty." An intricate system of checks and more checks developed; even then, certain key actors within the monopoly media (both print and broadcast) were able to exceed their own understanding of what was allowed and inflict their musical tastes on a general audience. Thus, despite the "invisible" system of IMs and the more obvious interventions of censorship and *Einstufung* (classification, in this case, of the bands), there was a compelling independent music scene in the GDR before the fall of the Berlin Wall.[5] It is this *Indie-Szene* and its explicit critique of GDR socialist rhetoric that I examine below.

Of Borders and Boredom

Seen the same country too long,
Heard the same language too long,
Waited too long, hoped too long
Honored the old men too long
I've been run around . . .
—"Langeweile" (boredom),
Pankow, 1988[6]

In the search for a popular GDR identity, rock (and punk rock) music constitute one sign system among others, equipped with a style, a sound, a language, and dance, as well as various public and private spaces, to designate or define a group or "scene."[7] Performance always engaged the attention of the state, especially when one aspect of that performance was everyday appearance, from long hair to no hair. To set the stage, an abbreviated history of the relationship between the party and the performers of rock music follows. Early on in its existence, the SED took note of and attempted to control or direct the production of rock music; specifically, the party leadership was invested in resisting the Americanization of popular culture. As early as 1958, Walter Ulbricht called for an end to the influx of ". . . currently mass produced (musical) products of dubious origin."[8] He wanted instead music that would contribute to the construction of the socialist personality.[9] The legacy of this caveat was evident even in the 1980s when punk was officially dismissed and also targeted as subversive, when functionaries suppressed the release of certain songs or expurgated albums because there were residual bits of text deemed inappropriate for socialist consumption. The 1950s witnessed the encouragement of "home-grown" music: the *Aufbauwalzer* (construction waltzes) thematized work and workers, examples of which include "Alle 105 Minuten" (every 105 minutes; about a streetcar operator) and "Stewardeß im blauen Dreß" (stewardess in the blue dress) about an Interflug camerade.[10] Music in the party and its institutions, the most significant of which were the monopoly record label AMIGA (VEB Deutsche Schallplatten), radio, and the youth clubs managed by Freie Deutsche Jugend (free German youth) or FDJ, responded to the infiltration of sounds from the West.

The history of official reception alternates between efforts at resistance and cooptation. Rock music was, for example, discussed at the eleventh meeting of the Central Committee of the Communist Party of the GDR, where none other than Erich Honecker attacked rock, insisting that, according to the rock historian Peter Wicke, ". . . rock music was not and could not be in accordance with the goals of a socialist society."[11] The 1960s brought changed attitudes, the Beatles craze, and renewed efforts at cooptation.[12] In 1967, the party started a "Sing-Bewegung" (song movement)[13] to encourage the music industry in East Germany, to compose in the style of folk music and the tradition of *Liedermacher* (singer-songwriters) such as Wolf Biermann and others. These performers, ironically, once encouraged, turned critical. In 1972, the party leadership made a further concession to *Jugendtanzmusik*, or youth dance music, to keep the "bread and circus" of socialism alive for a young generation. This period came to a resounding halt with the celebrated expatriation of Wolf Biermann in 1976.[14] According to Peter Zocher, a music scholar from Humboldt University who wrote for *Unterhaltungskunst* and later cofounded the fanzine *NM!Messitsch*, FDJ politically and consciously manipulated any musical trend that became popular; FDJ functionaries ". . . embraced it until they broke it."[15] The response to music was congruent with a general political profile: policy occasionally lifted the lid to let off a bit of steam, as was the case in the mid-to late-1980s. Eventually, the pot boiled over.[16]

Both the party leadership and the academics recognized the enormous potential of music for the controlled development of youth-group identity. In a 1981 article on "Unterhaltungskunst—fest mit dem sozialistischen Leben verbunden" ("Entertainment Art—Closely Connected to Socialist Life"), Dr. Jürgen Hagen of the department of culture of the Central Committee of the SED, emphasizes the lofty themes of honesty and love in popular music, and labels any aberrant forms of behavior as culturally retrograde.[17] In other words, the goals of utopian socialism would be echoed in its rock music.[18] While this piece calls for improved and enhanced conditions for performance, and while it highlights the shared roots of popular culture and the proletariat, its message remains one of regulation.

Somewhat prophetically, Hagen calls for a heightened quality and influence of "entertainment" music, though under the leadership of the party.[19] It is safe to say that in the course of the 1980s, in spite of this official shift in attitude, music got out of hand. In 1983 the party instituted "Rock für den Frieden" (Rock for Peace): in 1987, Pankow, a Berlin band led by vocalist André Herzberg and quoted at the beginning of this section on the politics of boredom, directly challenged that caveat, exposing the SED hypocrisy of encouraging peace while battling internal peace initiatives.[20] And the walls of socialist utopia came tumbling down.

"Punk"—Rock and the Public Sphere

"Punk is the language people can use to protect their feelings from the civilization that has achieved independence."

—Key Pankonin (*Keynkampf*)[21]

Punk holds a peculiar place of honor in GDR history. The music, the look, and the lifestyle presented the authorities with a great practical and conceptual challenge. While the impetus resonated with the official, lofty goals of the party, the potential for uncontrollable and incorrigible politics, for a meaning beyond "entertainment music," posed a threat. In the reference work *Rock: Interpreten, Autoren, Sachbegriffe*, H.P. Hofmann defines punk's purpose:

> Profoundly social causes are the basis for the origin of punk rock: unemployment among young people, dim prospects for the future, but it was also the rise of racism and neo-fascism that widened the gulf between the gray reality of everyday life and the dazzling freedoms from obligation that were offered by a majority of the established rock-hierarchy with access to highly unaffordable equipment, to such an extent that young musicians felt compelled to counter it with a music of their own feelings, thoughts, attitudes, and (financial) possibilities.[22]

In this description of punk's conceptual and practical origins, the author locates the impulses in an almost noble critique of capitalist conditions, naming unemployment, racism, and a "no-future" outlook as the prime movers. Hofmann appears here almost as an apologist for the infamous "three-chord" ability of punk rockers and nearly implies that this often maligned quality of their musical performance is predicated on what (little) equipment they can afford. Indeed, the early reception of punk in the GDR was positive, emphasizing its raw social critique.[23] This opinion held sway until the style and sound were imported and tried out at home; then the object of criticism shifted to socialism with its own gray, everyday realities.

The insistence on bleak everyday reality as a legitimate object of rock-musical culture offsets the overwhelming force of rock designed to "shape" a socialist personality through affirmations and fictitious reinforcements of political rhetoric. Wicke, in a 1988 essay entitled "Rock Music and Everyday Culture in the GDR," addresses the inscription of the socialist-specific aspects of everyday life into music. While he notes the importance of routine and its capacity to foster connections beyond institutional social organization, he also widens the lens to include as well the ". . . casual and fleeting experiences such as dreams, desires, and hopes which reach beyond purposeful actions within a social framework." He continues:

> These disparate moments are not isolated events; they are embedded in a cultural pattern in which they are related to each other, where they crystallize into values and value concepts and thus continue the complex dynamics of life, the individual appropriation of social conditions.[24]

The reality of the everyday articulated along with the compensatory cognitive acts of the dream and desire expressed in rock constitute a crucial aspect of socialist youth culture.

Punk does not translate easily. Many bands had a "punk" phase that marked a rite of passage or a provocation. While the transnational genre of punk manifests itself differently within national or local cultures, GDR punk became associated with pugnacious, fast music that broke social and political norms specific to socialist culture. Punk was a synonym for subversion. Specifically political bands were persecuted; others were intentionally mainstreamed in order to accommodate and co-opt the discontent of a younger audience.[25] In spite of this cynical move by the state, the impetus to turn the status quo inside-out persisted among the bands. Two groups in particular, though not punk bands per se, achieved this critique by turning the rhetoric of the state against itself. They participated in the alternative music culture that occupied and criticized the idiom of a socialist utopian project. The myth of the GDR as a socialist utopia in the cultural production of such sources as the rock bands Sandow and Herbst in Peking points to the pervasiveness of the theme and an impatience with its historical disappointments. The generation "born into socialism" (Kolbe) held up the "real existing socialist" utopia to scrutiny in the mirror of their own reality—even if they never seriously believed the sayings of the state. For a generation of performers "born in the GDR," the myth takes a different form:

> I'd like to tell you about a country that a lot of people call never-never land, that some people call paradise. Really wise heads call the country communism,

but we just call it wonderland. That is the country where no weapons are needed. The country where you can really live and love and the country that we don't have yet (*Whisper and Scream*).

This introduction to a performance of the rock group Chicoree's song "Wunderland"—the band broke up in the course of the film shoot—is followed by an explanation of the lyrics and the sentiment. In the context of the documentary film, the lead singer says: "It's a feeling of warmth. It's my naive idea of communism" (*Whisper and Scream*). In this quotation, the speaker expresses a sentiment close to the party line; the country is on its way to paradise. Still, the calls for disarmament come from the mouths of rock singers. This is the country of the "not yet."

In a more speculative moment, the lead singer from Sandow (a radically different group), Kai-Uwe Kohlschmidt, asks questions in his lyrics that amount to an indictment of history, as well as of the present society and its politics. Sandow introduces a song called "It's the Day, It's the Way" with the statement:

> Right now what interests me, okay, the German nation or our people in general were once, as they used to say so nicely, a people of poets and thinkers, and I'm preoccupied with the question, which is that today? Who are the thinkers? Are we dealing with an iceberg without a tip? (*Whisper and Scream*).

The song, which the lead singer goes on to describe but not to perform, ends with the question: where are the heroes? In the world of official cultural policy, those questions remained unanswered. Sandow answered them in a song called "Born in the GDR," the ironic anthem of a generation, which will be discussed below.

Kohlschmidt and Chris Hinze founded the band in Cottbus when they were 14 and 13 respectively, taking the name from a section of that city. Sandow survived the *Wende*, and continued to perform for a decade. The band members, including Tilman Berg and Tilman Fürstenau since 1987, have always produced "innovative music" and developed independent of trends, though they passed through a punk phase. Sandow achieved an almost cult status in the former GDR. Early on, the band played at women's conferences and brigade parties—whenever and wherever they could find an audience. As most bands, Sandow had its own sound system, and they wandered from place to place (on bicycles or by train, referred to in the band's biography on their website as "die Zeit der Zug-und Fahrradtourneen, 1984[26]), followed by loyal fans. Under such circumstances, live perform-ances provided an opportunity denied to amateur bands by the painstaking process of obtaining permissions, *Einstufung*,[27] an effective form of censorship enforced by the record label with a nationwide monopoly, AMIGA. Sandow was represented on the AMIGA sampler called "die anderen bands," which is treated in more detail below. They produced a record for AMIGA with some difficulty. They also traveled with the film "Flüstern und Schreien" and did a tour. The band performed in the cinemas where the documentary was shown. "For the first time," according to Kohlschmidt,

> there was something like an open podium for the expression of personal opinions, which otherwise didn't exist at all. People were more or less ashamed of expressing an opinion. And the later it got, the longer the night, the more open the atmosphere. At first people were careful. Those were subversive nights. Under observation by the Stasi and the power of the state.[28]

Kohlschmidt describes an evolving "public sphere," the occasion for which was rock music. The relationship between rock and revolution gets a bit tighter.

The 1980s drove a wedge between the more adventurous experimental groups and those Christoph Tannert describes as a "Schlaf-Rock-Verbund mit genereller Wirkungslosigkeit" (Night-robe-rock group, generally ineffectual),[29] which, however, enjoyed "official" status as well as record contracts. Tannert puns on the double meaning of "Schlaf-Rock" as a night shirt, or, literally, sleeping skirt, and the resonance of Rock for rock music. In contrast to these sleeping musicians, he characterizes the aim of punk groups of the 1980s as one of aesthetic revolution as well as a new form of protest. Most of these bands remained unofficial, some through the refused recognition of the state, some by choice. The punks were generally associated with left-wing proletariat, and were thus the frequent victims of the violent right-wing radical skinheads.[30]

Tannert marks the change from the tame 1970s, dominated by the official bands, such as the Puhdys. A few songs in the early 1980s challenged the perception of socialist rock as impossibly functionary. Tannert writes,

> Whoever refused to be isolated by the hammer and sickle and the carefully circumscribed spheres of daily freedom of movement; whoever refused to be be driven out of the country, as so many musicians and their fans, that person could only hope with impatience for the waves of impatience already foaming around the world; for independence, open words and the increasing sense of self-worth.[31]

Tannert describes a situation in which change pended. By the mid-1980s, intrepid independent labels were available; a journal called *Unterhaltungskunst* (*Entertainment Arts*) wrote not only about some of the new bands, such as

Sandow and Herbst in Peking but about many others as well. One thing is clear: popular music, certain theater productions, informal readings, as well as the alternative scene, filled in the silences created by the disenfranchisement of the general populace through the authority of the SED state. The absence of a critical media or any other forum for public discourse was felt among the musicians and a few adventurous and strategically placed fans, such as Lutz Schramm at DT64, and Ebi Fischel and Ronald Galenza who wrote for *Unterhaltungskunst*, and who became allies in musical taste. Though it existed under the watchful eye of the Stasi, the music scene produced some of the most energetic, directly and indirectly political critique of the system, and some even had fun doing it.[32]

The attempt to provide a forum for new music was not motivated directly by politics. In his article about the "Indie-Nische," Schramm recounts the small and significant victories at DT64 and other venues for music that located itself outside the mainstream. He points to the "speed" of radio as a contributing factor to the difficulty in exercising censorship of broadcasts. Schramm describes the way his own project, Parocktikum—with the noble inclusiveness of seeing "all" in rock music and the sinister echo of *Panoptikum*, being seen—slipped through the "eye-of-the-needle" created by complete censorship on the one hand and selective prohibitions at DT64 on the other. Parocktikum began broadcasting in March 1986. According to Schramm, it became an "Informationsquelle und -börse" (source and exchange of information).[33] Like the concerts and meetings organized around the film discussed above, the show exceeded its function of playing music. As Schramm describes it, Parocktikum was "in der ersten Zeit nicht so sehr ein Musikprogramm, als vielmehr eine Art Minenräumboot" (at first not so much a music program as a minesweeper). Schramm responded to feedback from his audience that was interested in punk and also in GDR bands beyond the usual suspects. In 1987, more and more amateur bands sent cassettes, Sandow among them. That year, Walter Cikan, executive producer of youth music for GDR broadcasting, approached Schramm with the idea of financing several of the bands. In 1988, AMIGA released an LP, "die anderen bands," in the "Kleeblatt" series. The "Parocktikum" sampler as well appeared that year. By the end of 1989, the dance was over. Schramm's article, however, rehearses the exigencies of playing and producing independent music under the conditions of censorship; the conditions themselves politicize the effort.

While not overtly politicized like certain oppositional groups (Initiative for Peace and Human Rights, for example), some bands took risks both aesthetically and politically. The aesthetic dominance of Socialist Realism had as its goal the representation of everyday work and life in art. The East German everyday of the 1980s that was most desperately in need of general critical examination, is precisely what was often evacuated from the stages, screens, and pages of East German cultural production and political discourse. In their speculations on the existence of an alternative rock scene in the GDR, Baumgartner and others point to the themes of certain rock bands:

> In their own lyrics/music, but also in the processing of certain stimuli, even quotations from Brecht, Eisler, Kästner, and Mühsam, many groups took a stand on the problems of everyday life, as for example thoughtlessness, the "co-conspirator" or "follower" mentality, careerism, egoism, bureaucracy. Not least significantly, many pieces demonstrate a growing consciousness of threatening danger of war, ecological death, and neo-fascism.[34]

The authors of the study quoted above continue to compare the political function of punk in the early 1980s to the earlier effects of blues in the GDR. (Punk came to the attention of Mielke and the Ministerium für Staatssicherheit, in the early-1980s as discussed in an article by Peter Wicke and later documented by others.)[35] Though the authors point to the potential political implications of punk and other alternative groups, they stop short of asserting the important role such musicians played in providing a "positive" identification for GDR youth.

Before focusing on two bands, Sandow and Herbst in Peking, it is necessary to rehearse briefly the modest concessions made by GDR institutions to the rise of punk and other forms of alternative rock. The film cited above, *Whisper and Scream (Flüstern und Schreien)*, a DEFA production directed by Dieter Schuman and Jochen Wisotzki, documented the rock culture, its performances, its fans, and its bands, in 1988.[36] Significant is the willingness of a GDR institution, DEFA, the only film studio, to sponsor the documentary in the first place. As mentioned above, AMIGA released the album "Parocktikum, die anderen Bands," featuring the music of Hard Pop, Die Skeptiker, Feeling B, Sandow, die anderen, AG Geige, Der Expander des Fortschritts, and others. On the back cover, Schramm explains the appeal of the bands, which lies in an "unverlogene Beziehung zum Hörer ihrer Musik" ("genuine relationship to the listeners of their music"). Further, he writes, this relationship is determined by community:

> A relationship, which is characterized not by an applied image, rather by the fact that after the concert they ride home in the same subway and the next day, in the same cafe on the corner, they can talk about common problems, without being divided into autograph hunters and autograph givers.[37]

The accessibility of the bands, largely from Berlin and Leipzig, constitutes in part the success of the music, according to Schramm. The album bears the same name as the radio program on DT64, dating from 1986, as discussed earlier. In the print media, changes took place as well. *Unterhaltungskunst* published a series of articles focusing on the new bands. For example, in the eighth and the eleventh articles, Ronald Galenza and Ebi Fischel wrote about Sandow and Herbst in Peking respectively.[38] Thus a few people served to mediate between the bands and the audience.

Still, the direct relationship between the public and the bands, which Schramm describes on the Parocktikum album, marks a moment of GDR-specificity in the music scene. Zocher describes the dynamics of the band–audience relationship in the context of an absent public sphere: "We were a society living under a cheese-dome."[39] There was no intact public sphere, though he claims that in the 1980s an informal network of intrepid individuals who took responsibility for effecting change formed. In addition, couriers traveled through the country on bicycles; according to some fans, every type of music was available on a limited black market, with perhaps a one-month time lag. DT64 provided a *Mitschnittservice*, the continuous playing of an album that could be taped by the listening audience. Most important was the intensity of the live performances, the queues of people waiting to storm the record stores for a newly released album, and the possibility of establishing an understanding among the performers and the audience. This understanding could be signaled by a single word, such as "wall" or, according to Zocher, the word "teacher" from a Mixed Pickles song "Lied an eine ergraute Lehrerin" (song to a distinguished [gray-haired] teacher). Mixed Pickles had broken up at the time of our interview. Other bands went in search of an audience. In the 1990s, the audience went in search of a past GDR-identity, and many (re)discovered some of these bands and their music.

Sampling Socialism

The politicization of popular culture in the GDR contributed to the general unrest in that country in the 1980s, as Wicke and others have pointed out, perhaps attributing too much political intent to the individual bands. The emergence of rock groups, both amateur and professional, whose lyrics twisted GDR party rhetoric, pointed to the discrepancies between the mythical socialist utopia and the reality of life in socialism. The group Sandow produced an explosive song that rivaled Uwe Kolbe's poem as the banner of a generation. In "Born in GDR," an obvious reference to Bruce Springsteen's "Born in the USA" as well as to the 160,000 people in attendance at a concert in Berlin in 1988, Sandow combines the anger and resignation of a generation born into socialism, but with the intent of mocking the sentiment involved. The song, which was supposed to appear on an album under negotiation with AMIGA, effectively prevented the record's

release. The song remained controversial in GDR broadcasting. The text
follows:

> jetzt jetzt lebe ich
> jetzt jetzt lebe ich
> jetzt jetzt trinke ich
> jetzt jetzt stinke ich
> jetzt jetzt rauche ich
> jetzt jetzt brauch ich dich
> wir bauen auf und tapezieren nicht mit
> wir sind so stolz auf katerina witt katerina katerina
> BORN IN THE GDR (4x)
>
> wir können bis an unsere grenzen gehen
> hast du schon mal darüber hinweggesehen
> ich habe 160.000 menschen gesehen die sangen so schön
> sie sangen so schön sie sangen so schön
> BORN IN THE GDR BORN IN THE GDR BORN IN THE GDR[40]

> ["Born in the GDR"
> now now I'm living
> now now I'm living
> now now I'm drinking
> now now I'm stinking
> now now I'm smoking
> now now I need you
> we're building up and not decorating the walls.
> we're so proud of katerina witt, katerina, katerina,
> born in the GDR (4x).
>
> we can go as far as our borders
> have you looked beyond them?
> I saw 160,000 people, who sang so beautifully
> they sang so beautifully, they sang so beautifully,
> born in the GDR (4x).

"Born in GDR" (Sandow, 3:27)

With typical high energy from Sandow, this song is triumphant and
ominous, aggressive and self-satisfied. The anger of the stanzas is set off by
the return to the introductory music in the refrains. Sandow refers to the
narcotizing activity of an entire country that had no statistics on alcohol
abuse, drug abuse, or suicide. The repetition of "living" is self-impugning.
The progress from "drinking" to "stinking" to "smoking" culminates in
what can only be an ironic comment on the need to "build": "und jetzt jetzt
brauch ich dich wir bauen auf und tapezieren nicht mit." Here Sandow
allies the "speaker" in this song with the SED regime, for the GDR resisted
glasnost and perestroika. Party ideologue Kurt Hager made the point in a
speech that the GDR did not have to "hang wallpaper" just because the
neighbor, read the Soviet Union, was doing it.[41] Apart from the rupture in

syntax, the anacoluthonic twisting of the rhetoric familiar from the founding of the socialist state, the dictum *Aufbauen*, of having to "work" on the foundation of a socialist utopia, of *mittapezieren*, deflates the dream with its own vocabulary. Any stable interpretation of the song is disrupted by the things the band has said about it in interviews.[42] Even so, the song was elevated to the level of political protest, largely, one could speculate, because of the aggressive energy in the music.

Sandow uses the rhetoric of the socialist utopian vision against the reality of the SED state. The end of the first stanza indicates the degree of frustration with the discrepancy between theory and reality: the reference to Katerina Witt, the international ice skating champion held up in the GDR press as a heroine, who was booed when she introduced Bryan Adams at a concert, and blasted with criticism—based on privileges she enjoyed—after the *Wende*, marks the transition to the refrain. The singer virtually spits the name out, at the same time the lyrics claim how proud society is of her accomplishments. The words say one thing while the voice screams another.

This song has resonated since the *Wende* beyond the borders of the former East German state. It has also been anthologized on all "East German" record collections as the representative whisper/scream. In the Deutsche Schallplatten release "Aufbruch Umbruch Abbruch. Die letzten Jahre," Bongwater and Giwsoj write: "Sandow, the angry young men from Cottbus, described with precision in 'Born in the G.D.R.' the disgruntled mood of the last years of the GDR-era on its way out. Even if the band distances itself from the song today, the music remains rooted in a time when one shook hands upon meeting."[43] In an interview in a rock journal, Sandow indicates that the song was a "Spott-Lied auf die DDR" (song to mock the GDR) against what it called "verlogene Sentimentalität" (false sentimentality).[44] The interviewers ask about the tension between the sound and the message in the song, to which Kohlschmidt replies:

> Those were other circumstances. "Born in the GDR" was just a song making fun of the GDR, at least in our opinion. It was built up during the "Wende" by the media, not by us. I can show you texts I wrote in 1983, they are so moralizing, so full of dripping indignation about some sort of situation . . . I say, yes, it is a leap, and we still haven't landed, and we're leaving all that behind us, because I know, it's all so imperfect. Our only goal is to remain on our way.[45]

The song changes with historical circumstance and GDR identity. Sandow planned to sing the song again in the future:

> Our immediate future lies outside the GDR. That will also widen the scope thoroughly. I will announce GDR-identity when it has just been forgotten.

Then we will sing ["Born in the GDR"] again, not to mock as before, but rather as a grotesque, threatening hymn. (Since the fall of the Wall, we haven't sung it anymore, because its goal had been fulfilled.)[46]

Sandow has played a crucial role in the recognition of GDR rock music. For them, though, the relationship between music and society has changed. In a fax interview, Sandow responded to questions about this relationship in the following manner:

It (the relationship between society and music) can't be avoided, but I find it only attractive or necessary under totalitarian conditions.[47]

On political understanding came the response:

My political understanding begins with the RAF and, considering its fatality, ends there as well. I'm interested more in negative energy of every attempt of structural disturbances, as everything becomes a constitutive part, regardless of which nature or calling it had in the beginning.[48]

The band has since released several albums and toured the western part of Germany and elsewhere in Europe. It continued to compose and perform innovative music, taking the form of music theater, spoken music pieces, compositions of Artaud's texts, and a drum performance called NGOMA. Its eighth album, "Stachelhaut," appeared in 1998. Sandow's initial post-Wall success can be attributed in part to an adventurous and dedicated producer located in West Berlin. After the fall of the Wall, Jor Janka went East to avail himself of the cassette collection at DT64. He signed the band whose music he describes as "pure rock and roll" and whose musicians he said were "living for the music." Below I will return to his points, and to Sandow's activities at the end of the millennium.

Bakschischrepublik

Perhaps the most fed-up of all the GDR bands of the 1980s was Herbst in Peking. More clearly than any of the bands described above, Herbst in Peking indicts the Stalinist state for its failures, its illusions, and its lies. Also highly anthologized, the song constitutes ". . . der Abgesang auf eine deutsche Republik im Zustand der Agonie" (the final stanza to a German republic in a state of agony, quoted from "Aufbruch . . ."). The song, introduced by strains from the socialist anthem "Internationale" and mixed with a speech by Walter Ulbricht combines dissonance, disrupted rhythm, and accusational tones of voice to make the point that there is a radical disjuncture between the sentiment of the "Internationale" and the nation that was the GDR:

> Wir leben in der Bakschischrepublik und es gibt keinen Sieg.
> Die Hoffnung ist ein träges Vieh und nährt sich an der Staatsdoktrin.
> Man wird die roten Götter schleifen, viele werden das nicht begreifen.
> Der Götzendiener, pißt sich eins, so einfach ist es Mensch zu sein.
> Wir leben in der Bakschischrepublik und es gibt keinen Sieg.
> Schwarz rot gold ist das System, morgen wird es untergehen.
> [mixed with a speech by Walter Ulbricht]
> Das Volk, es wird in Trance verfallen und eine alte Hymne lallen.
> Schwarz rot gold ist das System, morgen wird es untergehen.
> Der Götzendiener, pißt sich eins.
> Es könnte alles falsch gewesen sein.
>
> [Bakschisch Republic
> We live in the bakschisch republic and there is no victory.
> Hope is a lazy dumb cow and feeds on state doctrine.
> We'll grind the red gods, many won't understand it.
> He who worships false gods, piss off!
> It's so simple to be human.
> We live in the bakschisch republic and there is no victory.
> The system is black red gold, tomorrow it will collapse.
> [speech, mixed with the International playing in the background]
> The people will fall into a trance, and mumble an old hymn.
> He who worships false gods, piss off!
> It could all have been wrong.]

"Bakschischrepublik" (Herbst in Peking, 2:35)

Finally, Herbst in Peking declares that the Kaiser is wearing no clothes, and that there is no victory over history in the republic that is dominated by corruption and petty bribes (*Bakschisch*). The red, communist gods, the old heroes, and those who worship them, are finished, for the system is going under. The final stanza, separated from the opening of the song by a parody of a state address in which a voice declaring that socialism will be constructed according to plan (*planmäßig aufgebaut wird*) hollows out the superlative history of the GDR.

The band arrived on the scene without a prehistory, according to an interview with Jürgen Winkler and Aram Radomski. Their musical roots include Velvet Underground and Lou Reed.[49] Herbst in Peking broke up after "Internationale," though they were known even before its release for their music as well as their self-assured performance style perceived as unusual in the GDR. After the *Wende*, Rex Joswig, the lead singer, founded the label Peking Records, which is currently on ice due to legal complications, but he is still with the band, which broke up in December 1990 and performed again for the first time in 1993. They have taken on Trötsch, whose Stasi involvement during his time with the band "Die Firma" certainly alienated some fans, but their goal is to make music. A later project, "Terrible Herbst," was released on "Stay Hip Records." The band's first album, "To be hip," was recorded live in Paris at Espace LSC and Live in Ebersbrunn at the Gasthaus zum Löwen in 1990. It includes a song "Parade," the lyrics of which alliterate on words beginning with "p," from "paradox" to "paradise" to "police state" to "panopticum," and an instrumental entitled "Leon Trotzki." In an interview with Joswig, he mentioned the band's one-time plans for the future, which included an open-air concert called "Amnesty for Mecklenburg," and that he himself hosted a radio show for years. The band released records throughout the 1990s, among them "Das Jahr Schnee" (Plattenmei [EFA], 1996), "La Dolce Vita" (Maxi Single, Plattenmei [Indigo], 1998), "Feuer Wasser und Posaunen" (Moloko, 1998), and "Les Fleurs du Mal" (Moloko Plu [EFA], 1999). Like other surviving bands, Herbst in Peking was constantly pushing the limits of "entertainment" music, covering their own songs, experimenting with a variety of musical idioms, but maintaining a critical stance. "Every country gets the entertainers it deserves," he said, speaking his own words of wisdom.[50] The declining GDR certainly deserved his criticism. The band's declaration became an anthem for the political death of a nation.

"Es könnte alles falsch gewesen sein." The interviewers describe the song as follows: " 'Bakschisch-Republik' is until today the definitive song about the situation of the nation. It is as inflamed as the time between *Wende* and annexation, between awakening and lethargy."[51] Finally, after half a century, the lyrics of the sarcastic song suggests an inkling of an admission of error. That which was utopia, which was claimed to be utopia, has been recognized—in rock lyrics—as the opposite. For the generation of musicians born into the GDR, the self-proclaimed socialist utopia of the East, the possibility that the regime had made a mistake resonates throughout their work. Their critical stance, their capacity to use the persuasive power of the Party against itself, and their ability to empower themselves and their fans through that co-optation of language attest to the political significance of rock music in the GDR. When the official cultural representatives had abandoned utopia, the unlikely successors made it their mission to explore the nature and nation of their own ideal commonwealth; to hold that image up to their daily encounters with the regime as well as the pathology of everyday life; and to declare the reality of "real existing socialism" illusory and transform their illusions into reality.

Now, while GDR history is "under erasure," many look back on the time between the fall of the Wall and reunification as a period of productive anarchy. During that time, many bands enjoyed the fleeting interest of a new audience; many now lament the loss of *Verständigung* with the old audience. Few survived the transition to a market economy; fewer the dawn of a new millennium. Sandow was one of few bands with a West Berlin label in the immediate post-Wall era. Herbst in Peking founded a label, had an extremely unpleasant encounter with capitalism, and went on to establish another label. The band members, who shifted around, found day-jobs. Other bands have become so successful that no one cares about their birth certificates. The band Rammstein, which has musicians from Berlin and Schwerin who played for other GDR bands, for example, has achieved success both nationally and internationally. Their records have gone gold: their music goes beyond the realm of the socially and politically acceptable, which has its own appeal. Other bands enjoyed a period of regained popularity within a local club scene even though economic realities hit fans hard. Until recently, record distributors seemed to be pulling out of the Eastern states. In the early 1990s, Jor Janka saw a bleak future for GDR bands and fans alike: he predicted a time when a kid in Rostock would only be able to order records by mail. There was little to no response to the new music from the East in the former West. The initially exotic, unknown aspects of the music disappeared or lost their attraction for a West German audience, which politicized the reception of those groups. With the passing of the political moment came the loss of interest in anything and everything, even the most stunning examples of innovative music, from *drüben*. Though Deutsche Schallplatten has rereleased much of what constitutes GDR rock in the series "Rock aus Deutschland (Ost)," and anthologies of *Wende* music have appeared, the very availability of the material seems to have lessened its value. Only that which remains inaccessible seems to be worthwhile.

Indeed, there was generalized cynicism about the future of the music produced in the former GDR. Little to no interest exists in the former West for this music, due, according to Jor Janka (Modern Musik), to the politicized reception of the bands immediately after the fall of the Wall. They were exotic; they were politically oppressed, and they lost the claim to that status during the transition to a market economy. The initial optimism about signing with new, established labels and going on tour faded in the first year. The scene still exists in the local clubs. The unfamiliar has become the norm; the market functions differently from the former censors, though the end result, silence or marginalization, is the same. Many of the labels founded in the early 1990s went under; with the exception of Freygang, the bands that once enjoyed a cult status in the East have broken up and gotten day jobs. There is, however, some East German influence on the public sphere, in the broadcasting media. Still, in the first year after the *Wende*,

Zocher indicated, no newsstand would sell East German publications, such as fanzines devoted to new music from the East. Janka pulls no punches: "The press is completely fucked up. People in Hamburg don't know where East Germany is. They pick out the politics. For some reason, they all focus on the politics . . . . Elsewhere, people judge groups like Sandow for the music. They get positive reviews all over the place . . . . Not in West Germany."[52]

A shift in the ground of identity does seem to have taken place. There are both positives and negatives to this politics of particularly German pop-cultural identity. In the 1990s, bands who made the transition from the GDR to the FRG succeeded because they do not explicitly thematize the content and politics of what has become their private history. Successful bands included "Bobo in White Wooden Houses" whose songs were in English and who could be seen on MTV. And, to paraphrase Peter Zocher[53] with reference to the "Prinzen," a band which enjoyed a certain crossover success—no one knows where they come from. As the tenth anniversary of the fall of the Wall approached, there was a brief resurgence of both cele-bratory and defiant GDR identity. Some things were again "staying the same." In 1997, Sandow released a CD entitled "Born." On it, they sang "Born in the G.D.R."—again. Apparently the time had come to cover their own song in a post-socialist and post-satirical way. But Sandow performed its farewell concert in 1999. Kohlschmidt continues to perform in a band, and he is involved in a range of other projects from sound-editing on the also popular "Lola rennt" to the production of radio plays. But an era came to an end.

The late 1990s did witness the recuperation of positive associations with a lost GDR identity, especially in the realm of popular culture. The use of GDR music in the hit film "Sonnenallee" points to a certain distanced nostalgia for the soundtrack with which a generation came of age. More recently, the widespread success of Wolfgang Becker's "Good-bye Lenin" both in Germany and abroad was shored up with critical acclaim. That film, however, walks a finer line between loss and critique. The critical impulses associated with the GDR music of the late 1980s can still be heard in pop-ular idioms of German music. A highly politicized punk culture still thrives marginally in Germany. Alongside a more mainstreamed genre that include such established bands as Die Toten Hosen, are bands such as SPN-X, from Cottbus, a band that dedicates songs to violence against skinheads as well as to their own sex drives and need for media recognition. Other contempo-rary bands access a wide range of popular genres, from rap and hiphop to reggae and soul, to voice against the economic, social, and political targets the globalizing Federal Republic of Germany continues to provide.

Notes

I would like to thank the Institute for the Humanities and the International Institute at the University of Michigan for support during various stages of work on this article. In addition, I owe thanks to Belinda Cooper, Ina Merkel, Felix Mühlberg, Tim Taylor, Frauke E. Lenckos, Kai-Uwe Kohlschmidt, Rex Joswig, Jor Janka, Konstanze Kriese, and Peter and Ursula Zocher, for their generosity of time, material, and spirit. I offer special thanks to Michael and Birgit Rauhut for continued friendship and support.

1. One of the first to comment on the divide between official and unofficial culture in the GDR was Peter Rossman. See his "Zum 'Intellektuellenstreit': 'Intellectuals' in the Former GDR," in *Gegenwartsbewältigung: The GDR after the Wefnde*, Patricia A. Simpson, guest editor, *Michigan Germanic Studies* v.21, n.1/2 (Spring/Fall 1995): pp. 32–36.

2. Uwe Kolbe, *Hineingeboren. Gedichte 1975–1979* (Frankfurt am Main: Suhrkamp Verlag, 1982 [Berlin and Weimar: Aufbau-Verlag, 1980]). The poem has come to signify a feeling of generational affiliation among those "born into" socialism.

3. The difference between a "professional" and an "amateur" band was significant in the GDR. Everything from permission to perform to getting paid depended on that distinction. For the purpose of this article, these designations are primarily heuristic devices; the bands discussed here frequently obtained official permission in order to perform, yet their songs are often implicitly or explicitly critical. In some cases, going through the process of *Einstufung* (categorization) meant alienating an audience. The bands should be treated on an individual basis, for they do not sing with one voice.

4. See Peter Wicke, "The Role of Rock Music in the Political Disintegration of East Germany," in *Popular Music and Communication*, 2nd edition, James Lull, ed. (Newbury Park, London: Sage Publications, 1992), pp. 196–206. He makes similar points in "The Times They Are A-Changin'. Rock Music and Political Change."

5. See Lutz Schramm, "Sonderstufe mit Konzertberechtigung—die DT64 Indie-Nische zwischen sanfter Zensur und Szene-Belebung," Internet website (www.fritz.de/team/lutz), taken from *DT64 Das Buch zum Jugenradio 1964–1993*, Andreas Ulrich and Jörg Wagner, eds. (Leipzig: Thom Verlag, 1993). I refer to this article with the kind permission of the author.

6. "Dasselbe Land zu lange gesehen,/ Dieselbe Sprache zu lange gehört,/ Zu lange gewartet, zu lange gehofft,/ Zu lange die alten Männer verehrt Ich bin rumgerannt . . . ." Pankow, "Langeweile," from "Pankow 10 Jahre," v.10 of "Rock aus Deutschland Ost," Deutsche Schallplatten GmbH (1991). I treat this song and the band in greater detail in "Retro-Nationalism? Rock Music in the Former German Democratic Republic (GDR)" in *Rock Music and Nationalism: A Multinational Perspective*, Mark Yoffe and Andrea Collins, eds. (Amersham: Cambridge Scholars Press, forthcoming in 2006).

7. As defined by Manfred Stock and Philipp Mühlberg in their insightful book *Die Szene von innen. Skinheads, Grufties, Heavy Metals, Punks* (Berlin: LinksDruck, 1990), the "scene" ". . . erscheint hier als eine spezielle Organisationsform kollektiver Bindung, die sich von anderen Formen, beispielsweise von der festen gefügten Gruppe, unterscheidet. In der Szene herrscht eine Balance zwischen

Intimität und Anonymität. Man kennt sich teils persönlich, teils vom Sehen, aber auch als Unbekannter stößt man nicht gleich auf Ablehnung. Entscheidend ist nicht, daß jeder jeden kennt, sondern daß man davon ausgehen kann, in der Szene Gleichgesinnte zu treffen, Bekannte, über die sich rasch Kontakt zu weiteren Personen herstellen läßt" (p. 240). In a substantial scholarly and highly readable work, Olaf Leitner argues against the existence of a "scene" in GDR rock music in the early 1980s, suggesting that it would be a bit "euphoric" to do so. See Olaf Leitner, *Rockszene DDR. Aspekte einer Massenkultur im Sozialismus* (Reinbek bei Hamburg: Rowel Taschenbuch Verlag, 1983), p. 412ff. "Denn 'Szene' verpflichtet auf ein künstlerisches Environment, das Literatur, Film, Fotografie, Malerei, Graphik (Poster, Plattencover, Werbeprospekte), Presse (Fanzines, Rockzeitschriften), Theater, Mode und immer stärker Video einbezieht," pp. 412–413. Precisely these aspects of the GDR's alternative culture—however problematic this term remains in light of the degree of Stasi involvement—developed during the mid- to late 1980s.

8. "Tingeln für den Sozialismus," Elmar Kraushaar in *die tageszeitung* (August 10, 1991), p. 12. See also Timothy W. Ryback, *Rock Aroung the Bloc: A History of Rock Music in Eastern Europe and the Soviet Union* (New York: Oxford University Press, 1990), p. 9. The party ideologue Kurt Hager compared the bouffant hair style to the mushroom cloud that rises from an atomic bomb and, to quote Ryback's assessment, amounted to ". . . a subliminal inducement to war hysteria" (p. 9). For a more complete history of rock in the GDR, see Leitner, "Unterhaltungskunst statt Vergnügungsindustrie," p. 21ff. I cite newspaper articles from the time following the fall of the Wall to indicate a level of interest in the GDR which since seems to have lapsed.

9. Ibid., "Tingeln für den Sozialismus," p. 12. See also Ryback, *Rock*, p. 8.

10. Ibid., "Tingeln," p. 12.

11. See Wicke, "The Times," p. 82. See also Ryback, *Rock*, p. 28ff. The author discusses the party's "war" on rock, declared in 1958. Ryback cites the 60/40 clause—or the regulations for playing or performing music, 60 percent of which had to come from the East, the other 40 percent from the West pending prior approval. In the late 1980s, the intrepid found ways around this percentage, with what Felix Mühlberg described to me as *Prozente abspielen*. In at least one anecdote, the club played the 60 percent East during intermissions.

12. See Ryback, *Rock*, pp. 4, 51, 61ff. on Beatlemania in the GDR. He points to the founding of a Western style radio station, DT64, p. 87. For an account of the Rock Plenum, see p. 88ff.

13. Wicke, "The Times," p. 83.

14. Ryback discusses the period following the June 1953 uprising, *Rock*, p. 27ff. For his analysis of the Biermann case, see p. 39ff.

15. Interview with Peter and Ursula Zocher, Berlin, July 5, 1993. I thank both for their cooperation.

16. For a comprehensive narrative about rock music in the GDR, see Michael Rauhut, *Beat in der Grauzone. DDR-Rock 1964 bis 1972—Politik und Alltag* (Berlin: BasisDruck Verlag, 1993); see also Rauhut, *Schalmei und Lederjacke. Udo Lindenberg, BAP, Underground: Rock und Politik in den achtziger Jahren* (Berlin: Schwarzkopf & Schwarzkopf, 1996).

17. See also Leitner, p. 297. Hagen is described as "Verantwortlicher Mitarbeiter für den Bereich Unterhaltungskunst in der Abteilung Kultur des ZK der SED," and interviewed in *Rockmusik und Politik. Analysen, Interviews und Dokumente*, Peter Wicke and Lothar Müller, eds. (Berlin: Ch. Links Verlag in Zusammenarbeit mit der Berliner Zeitung, 1996), pp. 165–178.

18. Jürgen Hagen, "Unterhaltungskunst—fest mit dem sozialistischen Leben verbunden," in *Praktische und theoretische Fragen der Entwicklung von Unterhaltung und Unterhaltungskunst in der DDR*, ed. Informationszentrum beim Ministerium für Kultur v.4 (1981): pp. 1–32. His specific discussion of themes can be found on p. 16.

19. Hagen, "Unterhaltungskunst," p. 26ff. I treat this essay in greater detail in my "Retro-Nationalism? Rock Music in the Former German Democratic Republic," see note 7.

20. Wicke, "The Times," p. 86. Pankow, named after a part of (East) Berlin, is known, among other things, for its rock spectacles "Paule Panke" and "Hans im Glück," which, according to Olaf Leitner, ". . . stellten Szenen aus der spießig-brutalen Arbeitswelt auf die Bühne (brought scenes from the petit-bourgeois-brutal working world to the stage). Liner notes, "Pankow 10 Jahre," v.10 of Rock aus Deutschland, 1991, Deutsche Schallplatten, Berlin.

21. Key Pankonin, *Keynkampf* (Berlin: Unabhängige Verlagsbuchhandlung Ackerstraße, 1993), p. 26. Pankonin is described as the guitarist and singer of the "Trashfoodpunk 'n' Roll-Band" IchFunktion. He wrote songs for the "Firma," a band implicated in the Stasi network. His book is an autobiographical narrative about life in the "scene." For more on Pankonin and the band, see my "Soundtracks: GDR Music from 'Revolution' to 'Reunification,' " in *The Power of Intellectuals in Contemporary Germany*, Michael Geyer, ed. (Chicago: University of Chicago Press, 2001), pp. 227–248.

22. H.P. Hofmann, *Rock: Interpreten, Autoren, Sachbegriffe* (Berlin: VEB Lied der Zeit, 1983), p. 186: "Es sind zutiefst gesellschaftliche Ursachen, die dem Entstehen des Punk Rock zugrundeliegen: Jugendarbeitslosigkeit, trübe Zukunftsaussichten, aber auch aufkommender Rassismus und Neofaschismus hatten die Kluft zwischen grauem Alltag und dem, was von einem Großteil der etablierten Rock-Hierarchie unter Einsatz von kaum erschwinglichen Gerätschaften an glitzernden Unverbindlichkeiten angeboten wurde, derart vergrößert, daß sich junge Amateurmusiker angesprochen fühlten, dem eine Musik ihrer Gefühle, Gedanken, Haltungen und (finanziellen) Möglichkeiten entgegenzusetzen."

23. There are many references in the journal *Unterhaltungskunst* to Patti Smith, the Ramones, et al.

24. Peter Wicke, "Rock Music and Everyday Culture in the GDR," in *Studies in GDR Culture and Society* 8, Margy Gerber et al., eds. (Lanham, New York, London: University of America Press, 1988), pp. 171–178.

25. See my "Germany and Its Discontents: The Skeptiker's Punk Corrective," in *German Matters in Popular Culture*, Christoph Lorey and John L. Plews, eds., Special Issue, *Journal of Popular Culture* v.34, n.4 (Winter 2000): pp. 129–140.

26. From Sandow's website at www.sandow.de.

27. See Leitner, p. 138.

28. Interview with Kai-Uwe Kohlschmidt, Berlin, June 21, 1993. Again, I express my gratitude to Kohlschmidt for his help.
29. Christoph Tannert, "Post-Punk, auch ohne rote Sterne. DDR-Rock aus dem Unterholz. Die 80er Jahre." Unpublished manuscript, p. 1. I thank Tannert for his generous help and for permission to cite this piece. See also his "Rock aus dem Unterholz," *Jenseits der Staatskultur. Traditionen autonomer Kunst in der DDR*, Gabriele Muschter and Rüdiger Thomas, eds. (Munich: Carl Hanser Verlag, 1992), pp. 155–178.
30. Tannert, p. 3. In the interview with Zocher, indicated that the state seemed unable to differentiate between youth groups, "tossing them all into the same pot." He pointed to some class differences; punks had intellectual, aesthetic aspirations of subversion; the children of the working-class tended to prefer the "hit-parade" and heavy metal (Zocher interview, Berlin, July 6, 1993).
31. Tannert, p. 5. "Wer sich durch Hammer und Sichel und die säuberlich abgezirkelten Bereiche alltäglicher Bewegungsfreiheit nicht hatte isolieren oder außer Landes treiben lassen, wie so manchen Musiker und seine Fans, der hoffte nun ungeduldig auf die bereits weltweit schäumenden Wogen der Unduldsamkeit, Unabhängigkeit, der offenen Worte und des gesteigerten Selbstwertgefühls."
32. I must stress here that those overtly political bands who in their music took aim at the Wall, the Stasi, and specific state institutions were harassed, jailed, drafted into the National Peoples Army (NVA), or sent to the West. Fun was definitely not had by all.
33. Lutz Schramm, "Sonderstufe mit Konzertberechtigung," see website article, which is the source for this information unless otherwise noted.
34. See Baumgartner et al., " 'Alternativrock' in der DDR?" (Berlin: Forschungszentrum populäre Musik, FPM-Publikation 27, 1989), p. 12. "In eigenen Texten/Musik, aber auch bei der Verarbeitung von Anregungen, selbst Zitaten von Brecht, Eisler, Kästner und Mühsam nehmen viele Gruppen Stellung zu Problemen des Alltags, als da sind Gedankenlosigkeit, Mitläufermentalität, Karrierismus, Egoismus, Bürokratie. Nicht zuletzt zeugen viele Stücke vom wachsenden Bewußtsein drohender Kriegsgefahr, ökologischem Tod und Neofaschismus."
35. Peter Wicke, "Pop Music in the GDR between Conformity and Resistance," trans. Margy Gerber, in *Studies in GDR Culture and Society* v.14, n.15, Margy Gerber and Roger Woods, eds. (Lanham, New York, London: University Press of America, 1996), pp. 25–35, here p. 27. Wicke demonstrates the degree to which party officials were at a loss when it came to understanding the vicissitudes of "youth music" in the following: "When in 1984 the Mielke ministry began to take notice of punk music, it was not reacting to developments in the GDR—there were no signs of punk music at that time—but instead to an article on this form of youth culture in the Federal Republic which had appeared shortly before in *Der Spiegel*. The influences were ridiculously slight, but the apparatus had one more category for determining 'negative' developments. This notwithstanding, up to 1989 Party functionaries who still had not learned to pronounce the word properly made public speeches in which they denounced 'Western punk,' not noticing that punk existed under their very noses [. . .]" (p. 34).

Since that article appeared, several books have documented the excessive state response against punk in the former GDR. See, e.g., Ronald Galenza and Heinz Havemeister, eds., *Wir wollen immer artig sein . . . Punk, New Wave, HipHop, Independent-Szene in der DDR 1980–1990* (Berlin: Schwarzkopf & Schwarzkopf Verlag, 1999).

36. See Christoph Dieckmann, *My Generation. Cocker, Dylan, Lindenberg und die verlorene Zeit* (Berlin: LinksDruck, 1991), pp. 250–252, for a review of the film "Flüstern und Schreien."

37. "Eine Beziehung, die nicht durch ein aufgesetztes Image gekennzeichnet ist, sondern dadurch, daß man nach dem Konzert in der gleichen U-Bahn nach Hause fährt und am nächsten Tag im gleichen Café an der Ecke über gemeinsame Probleme reden kann, ohne in Autogrammjäger und Autogrammgeber unterschieden zu werden."

38. See Galenza/Fischel, "Die neuen Bands," 8 and 11, in *Unterhaltungskunst* v.9, n.88, pp. 9–10; and v.12, n.88, p. 10.

39. Zocher, interview, Berlin, July 6, 1993.

40. This version of the text, which varies depending on performance and recording, is taken from the liner notes of the CD "Stationen einer Sucht," Fluxus, LC 6732, 1990. The text posted on Sandow's website also differs slightly, referring to 120,000 people instead of the original 160,000.

41. I thank Ina Merkel for the reference.

42. See "Gegen verlogene Sentimentalität: Sandow," in *Messitsch* (4/1992, August/September), pp. 28–33.

43. See "Aufbruch, Umbruch, Abbruch. Die letzten Jahre," from the series *Rock aus Deutschland*, v.20, Deutsche Schallplatten GmbH., Berlin (1992). "Sandow, die zornigen jungen Männer aus Cottbus, beschrieben mit 'Born in the G.D.R.' sehr genau die Verstimmung der letzten Jahre im ausgehenden DDR-Zeitalter. Auch wenn sich die Band heute von dem Song distanziert, bleibt es Musik aus einer Zeit, als man sich noch die Hand gab, wenn man sich traf" (CD cover).

44. "Sandow," Jürgen Winkler and Rocco Gerloff, *NM!Messitsch. Das Rockmagazin*, 4/1992 (August/September), pp. 28–33. Cover story.

45. "Gegen verlogene Sentimentalität," p. 33. "Das waren ja andere Bedingungen. 'Born in GDR' war von uns nur ein Spottlied auf die DDR. Das ist von den Medien in der Wendezeit hochstilisiert worden, nicht von uns. Ich kann dir Texte von mir zeigen von 1983, die sind so moralisierend, so voll triefender muggerhafter Entrüstung über irgendwelche Zustände . . . ich sage ja, es ist ein Sprung, und wir sind immer noch nicht gelandet, und wir lassen das alles hinter uns, weil ich weiß, es ist alles unvollkommen. Unser einziges Ziel ist es, unterwegs zu bleiben."

46. Fax interview with Kai-Uwe Kohlschmidt, Sandow, April 27, 1993. I thank him for his help. "Unsere nächste Zukunft liegt im Ausland. Das wird auch den Blick nachhaltig weiten. DDR-Identität werde ich aussprechen wenn sie bereits vergessen ist. Dann werden wir 'Born in the GDR' wieder singen, nicht als Spott wie einst, sondern als groteske, bedrohliche Hymne (Seit Mauerfall haben wir es nicht mehr gespielt, weil sein Zweck erfüllt war)."

47. Fax interview, May 1995. "Das läßt sich wohl nicht vermeiden, finde es aber nur unter totalitären Bedingungen für reizvoll oder notwendig."

48. "Mein politisches Verständnis beginnt bei der RAF und endet auch angesichts derer Fatalität dort. Mich interessiert eher Negentropie (negative energy) jeglicher Versuche von Strukturstörungen, wie alles Bestandteil wird, gleich welcher Natur und Bestimmung es zu Beginn war."

49. "Herbst in Peking," interview in *NM!MESSITSCH*.

50. Interview with Rex Joswig, Berlin, July 2, 1993.

51. Winkler/Radomski interview with HiP, p. 59.

52. Interview with Jor Janka, July 1993, Berlin.

53. Follow-up conversation with Peter Zocher in Berlin, March 8, 1994.

CHAPTER SIX

SPIES, SHELL GAMES, AND BANANAS: EVERYDAY SYMBOLS AND METAPHORS IN THE PROCESS OF CULTURAL INTEGRATION OF EAST AND WEST GERMANY

Gottfried Korff

"Spies everywhere," this leitmotif was a standard flourish in one of the intelligent and seemly short stories on the GDR by the German American Irene Dische. Here she precisely outlines the reasons for a flight from the Republic, among others the ubiquity of "spies." The story is contained in the collection *Fromme Lügen* (Pious Lies) from the year 1989 and envisions the time before the fall of the Wall.[1] The formula "spies everywhere" is a concise gloss into everyday-language for a state system of control that first became visible in its complete repressiveness and absurdity in the post-*Wende* years.

"Spies everywhere," this formulation would also be imaginable in a hitherto unwritten story by Irene Dische or whomever else. There it might be explained how the GDR population established itself in a new political and economic system after the collapse of its regime. During 1989 and 1990, a vigilant observer might have discerned an increase in "spies everywhere." Of course, these are different spies from those described by Irene Dische. For these "new" spies were not agents, Stasi informants, or manipulators of opinion, but rather things, namely spy-holes.[2] Mounted on apartment doors, they allow a perspectively widened view of the area around the doorstep from within through an optically excogitated set of lenses. Along with other security devises, spy-holes of this kind encountered a voracious market in the former GDR in 1990–1991. It seemed that the almost frenetic demand for spy-holes, security chains, and locking apparata placed on the market by West German locksmiths and requisitioners was a symbolic rejection of the deposed system of patronage. Marking the border between public and private space, this inconspicuous device, the built-in spy-hole, became an indicator of social and cultural reorientation and reevaluation.

The spy spoken of in the title is not, therefore, a political emissary or someone employed in intelligence, but rather an instrument that in turn served secret observation. In this form the spy joins the other expressions in my title as designations for things and situations that can now be read as metaphors of the *Wende* and German unification, and of the conflicts and fears they caused and conditioned. "Spies, Shell Games, and Bananas" are not only indicators, but also confirming interpretive elements accompanying the cultural and symbolic transformations in Germany. As we know and have been able to observe with intensity in the last few years, symbolic conversions do not only occur in the official political significations of states and social orders. They are not related only to the liquidation of the hammer and sickle, of hands of unity, street names, and monuments to Lenin. Such conversions are also tangible in the sphere of diminutive symbolic forms which emerge in rather unpolitical and primarily unreflexive contexts of everyday life and provide images and meanings, which help to designate and confront new and unstable situations by asserting themselves as temporary and tentative instruments to comprehend unusual challenges and insecurities. Standing behind the words, concepts, and categories presented by politicians, academicians, and cultural producers (to use Bourdieu's term) are images, metaphors, actions, and rituals that furnish modes of orientation and help to make altered realities comprehensible. "For what is happening in Eastern Europe there is still no language except the images that show what is happening . . ." Here, one of the most precise and sensitive observers of the epochal changes in the east, the East European historian Karl Schlögel, has pointed out that the "concepts that once meant something are all used up," noting in addition that even historical analogies have little explanatory power because they lead astray.[3]

With the title words "spies, shell games, and bananas" we are thus confronted with metaphors—or what I call "material metaphors"—that do not definitively disclose altered realities, but do, however, help to understand and interpret them. These are expressions that relate first to the things themselves, then to the import of the things, that is to meanings that are collectively and symbolically enclosed in these things. In his posthumously published *Phänomenologische Skizzen*, Vilém Flusser commented that one can "see things in two ways: observing or reading." If we observe things, then "we see them as phenomena . . . If we read things, then we assume that they mean something and try to decode the meaning."[4] Beyond naming of factual and interactive aspects, "spies, shell games, and bananas" point to cultural meanings that reciprocally illuminate the things and facts themselves and the social actions related to them. For this reason the concept of "material metaphor" seems appropriate, since the observer encounters the spies, shell games, and bananas as factual evidence, as perceptible things, and as actions by observers; yet they additionally contain metaphoric resources of meaning and associations that are actualized in individual situations and finally can be bound and secured in a collective symbolic system.

In historical situations, such as German unification, occurring with such unprecedented speed—at least as far as political negotiations were concerned—informal symbols and signs, though created for the moment, still carry iconic energies or semantic impulses, playing an important role in the social construction of new realities.[5] Spies, shell games, and bananas are shortened lexica of meaning; in situations in which economic and political orders change rapidly and in which various value and normative systems collide, they become elements and instruments of social construction. They function as media of association for self and other and thus serve as extralinguistic media in a discourse that is characterized by a deficit in applicable concepts.

Material metaphors along the order of spies, shell games, and bananas are especially informative in the reconnoitering of changes in political symbolism insofar as their analysis makes perceptible those moods, colorings, and polyvalences that characterize cultural orders and mental conditions of a society just as well as do the contours of political systems and political culture. The occupation with symbolic "diminutive forms" is also enlightening because they involve social forms of expression that, because of their equivocal meaning, must always be examined in context. The intensified consumption and discourse of bananas in 1990–1991 not only reveal the mental consequences of a socialist planned economy, discernable in the heightened demand for southern fruits shortly after the fall of the Wall, but also expose a style of self thematization in accordance with a different political system, manifesting itself in the figures of speech and thought relating to bananas.[6] In interaction with bananas, both in their utility and discursive elements, differing acquired conceptions of the world are validated, conceptions that with good reason can be described as "tragic" (with respect to the old GDR) and "ironic" (with respect to the old FRG).[7]

Their confrontation produced not only an assortment of symbols of distinction or, more precisely; distinctive material metaphors such as bananas, but also the Trabi or the left turn-arrow, all metaphors that are treated and evaluated differently in West and East Germany—either ironically or tragically. Whoever considers only the formulations of pathos in official political symbolism can all too quickly overlook the production patterns of authentic meaning which are incorporated into the "low symbolism" of spies, shell games, and bananas, which perhaps reveal more of the affectivity, fears, and hopes than do the discourses of politics and the media. Whatever is not discursively anchored demands interpretation and thereby brings to light— at least it can be assumed—those colors and multivalences that are just as characteristic for the "new" Federal Republic as the frequently diagnosed trends of westernification toward a society of experience, postmodernity, and so on.

To return to the spy-holes: The impression that the observer had in 1990–1991 of the many boisterous marketplaces in the former GDR can now be documented with economic statistics. The demand for security technology, for fittings, locks, and also spy-holes was so great that lock and key producers speak in retrospect of "distribution bottlenecks." The numbers for the year 1990–1991 provided upon request by the Association of Lock and Fitting Manufacturers show a clear rise of about 20 percent in the production of self-installable cylinder locks and padlocks, a percentage far surpassed in the case of spy-holes.[8] Exact spy-figures from the Association are not available because the production of spy-holes is limited to only four firms. What appears retrospectively in the Association's comments under the catchword "unification boom" had already impressed me during my informal market research during 1990–1991. In the first week of October, 1990, two lock and ironworks salesmen on the Dresden street market informed me of their daily sales of spy-holes—I calculated the weekly sales at almost 650 viewing instruments of varying quality and make. These numbers were partially confirmed by a number of Dresden suburbs and the city center where numerous locksmiths and lock firms were established that constantly referred to self-installable spy-holes in their advertisements.[9]

In discussions with locksmiths, street merchants, and not infrequently with spy-hole customers, it became clear that after the opening of the border, the east rising insecurity accounted for the purchase of lock and security devices both on the west and on the east. Reasons given for the insecurity were not only the increase in burglaries and, more generally, in property crimes, disturbances by peddlers, representatives, and insurance agents, but also a general fear of the new. "We are being overrun by everything coming from the West": this or similar remarks were given when I inquired about the purchase of security locks and spy-holes. It was said that with these viewing holes one could control who or what one was dealing. Whoever intended to protect themselves from unwanted disturbances could do so, unnoticed, with such a viewing device.

At the time of my inquiries in Dresden, in October 1990, there was indeed a steep increase in insecurity due to a drastic rise in burglaries. Radio and press reported daily—at times sensationally—about break-ins, robberies, fraud, and all kinds of scams.[10] There were emotional complaints that along with freedom, human rights, and the market economy came criminality, speculation, and "predatory capitalism"—as citizens of the GDR had been warned for years—indeed right up through the GDR front door. Inquiries in the eastern part of Berlin and again in Dresden in January 1991, revealed that following the political unification in October 1990, there were additional fears relating to land and home ownership, including the reclamation of property by West Germans, and especially relating to the threatening mass unemployment and to the more general loss of legal security. In the summer of 1990 the historian Christian Meier, who has given us an array of astute observations on the mental process of unification, spoke of an "alliance of fears," and described this as a typical transition-syndrome of a society that finds itself in a stage of systemic transformation.[11] Securing one's own four walls and partitioning oneself from the world—accompanied by the possible one-sidedness of visual contact with the outside via the spy-hole—were understandable reactions in this situation. With the installation of a spy-hole one could secure oneself, repulse the foreign and the new, or at least control them.

With this security technique the withdrawal into the private sphere was perfected. After the period of collectivized forces in socialization, education, career, and recreation, the spy-hole offered not only the opportunity to cultivate a familiar internal living space, but also the possibility to reject the social guides and values belonging to the recently collapsed regime. This observation is supported by a spring 1991 survey in East Germany in which the desire for "better living," at 33 percent, surpassed even the desire for a new car (30 percent) and vacation travel (18.5 percent).[12] With the spy-hole, the lock, and the bolt, the border of the domestic sphere of leisure was clearly demarcated—a spatial arrangement that contracts with the omnipotence of the Stasi. Following this interpretation, the purchase of spy-holes and door chains serves not only to defend property, but also as a symbolic action by which the authoritarianism and the dogmatism of the old political system of the GDR could be negated.

One can surmise even more: Through its function and especially through its name, the spy-hole was particularly well suited to become a material symbol that exhibited the pattern for an image opposed to the ubiquitous informant and control apparatus of the SED regime. The spy-hole is not totally isolating. Rather, it allows a view of the outside; it at least potentially allows the observation by those who were hitherto being observed. The peephole in the door provided the possibility of a material-symbolic opposition to the control operations of the state firm "Listen and Look."[13] The individual no longer sees him or herself as the object but rather as the subject of observation, all from the vantage point of a secure private sphere. On the level of individual action the spy-holes thus provide a subtle inversion or reversal of a perfectly organized state system of control and repression. This lens was, therefore, not only a sign of an altered relationship between private life and political power, but also the instrument of a largely unarticulated, perhaps even extra-cognitive opposition to the system of informants, denunciation, and control that was endured over many years. I am suggesting that the purchase of the spy-holes was more than the acquisition of a useful item and can be interpreted as a symbolic action that is tied to strategies for understanding the new political and social reality. The name "spy" itself is not without influence in this process, which was finally accomplished in the form of action. This name provides this observation device with semantic energies that go beyond its function, providing what one could call a semiotic of inversion. Making an additional conceptual link, one could say this name allows an anti-structural collective symbolic negation of the GDR's apparatus of repression.

As opposed to spy-holes, the shell games we are dealing with have a symbolic system that is formed ritually rather than as a material object and that is, above all, highly superimposed with discourses both from the hermeneutics of everyday life as well as from political attributions. Like the material symbol of the spy-hole that reveals its metaphoric meaning in contextualized actions, the ritualistic symbol of the shell game can be linked to the "alliance of fears" and to the syndrome of insecurity. The conceptions and fears captured by the image of the shell game, illustrated on the street in both political and administrative measures, are directed against threats from the east—however diffusely understood—rather than from the western part of the new state, as was the case for the spy-holes. The threat presents itself in the form of asylum seekers, immigrants, and refugees from Southeast Europe coming into the new Federal Republic across the former border that was, if not entirely hermetic, at least, controlled. What was seen as a fascinating bit of folklore from southern countries playing out on the streets of Berlin in the winter of 1989–1990, or immediately after the opening of the Wall, was, in the spring and summer of 1990, beginning to be perceived as a threat. The reason for this was most certainly the rapid expansion of the shell games on the one hand, and, on the other hand, the reports in the media and, in particular, the police actions against the groups of players.

Prior to the winter of 1989–1990 the game was almost unknown in Germany, even in Berlin. Only a few West Germans were familiar with it from their travels to Mediterranean countries such as Italy, Greece, and Turkey. In the winter semester of the academic year 1990–1991, a small survey presented in a lecture at the University in Tübingen revealed the following: Of the sixty-four people questioned, approximately half claimed to be familiar with the game, a third of these through their own travels before the opening of the Wall, the remaining two thirds through word of mouth and from trips to Frankfurt, Hamburg, and Berlin. More than thirty of those questioned in Tübingen had never heard of the game; a few apparently confused it with other games such as "Catch the Hat" ("As kids we often played that in our family on Saturday afternoons"). Another survey conducted for comparison at the Technical University in Berlin painted a different picture: With only one exception, all of the fifty-three questionnaires returned showed a familiarity with the game. An overwhelming number of respondents indicated that the source of their familiarity with the game was Berlin, both the eastern and the western parts of the city, though there was also mention of Milan, Marseille, and Istanbul. Participants in neither surveys said they actively participated in the game.

The shell game is, as a rule, a game of slight of hand in which an animator seated on the ground, usually on a textile mat, shifts around a small ball of wood or tin under three overturned matchboxes or other hollow objects with quick and agile movements in such a way that it is unclear to the players and audience where the ball is. Whoever is able to guess under which matchbox the ball is hidden receives double the wager. Whoever guesses incorrectly loses the bet. The wager is usually 100 marks. Since the summer of 1993 more and more groups have been playing for two century notes. Decoys and attendants, whose job it is to attract passersby by feigning a win and thereby encouraging them to bet some money, always accompany the man shuffling the ball. If they have a command of their game and have achieved a certain virtuosity, the group of players is generally surrounded by numerous passersby who watch the game pieces and money transactions with a mixture of fascination, irritation, and anxiousness. In the beginning—that is, in December 1989 and early 1990—the number of those drawn in by the game was larger than today, as was the corresponding level of excitement on the part of the passersby. The widely spread desire to play once more has declined due to people admonishing themselves and others.[14]

Nonetheless, the shell game players have continually been able to draw in passersby and convince them to wager some money. In March, 1993, I was able to observe thirteen passersby lose bets during a four-hour period (interrupted six times by the police) of watching a troop of players on Tauentzienstraße in Berlin. To be precise, I should say allegedly thirteen losses since I was able to interview only eight of the losers because my vantage point was the second floor of an insurance company office: five tourists from western Germany (two of whom were high school students on a class-trip), and three visitors to Berlin from other parts of the former East Germany. All of those questioned said that, despite intensive warnings beforehand, they had "fallen for" the ease of the game and the animated back-and-forth of money.

According to information obtained from the Berlin Police Department and the descriptions in the pertinent literature on the subject, it is not possible for players from the outside to win. They are always victims because, through simple tricks, slight of hand, and manipulation, the animator can either cover up or alter the location of the ball. Even according to descriptive and analytic literature on games, the shell game is considered a fraud. According to the *Dictionnaire des Jeux*, "Le bonneteur (from *le bonneteau* = game of hats, *le bonnet*, in turn, meaning "cap") était devenu jadis synonyme de tricheur."[15] Even German linguistic tradition recorded in the Grimms' German Dictionary associates "Hütleinspiel" with the dishonest guild of jugglers. According to the dictionary, even at the beginning of the sixteenth century "Unterm hütlein spielen" (playing "under the hat") was considered the proverbial paraphrase of an undertaking "conducted secretly and with the intention of deceiving."[16] In France, unlike Germany, "shell game" has even made its way into an encyclopedia. In *La Grande Encyclopädie. Inventaire raisoné des sciences, de lettre et des arts* "le jeu du bonneteau" is extensively described as a phenomenon of the big city and the metropolis. Portrayed as a "phenomenon of cultural interchange," in social historical terms the game is considered a part of the process of urbanization.[17] The street, the masses, the dialectic of cultural constrast and cultural contact, playing games with the foreigner or foreigners, all this is seen as constitutive of this game of sleight of hand. The definitive characteristics of the shell game captured in *La Grande Encyclopädie* could also be found in Berlin during and after the *Wende*. In this case one must distinguish between two phases in the reaction to the shell game. Observable from winter to early summer, 1990, the first phase was characterized by a fascinated curiosity that saw in the shell game an element of the now open city where, after a long division, there was a possibility for continual cultural exchange between eastern and western Europe. The shell game served as an exotic, folkloric contribution to the historically new situation and to the changed image of the street. Beyond this, it was considered a symbol especially appropriate to the historical situation: this game of luck and skill (no one had noticed the tricks yet) expressed a feeling between anxiety and hope— a game to parallel the new era.

Just as the German-German reality was seen as full of possibilities for a promising future, the prospect of real monetary profit, unlike the play money of a family room monopoly game, made the risk attractive. With its promise of quick winnings, the shell game was an impressive expression of contemporary feelings. With its mental characteristics of momentary intoxication, its devotion to the principle of hope, its desire for adventure (as the mark of a new beginning), and its freedom to succeed, the open situation of the *Wende* was projected onto the shell game. Mixed with all of these characteristics from the beginning were, of course, feelings of hesitance, fear, and insecurity, as is typical of any new beginning or game. The shell game thus emerged as a mirror to the new Germany in which success and failure, market economy, and the economy of scarcity were drawn together, as they are in the game itself, into an aggregate of possibilities. Analogous to the historical situation, the game offered itself as a scenario of indeterminants.[18]

Just as evaluations of the process of German unification itself changed over time, so too did evaluations of the shell game. The second phase of the shell game is characterized by its negative stigmatization. After 1992 the shell game players were denunciated more and more within the context of a generally rising discrediting of the East and, in the course of being discredited, the activities associated with the game have been criminalized. The shell game has become the central topic of an intense public discourse in which—in addition to the public—the media, the police, and the judicial system have participated. In the course of this discourse, the shell game mutated into a symbol of threat from foreigners, particularly the fugitives and asylum seekers from eastern and southeastern Europe who had been hitherto unknown in Germany. The relatively rapid expansion of the shell game, and especially its appearance in public as a crowd-pleaser, made visible in the everyday world of experience what had already been recorded in police reports and newspapers articles—that these shell game hawkers were asylum seekers from the former Yugoslavia, primarily the so-called Kosovan Albanians who had allegedly been trained for their activities in western Europe, especially West Berlin, in schools for slight of hand they had set up in Macedonia or Kosova. In newspaper reports the shell game players were named along with black marketeers, drug dealers, and pickpockets. With the headline "Every Day Shell Game Players Rip-off Well-Intentioned Passersby," even the liberal *Tagesspiegel* constantly referred to the enormous amounts of money seized during raids of the game (in early November 1991 there were reports of amounts as high as 70,000 and 102,500 marks). In December 1990, the Berlin Police had already distributed large numbers of a flyer with the caption "This is how they want to cheat you" warning people of the shell game players in seven languages.[19] A comic strip with eight illustrations of characters with strikingly southern physiognomy of the players suggestively exposed the shell game as a deceptive and deceitful operation. The iconography of the images unmistakably shows how the shell game was being used for obviously xenophobic stigmatization. The portrayal of the players indicted the Balkans as offensive, criminal, and uncivilized: a threat to Western civilization, normality, and security. In the case of the shell game, the dreams of promised fortune became the trauma of destabilization through the "great migration" from eastern and southeastern Europe.[20]

What had been the opportunity of free action through a game of risk during the euphoria of the period of transition and unification, became, by the start of 1991, the menacing image of the foreigner and the fear that uncontrollable, uncanny, and irrational forces would break through. The shell game figured as a rising xenophobic metaphor of the rising fear of the Balkans, a region seen as the unpredictable, fervid locus of eruptions and aggressions: the dark "id" of the continent compared to the civilized and thoroughly rationalized "ego" of Western Europe.[21] In the image of the game, Berlin saw a kind of Street-Corner-Sarajevo. The police flyer implies that the Balkans are right around the corner, showing that geopolitical coordinates have been transposed.

If remains of a fascination with the shell game are nonetheless still discernable—and watching the reaction of audiences on the street one would still get this impression—then this is most likely because of the positive interest that this sidewalk game once generated, and still does in a much reduced form. In addition, the police believe that the game received substantial impetus from an exhibition on one of the most popular shows on RTL, a private television broadcaster, in which an Italian named Salvatore, dressed mafia style and speaking broken German, uses stylized gestures to indicate he is concerned not only with the winnings, but also with the image of the discredited game. The TV game achieves what also applies to the real game: a contrary fascination which ironically counterbalanced the seriousness of the political and administrative discourse. And this was accomplished with the same means: the Mediterranean habitus and the gaming attitude were staged as a completely stereotypical portrait.[22]

Like the shell game, bananas also belong to the first images created by the German-German unification process. "Il faut parler des bananes," one must talk about bananas, if the end of Germany's double-statehood is to be made clear. This is what the French journalist Eric Onnen wrote in his diary published in *le débat* in 1990.[23] Bananas, Onnen says, were in everyone's mouth, literally and metaphorically. However, unlike the sidewalk-roulette, during the unification process the banana went through a semantic transition that was linked (here also there are parallels with the shell game) to the role of this tropical fruit in intellectual systems of discourse. If in November–December 1989 the banana was a symbol of the German–German distinction insofar as it characterized the desire of "Ossis" for tropical fruits, then no later than spring 1990 the banana became a metaphor for the sell-out of the GDR to Bonn politics. This occured especially in the cynical commentary by Otto Schily during the March elections. Asked about the success of the CDU, he pointed at a banana that he had brought with him into the TV-studio for this reason.[24] Schily's rebuke qua banana of consumerism had been prepared by the now legendary cover of *Titanic* on which a beaming "Zonen-Gaby" extended to the viewer a pealed cucumber as a banana,[25] and also by a poster by the the pop-artist Klaus Staeck, which combined a banana and a sausage wurst with a statement of Willi Brandt underneath—"What belongs together will now grow together."[26]

During the years of unification, portrayals of bananas appeared with additional symbolic connotations, for example, the sexual metaphoric of a placard for AIDS relief in which a banana was exhibited covered by a condom; or, with religious-cultic associations, caricatures in which the banana as a devotional object was criticized with a certain sarcasm. After the political unification in October 1990, the additional motif of the act of slipping on a banana skin was added, a motif which can be traced to cartoons and figures of speech in the former GDR.

The point of departure for the banana metaphors, which at first were nothing more than an expression of the everyday hermeneutic perception of difference, thus functioning as a means of orientation within the German-German intercourse, was the onslaught by East Germans on the tropical fruit shortly after the fall of the Wall. In Berlin and along the German-German border, fruit dealers did the business of their lives,[27] while Chiquita even developed its own advertising strategy for East Germany: A "Chiquita Energy-Mobile" drove through villages and towns, attracting attention with huge inflated banana balloons. Merchants and marketplace salespeople perceived in the banana the "currency of the East."[28] Within only two years of unification the amount of bananas imported into Germany increased by almost half: from 57.5 million cartons (each eighteen kg) in 1989 to 71.7 million cartons in 1991. The hunger for bananas in East Germany was significantly greater than in the old Federal Republic. "With the consumption of 25 kg per person," wrote the the *Sächsische Zeitung* in May 1992, "the new federal states are the world champions in the consumption of bananas."[29]

The meanings invested in the spectrum of banana symbols do not need to be discussed here in detail since they have been collected elsewhere. The dominant concerns between 1989 and 1992 revolved especially around consumerism, greed, and exoticism, and carried associations with the infantile, the savage, and the uncivilized. Codified in the hunger for bananas was the nourishment for children and monkeys, as well as the puerile and the colonialized. Those on the West German left, so it appears, conceived the banana as a symbol of the lower needs and instincts; with the metaphor of the banana they criticized on the one hand the political-ideological deficits of the "delayed revolution," as Jürgen Habermas perceived the transformations in the East,[30] on the other hand the political-economic system of the FRG that emerged as a banana republic because it could offer nothing more than the potency of the economy (here there were cross-codifications with sexual symbolism). This banana argumentation was constantly, and often emphatically disputed on the East German side. "We aren't monkeys" was printed on demonstration placards in Berlin during the winter of 1989–1990. In an article in *Die Zeit* from August 1990 Barbara Sichtermann vehemently repudiated the denunciation of the East Germans through the metaphor of the banana. She charged that, with their moral-political objurgations of bananas, the western critics of consumerism were trivializing the everyday consequences of the economy of scarcity. With the bananas they were constructing a distinction, even an opposition, between consumerism and culture. Sichtermann's article was entitled "Die Bananen von Wandlitz," which suggests that her argument that from the point of view of the East Germans the West German criticism of this consumer good was nothing more than the attempt "to discipline retroactively cultural standards in their elementary form through a differentiation of the five senses."[31] The often cynical use of the banana-metaphoric in the West and the rebuttals from the East document those early difficulties and misunderstandings in the dialogue between two cultures that had arisen during forty years of dual statehood and that had as much influence on the varied use of things (as a point of departure for symbolic distinction) as it did on the discursive style which made use of these material symbols.

Meanwhile the banana metaphorology has moved on. From a symbol of economic unification, the banana has become a symbol of economic protectionism. In the first case, the banana was related to the integration of the East; in the case of the immediate present, it is related to the integration of the West, but here again, it serves as a metaphor of distinction: this time directed against the interests of other members of the Economic Community. The West German Left no longer interprets the symbols and dominates the discourse over the dollar and colonial bananas, instead the representatives of German economic and trade interests do. It is no longer *TAZ* and *Titanic* who perpetuate the banana-metaphoric, but rather the *Frankfurter Allgemeine* magazine and *Focus*.[32] During 1989–1991 the metaphor of the banana served to characterize cultural differences related to the eastern part of the nation, in 1992–1993 it characterized the economic differences in Western Europe. And while the banana stood as a symbol of the opening of the border during the German–German unification, in today's discussions it stands for the closure of trade borders and for the "fortress Europe" to which Brüssels aspires.[33] This symbolism is also similar to the discourses of the shell game: in both metaphors of the banana the West is taken as the status quo of Europe. One can be sure, in any case, that the banana metaphoric at the time of the unification imparted impetus and the force of images to the new banana discourse, which is being conducted much more seriously and with greater validity in the business sections of the daily press.

The collapse of the GDR and of the unification were, as subsequent publications attest, processes of intense generation of symbols. Especially in the realm of everyday thought and action there were semiotic, pictorial, and metaphoric systems produced, all of whose purpose it was to offer communicative possibilities to a situation that was shaped by transformations, the dissolution of the accustomed and the trusted, and tentative reorientations. In a situation in which accepted concepts about contemporary events and perspectives for future action were lacking, and in which action and the perception of action had been destabilized by the erosion of routinized relationships of thought and praxis, important perceptual, orientational, and communicative assistance was provided by signs and symbols, especially those which relied on either material things or concrete images. Here the material metaphors and symbols could function in varying ways: as rather gentle instruments of nonverbal opposition, as silent operators of a symbolic inversion (as in the case of the spy-hole), as a semiotic system gradually surrendered to public discourse whose double-coding is thereby in no way compromised (as can be observed in the shell game), or finally as a material metaphor whose semantic field varies according to the intellectual discourses of changing intellectual elites (as in the case of the banana).

The destruction, transformation, and new constructions of symbols which can be observed during the period of heightened cultural and political change from 1989 until the present can perhaps be described with the categories and schematizations of the theory of liminality developed by the British anthropologist Victor Turner.[34] Turner's theory of liminality is part of a larger symbology he has outlined in an attempt to explain the rise and function of symbols and rituals in various types of societies. Liminal situations are distinguished by a strong symbolic dynamic because they are characterized by destructuration and liquefaction. Liminality means on the threshold and thus indicates a cultural constellation in which the accustomed norms and forms, which make us feel secure in our lives, are sublated. This liminal state (because it is, according to Turner, characterized by an anti-structure) produces cultural inversions and innovations that are, however, not yet consistently politically proficient or completely stable. They therefore seek consensus and interpretation by experts and elites in order to reach a level of stability that makes them into routinized patterns of normal discourse. Because it is related to a state of suspension on a threshold, the liminal discourse relies on symbols and rituals for incorporating power and the material stabilization of concrete and living experiences. The discourse of routines, on the other hand, relies on concepts, categories, and figures of meaning.

Victor Turner's theory of liminality allows for three additional observations concerning spy-holes, shell games, and bananas which make more clear the attributes of the German-German cultural contact in the unification process.

First: Turner juxtaposes liminal with liminoid phenomena. The latter are characteristic of industrial and, especially, of advanced societies. Liminoid phenomena are more blithe, playful, and fluid than liminal ones. The liminoid emphasizes what is creative in political interpretation and action. This contrasts with the liminal, which is related to the necessities and dangers connected to a process of transformation. In 1989–1990 there was a confrontation between the liminoid (West Germany) and the liminal (East Germany). The liminal symbol of the banana, symbolic of the economy of scarcity in the East, was cynically reconstructed by the liminoid symbolic strategies in the West, which was met in turn by noncomprehension in the East. The tendency toward liminality and the attribute of liminoidality were cultural patterns that developed analogously to the political division. This is a finding that, as was mentioned earlier, has since been described by political scientists with the terms "ironic" and "tragic" as systemically specific patterns of social self-thematization.[35]

Second: liminal situations strive for stability and normalization. The shell game is permitted as long as it is seen as an attractive folkloric indicator of a new situation. In a normalized situation it becomes discredited, is criminalized, and subjected to the existing public order. This is what befell other "liminal rituals of transformation" during the *Wende*: they experienced their demise along with the normal East German political system and then became liminoid and are commented upon and caricatured.

Third: this confirms Turner's thesis that is expressed in the title of his book on liminality: "From Ritual to Theater."[36] Complex societies only allow liminal states during exceptional situations. Their institutional formation and inclusion is the rule. The reality of the ritual is dissociated from the context of action within a life-world and is delivered over to the institutionalized discourse and finally reworked in stagings by the media. In the RTL program "Pronto Salvatore," the shell game is permitted as a licensed game show and not subject to any criminalization, just as the banana metaphors can be taken to ironic and sarcastic extremes in caricatures and advertising campaigns.

Spies, shell games, and bananas: three banal phenomena of contemporary German culture. Despite their banality, however, they allow for instructive observations about the constitution and dynamic of the culture emerging from a society that finds itself in a period of transformation.[37] Spies, shell games, and bananas are phenomena of contemporary culture, and I believe that deciphering them within the framework of a scientific study of reality and the historical perception of ongoing events contributes to a better understanding of the forces and fears, hopes and efforts in contemporary

Germany, a Germany that still faces the difficult phase of integrating two different cultures. Even such trivial and harmless things as spy-holes, shell games, and bananas can reveal that even after October 1990 expressions of difference and division unmistakably asserted themselves alongside feelings of commonality in the everyday culture and mentalités of Germans.

Translated by Brett Wheeler and Peter Tokofsky

Notes

Shell game is a possible translation of the German *Hütchenspiel* (literally "hat game"). The game is explained below—trans.

1. Irene Dische, "Hintergedanken eines Überläufers," in *Fromme Lügen. Sieben Erzählungen* (Reinbek bei Hamburg: Reclam, 1992), pp. 116–129.
2. The German *Türspion*, most appropriately translated as "peephole" in English, is rendered here as "spy-hole" to preserve the play on the word "spy"—trans.
3. Karl Schlöder, "Die stille Revolution," *Der Spiegel*, February 15, 1993.
4. Vilém Flusser, *Dinge und Undinge. Phänomenologische Skizze* (Munich: Carl Hanser, 1993), p. 123.
5. Cf. Gottfried Korff, "Rote Fahnen und Bananen. Notizen zur politischen Symbolik im Prozeß der Vereinigung von DDR und BRD," *Schweizerisches Archiv für Volkskunde* v.86 (1990): pp. 130–160.
6. Cf. Gottfried Korff, "Banane," in *13 Dinge, Form, Funktion, Bedeutung*, Gottfried Korff et al. (Stuttgart: Württembergisches Landesmuseum, 1992), pp. 153–166.
7. Cf. Heinz Bube, "Das Ende einer tragischen Gesellschaft," in Hans Joas and Martin Kohli, eds., *Der Zusammenbruch der DDR. Soziologische Analysen* (Frankfurt am Main: Suhrkamp, 1993), pp. 267–282.
8. In his letter of April 6, 1993, August Börkey states "that there was a super elevated demand for spy-holes in the new states for the years 1991–92." He continues: "The demand was so high that there were distribution bottlenecks in all firms. The backlog was eliminated by 1992, and some orders were cancelled."
9. On April 14, 1993, August Bremicker Söhne KG Lock Factory (Wetter-Volmarstein) wrote: "In the new states there was an heightened demand for spy-holes as well as security technology for houses and apartments. We can speak of a high wave of demand in the first months that already significantly receded, however, by the start of 1991. This high early demand that was apparent to many insiders and outsiders in the trade caused many people to open stores for key services and security technology. In the meanwhile, however, many businesses no longer have a basis for their livelihood. A certain number have already been liquidated, others are still vegetating away." In a note from the company ABUS on June 7, 1993, the information was more precisely defined: "We registered up to four times the amounts compared to the amounts before the opening of the border. In the spring 1991, however, this boom abated just as fast as it had risen."
10. Cf. "Wildwest in Südost," the lead article in the local section for Dresden of the *Sächsische Zeitung* on October 11, 1990; "Ambulente Händler" *Dresdner Neueste Nachrichten*, October 11, 1990; "Sieben Einbrüche an einem Tag," *Dresdner Morgenpost*, October 10, 1990.

11. *Frankfurter Allgemeine Zeitung*, June 7, 1990.
12. "Was die Ostbürger wünschen," in *Der Morgen*, May 28, 1991 (report on a survey conducted by the Society for the Promotion of the Study of Recreation [DGFF]).
13. The "Firm Listen and Look" ["Horch und Guck"] was a widespread, ironic designation for the state security agency (Stasi) in the everyday language of the GDR.
14. Until now there have been very few portrayals of or reflexions on the shell game. Some initial remarks can be found in Michael Reinhard, "Wir können nicht jeden vor seiner Dummheit schützen," *Der Tagesspiegel*, November 2, 1991; "Beichte eines Hütchenspielers," *Magazin* 11/1991 (November 11, 1991); "Rätsel Hütchenspiel," *Titanic*, January 29, 1992.
15. Entry: "le bonneteau," in *Dictionnaire des Jeux* (Paris: Tchou, 1964), p. 64.
16. Entry: "Hütleinspieler," in *Grimmsches Wörterbuch* v.4, n.2, col. 1992 (Leipzig: S. Hirzel, 1877).
17. *La Grande Encyclopädie. Inventaire raisoné des sciences, de lettre et des arts* v.7, col. 330. In French literature (as in the *Dictionaire des Jeux*, see note 16) the shell game is generally described as a card game, in which the principle of mixing up cards and guessing the location of one is identical to the manipulation of the ball under matchboxes. In Berlin there are also groups (mostly of Polish players) who "work" with cards rather than matchboxes.
18. Cf. Carlo Mongarini, "Die Stellung des Spiels zwischen Kultur und sozialem Handeln," in Hans Haferkamp, ed., *Sozialstruktur und Kultur* (Frankfurt am Main: Suhrkamp, 1990), pp. 311–327; on the anthropology of games in general, see also Jean-Pierre Martignoni, "Jeux, joueurs, espace de jeu," *Ethnologie Française* v.22 (1992): pp. 471–489, which uses horse-racing as its example.
19. "Bulletin of the criminal police advisory department in Berlin," President of the Police in Berlin, ed., December 1990.
20. Hans-Magnus Enzenberger, *Die große Wanderung* (Frankfurt am Main: Suhrkamp, 1992).
21. Cf. Alexander Kiossev, "Mitteleuropa und der Balkan. Die Images zweier Regionen in den westlichen Massenmedien," *Neue Literatur. Zeitschrift für Querverbindungen* v.1 (1992): pp. 102–119; see esp. p. 115.
22. The publicity surrounding the "Salvatore" show was remarkable; witness the voluminous press articles that were generously made available to me by the press division of RTLplus/Cologne; see, e.g., "Hände Hoch. Ein Mann mit Profil," *Stern-TV*, August 1, 1991, pp. 7–9.
23. Eric Onnen, "Notes berlinoises," in *le débat* v.60 (1990): pp. 38–54; see esp. p. 41.
24. Cf. Helmut Karasek, "Mit Kanonen auf Bananen?" *Der Spiegel*, March 26, 1990, p. 56; Uwe Wiesel, "Innerlich erröten," *Kursbuch* 100 (1990): pp. 42–53 (esp. the chapter "Otto mit der Banane," p. 44).
25. *Titanic*, November 1989 ["Zonen-Gaby" is cliché for a typical resident of the eastern zone of Berlin, i.e., East Berlin—trans.].
26. *Der Spiegel*, February 19, 1990, pp. 52, 56.
27. For an impression of the initial scene, see Gottfried Korff, "S-Bahn-Ethnologie," *Österreichische Zeitschrift für Volkskunde* 93 (1990): pp. 5–26; esp. pp. 12 and 16.

28. "Erfahrungen eines Händlers mit den Wochenmärkten im Osten," *Frankfurter Allgemeine Zeitung*, August 31, 1991.
29. *Sächsische Zeitung*, May 14, 1992.
30. Jürgen Habermas, *Die nachholende Revolution* (Frankfurt am Main: Suhrkamp, 1990); see also Dietrich Geyer, "Geschichtskonjunkturen. Zum Interesse an der Geschichte in der jüngsten Vergangenheit," *Saeculum* v.43 (1992): pp. 5–20, esp. p. 13f.
31. *Die Zeit*, August 2, 1991.
32. The first two are alternative Berlin publications. The *Frankfurter Allgemeine* is a business-oriented daily, and *Focus* a recently-founded news weekly with what might be described as Yuppie perspectives—trans.
33. Cf. *Die Weltwoche*, February 18, 1993.
34. Victor Turner, *From Ritual to Theater. The Human Seriousness of Play* (New York: Performing Arts Journal Publications, 1982).
35. Cf. Bube, "Das Ende einer tragigischen Gesellschaft."
36. Turner, *From Ritual to Theater.*
37. For a possible interpretive model for such events, cf. Korff, "Rote Fahnen und Bananen."

CHAPTER SEVEN

CLUB COLA AND CO.:
OSTALGIE, MATERIAL CULTURE
AND IDENTITY

Martin Blum

On August 31, 2000, exactly ten years after the German Democratic Republic (GDR) had officially ceased to exist, *Die Welt*, one of Germany's national newspapers, announced nostalgia causes rising popularity of Eastern [German] products (Wolber 4)[1]. The newspaper article goes on to comment on the products and brands particular to the former East Germany that enjoyed a surge in popularity. A surprising fact, given the well-known scenario ten years earlier when access to the desirable hard Western currency, and thus access to Western consumer goods was a major reason for speeding up the monetary union, and thus the political union of both German states. The consequences of the currency union are known well enough: built on entirely different economic and political parameters, the planned economy of the GDR was in no way ready to face the competition of its capitalist counterpart in the West and almost instantly imploded, wiping out entire industries and leading to widespread unemployment. Perhaps the first and, in some ways, also the most visible change was the vanishing of once familiar products, brands, manufacturers names, packages, and the entire communication design of the GDR from the store shelves as the vast majority of these products did not stand any chance against their more sophisticated and more attractively marketed new competitors from the West. The change in products available also signalled one of the profound initial changes in the everyday experience shared by all East Germans as consumers of products. East Germans experienced this radical change as a sudden overturning, literally overnight, of their situation as consumers. During the weekend preceding the monetary union on July 1, 1990, not only the shop windows but entire shops were completely cleared of GDR goods following a closing-down sale: these were replaced by Western goods (Nick 80). And yet, despite having ended up in the dustbin of history, like the rest of the GDR, these seemingly substandard and dowdy GDR products have made an astonishing comeback. Once familiar names, such as Florena Soap, Komet Foods, and even the once notorious Rondo Coffee have reappeared in the stores thanks to a healthy customer demand. In particular some brands of drinks, such as the once ubiquitous Club Cola or Vita Cola, or Rotkäppchen Champagne (Little Red Riding Hood Champagne) have even been elevated to cult status among the young: Eastern Products have suddenly become cool. But not only are small, independent companies trying to capitalize on this trend, even major manufacturers such as Henkel with its entry line of Spee laundry detergents, give a clear indication of the economic and cultural scale of this development. In addition to the renaissance of actual products, there are also a growing number of novelty and souvenir items, such as T-shirts, card-games and postcards that bear logos and pictures of brands and products that did not survive the transition, such as the Trabant, East Germany's subcompact car.[2] This obvious paradox, namely the resurgence of a part of the GDR's everyday culture that seems to coincide with the rapid disappearance of the physical remnants of the GDR, has brought on its own cultural phenomenon: *Ostalgie*, seemingly, the longing for the GDR. What makes the phenomenon of *Ostalgie* different from other more common types of nostalgia such as the longing for the simple pleasures of the country life, is the relative historical proximity of the GDR (Ostalgie set in barely a decade after its demise), as well as the obvious contradiction of the longing for a state that during its existence most of its citizens did not particularly like or downright despised. Most glaring is the paradox with respect to the longing for GDR's material culture, in particular its consumer products. Before the *Wende*, in fact, exactly the reverse was the case: Western products that were either bought for hard currency at the Intershop or received as presents from relatives and friends in the West, were commonly savoured and revered.[3] Western goods were not only considered to be of better quality, but more importantly, also provided their owners with an instant rise in status that put them above those who lacked such contacts and who had to rely entirely on domestic products. Most visible in private residences was the fairly unique practice of openly displaying everyday products of Western origin, instead of storing them in cupboards, away from public view. Most common packages such as beer or soft drink cans were given pride of place in the living room, thus demonstrating the occupant's status by indicating that s/he had access to these rare and desirable goods.[4] Considering the recent fascination with Eastern brands and products, what, one may ask, has prompted this seemingly radical reevaluation of East German past and its physical remnants? Is this a simple reversal of a cultural practice born largely as a result of the Eastern disillusionment with the united Germany during the last decade? Is the essence of *Ostalgie* simply the desire to create the fantasy of a defunct system—and hence only an expression of the denial of the new reality—by surrounding oneself with the paraphernalia of yesteryears? Or is the phenomenon of *Ostalgie* a telling cultural issue that has as much to do with the history of East Germany as with the present of the united Germany?

The objective of this article is to examine the transformation of artifacts of East German material culture into a repository of memories and its resignification from products of everyday life into sites of potential resistance. This paper will explore *Ostalgie* as a unique form of nostalgia, and will discuss in particular specific products as sites of remembering. Following the theoretical discussion of nostalgia, I shall claim that *Ostalgie* is less an obsession with the past than an embattled site of memory and of the legitimacy of this memory. Consumption, then, will be read equally as a form of discourse, following language specific rules. By claiming ownership to the memory of the specific rules of consumption in the GDR's planned economy, residents of the New Federal States can, if they wish, create a distinct discourse community on the grounds of other fundamental rules that applied to consumption, that is the successful shopping experience (or its opposite) under socialism, as opposed to the values and strategies of consumer capitalism. Hence, nostalgia for these old and now seemingly useless rules provides the community that remembers them not only with a register of once crucial knowledge, but more importantly, with a firm identity based on a common discourse that includes all those who once shared this knowledge, namely all those who once were consumers in a planned economy. In addition, despite the already mentioned lack of any practical use of this knowledge, I also claim that the act of remembering itself is a political act: by remembering the social practices of the GDR, here exemplified in its material culture, its proponents challenge the supposed and frequently unquestioned superiority of Western style consumer capitalism that has swept away the planned economy of the GDR, its brands, and its entire discourse. One proviso here is, however, that despite a legitimate counter cultural impulse, all this is played out in the capitalist marketplace. Thus, *Ostalgie* and its current fascination with the material culture of East Germany is as much a comment on the East German past, as it is on the German present.

The second part of this chapter discusses the significance of *Ostalgie* in the context of theoretical approaches to nostalgia in order to provide a theoretical foundation for my reading of the cultural and social relevance of the material culture of the GDR. The third part will discuss the significance of material culture of this particular form of nostalgia. Following current scholarship in material culture and consumption studies, I propose to read consumption as a form of language that as a distinct sign system follows specific rules that in turn allow us to document its cultural valences and ultimately make visible its ideological and political nature .The fourth and the last part will discuss specific examples of GDR products. A central aspect of this discussion will be the relationship between the consumers and the material aspects of their products. A reevaluation of these GDR products after the unification and a discussion on their subversive potential in Western consumer capitalism will conclude this project.

I

Considerable insight into the cultural relevance of such mundane tasks as shopping and brand selection has been gained in the field of material culture and consumption studies. In particular the connection between the objects of material culture, its artefacts, and their varying interpretations in different cultural contexts have been of interest to practitioners of material culture studies. In particular the complexity and often contradictory nature of material culture can reveal the various meanings and messages that are embedded in its products. Reading the language of material culture enables us to determine the valences of its products as texts of everyday experiences (Brummett 51). By applying Saussure's concept of structural linguistics to material culture, Jean Baudrillard emphasizes a consumer product's Asign exchange value . . . a theory of objects . . . based upon . . . social presentations and significations (*Critique* 29–30). Countering empiricist notions that seek to determine a product's value simply by its use value, and Marxist approaches that mainly focus on the labour involved in its production, Baudrillard's approach centers on a product's social exchange value that is constantly under negotiation. In fact, according to Baudrillard, products, like linguistic morphemes, are inherently devoid of meaning. It is only by the ordering concept of consumption (such as that of language's grammar) that products are endowed with meaning in a materialist society: Consumption is a system which secures the ordering of signs and the integration of the group: it is therefore both a morality (a system of ideological values) and a communication system (*Consumer Society* 78). Taking the concept of capitalist consumption as a sign system one step further, Baudrillard then posits that it can be read as a social determinant: The circulation, purchase, sale appropriation of differentiated goods as signs objects today constitute our language—a code by which the entire society communicates and converses (*Consumer Society* 80).

It is precisely the inherently ambiguous nature of consumption as a communication system that accounts for a product's rapidly changing social value that can be affected by a myriad of factors, often entirely dissociated from the product *per se*, such as being the wrong colour or brand, or being associated with the wrong target group that suddenly make it uncool. Interestingly, the social value of a specific product can vary between different cultures, despite the efforts of a global economy to homogenize the world's tastes and predilections (which makes obvious marketing sense). The slippages within the system of consumption, however, show up as obvious contradictions that are part of material culture and consumption. In particular examinations of the way in which the products of Western capitalism are read by other cultures serves to illustrate this point. Daniel Miller has investigated the contradictions of a more and more homogenous global consumerism frequently embraced by many diverse ethnic and social communities that at the same time attempt to negotiate their very own, specific use of the blessings of Western consumerism, thus revealing the inherent contradictions in the cultural construction of mass products:

> Estonians, Trinidadians and Filipinas all seek to lay claim to what may be regarded as the modernity and style of Coca Cola or Marlboro cigarettes, but in all three cases they have developed a mechanism for disaggregating the qualities that they see as evil or at least inauthentic to themselves ... This emphasis upon material culture seems to offer important insights into the ability of groups to use variable objectifications available in a range of commodities to create a much more subtle and discriminatory process of incorporation and rejection than that allowed for in simple models of Americanization or globalisation. (18)

There may well be parallels to the way East Germans viewed what seemed the Western miracle of consumption before they had a chance to experience it first hand on an everyday basis. Never without a deeply political significance, especially in the days of the GDR, Western products, as demonstrated by the above mentioned displays in East German Intershops and people's living rooms, were deeply symbolic for a way of life that seemed tantalisingly close, thanks to Western TV commercials, and yet utterly unattainable for the average GDR citizen. These displays also highlight the inherently unstable relationship between product, social value and its cultural usage. As Arjun Appadurai demonstrates in a similar example, when ethnic products of everyday use, such as baskets or blankets, are taken out of their familiar context and placed as folk art in the living rooms of Westerners, these seemingly mundane objects automatically rise in status (28–29). In this context, Appadurai's emphasis on the cultural reuse of goods is central in understanding the significance of the recreated material culture of *Ostalgie*. These products and brands, despite their manufacturers efforts to create articles authentic to their Socialist predecessors, are by virtue of their changed social conditions endowed with a radically different meaning compared to those sold in the GDR. As such, consumption, along with its social and cultural context, is one of the prime determining factors of modern societies. Viewed from this angle, consumption as a form of discourse provides its own encoded language that in turn is a social regulative: it is therefore both a morality (a system of ideological values) and a communication system, a structure of exchange (Miller, *Consumer Society* 78). Hence, the complexity of meanings embedded in material culture and consumption defies simplistic binaries of local and global or Socialist and Capitalist material culture, pointing instead to an underlying and highly diverse and changing set of norm and values.

II

It is in particular the highly contested sphere of memory and nostalgia that forms the subtext for an understanding of *Ostalgie* since the norms and values—in particular with regards to commerce and consumption of East Germany—were frequently fundamentally different from those of the West. Thus, remembering these differences has become an integral part of East Germans in their search for their place in a changed society. In particular the issue of nostalgia, as indicated in the compound noun *Ostalgie*, plays a significant role in these acts of remembering. According to Ulbrich and Kämper, the word *Ostalgie* was first used by the stand-up comic Bernd Lutz Lange (111). The word's two compounds, *Ost* (east) and *Nostalgie* (nostalgia), denote this specific version of nostalgia that is firmly rooted in the East German experience. Despite its variety of uses and definitions, *Ostalgie* usually refers to the continuity or discontinuity of a specific identity associated with the other Germany (Keßler 101–103). Like many other forms of nostalgia, *Ostalgie* describes a sense of loss, while at the same time bestowing on an individual a sense of worth derived from his/her association with the past despite an adversity that may be currently experienced (Davis 34). In essence, nostalgia is an emotionally and socially meaningful strategy to make the present seem far less frightening and more assimilable than it would otherwise appear (36). In his examination of nostalgia, Davis emphasizes the notion of an idealized, highly selective view of the past in order to construe the appearance of a less threatening present that is frequently as inaccurate as the view of the past. Since nostalgia was historically[5] perceived as a physical condition, and later as an emotional affliction, it has always been seen in pathological terms, and hence dismissed as the symptom of a sick body and later of an addled mind. Although discredited as a historically inaccurate and invalid perspective on the past, the nostalgic view back in time can be read as an important register of the present and essentially as a democratic expression. In particular those whose official history has been marginalized, silenced, or has never been deemed worthy of official recognition find in nostalgic memories the only repository of their past. Not without coincidence has nostalgia been linked with the beginnings of mass culture in the mid-nineteenth century, when it reached its peak of popularity in Europe, particularly the salon culture of educated urban dwellers and landowners amongst whom it was a ritual commemoration of lost youth (Boym 16). The historical time is crucial here since the rapid pace of industrialization and technological development made people yearn for a simpler past in the midst of rapidly vanishing traditions that had no space in the scientifically dominated discourse of progress. As Pierre Nora suggests, a consequence of this yearning is the emergence of fundamental contradictions between history and memory:

> History . . . is the reconstruction, always problematic and incomplete, of what is no longer. Memory is a perpetually actual phenomenon, a bond tying us to the eternal present . . . in so far as it is effective and magical, only accommodates those facts that suits it; it nourishes recollections that may be out of focus or telescopic. (8)

From this premise Nora develops his notion of memory sites, or *lieux de mémoire* that signify a time of crisis when an immense and intimate fund of memory disappears surviving only as a reconstituted object (12). These moments of crisis are then equally an expression of anxieties about the present or the future as they are attempts to preserve the past and the meaning given to all forms of witnesses, even those usually deemed insignificant (13). Hence, Nora emphasises in particular material objects as one of the *lieux de mémoire*. Modern memory . . . relies entirely on the materiality of the trace, the immediacy of the recording, the visibility of the image. . . . The less memory is experienced from the inside the more it exists only through its exterior scaffolding and outward signs (13). However, Nora issues a caveat: even though materiality is crucial in the personal memory, it can only become a memory site if it is invested with the imagination and knowledge of the remembering individual (19).

Ostalgie is a perfect example to highlight these characteristic traits of nostalgia. Despite its often inaccurate and highly selective treatment of history, *Ostalgie* is nevertheless a reliable register of the fallout of these changes. Like nostalgia, *Ostalgie* is a personal reaction to what official history describes as impersonal historical developments. In particular it becomes symptomatic of the type of drastic changes that leave large parts of the population dislocated and experiencing a profound sense of loss that leads them to question the validity of their previous lives and their very identities. As an expression of the resistance to this loss, nostalgia can also be seen as a profoundly democratic expression. At this point history becomes memory and is reclaimed by the individual: the passage from memory to history has required every social group to redefine its identity through the revitalization of its own history. Frequently, this remembering is the only form of history available to disenfranchised groups whose past is not deemed important enough to be part of official history. Thus, *Ostalgie* as a very specific form of history is the visible expression of the transformation of the GDR into the New Federal States and of the erasure of the GDR from German history. Thomas Ahbe highlights this loss of identity that is so closely tied to the official dismissal of the achievements of East Germans, leading to the loss of their place in German history:

> *Ostalgie*, of course is closely linked to the ruptures which the East Germans experienced collectively. . . . Not surprisingly, a discourse of stigmatization against the different Eastern culture and experience as well as its agents— namely the East Germans—became commonplace. Thus, not only did the people of the East lose its illusions. It also lost its authority as a people who could say that it was *the* people. . . . The people of revolutionaries became a bunch of nostalgic fools.[6] (Ahbe)

Essentially, the end of the GDR also meant that individual biographies were disrupted and previous experiences under the old socialist system were considered worthless. The official discourse furthermore confirms this refusal of a recognition of a separate GDR identity. This leads to a taboo to touch anything connected with the GDR; it is deemed that East Germans have nothing to bring to the new, united Germany (ibid). Ahbe highlights the fallacy of this assumption by claiming that identities are shaped around a continuum of personal experiences and expressed in what he terms narratives of the self. As these experiences are, however, highly suspicious, or downright discredited in the official discourse of German history, many East Germans turn to the material culture of the GDR as their own *lieux de mémoire: Ostalgie* is a practice of the layperson (ibid.)[7]. Given the complex meanings and messages retained in material culture, it is thus no surprise that one of the predominant features of *Ostalgie* is its reliance on objects. Since the history of the GDR is still fraught with numerous anxieties that frequently result in the inability to sustain a neutral and unemotional discussion of this recent chapter in East German history, the focus on material culture makes sense. On the face of it, the products of everyday life seem innocuous enough and the often very personal memories surrounding these are on the surface deeply apolitical moments of individual acts of remembering. As such, the products of material culture are not fraught with nearly as many anxieties as other aspects of life in the GDR, such as culture or politics. The undeniable moral failure of the dictatorial regime and the GDR as well as the resulting grave violations of the rights of its citizens foreclose, at least for the foreseeable future, an unemotional engagement with the East German past and the reality of everyday life. In addition, the focus on the material culture of the GDR can also be seen as a form of resistance to the physical erasure of everything that is connected with the GDR. In 1990, the year of the monetary union, the East Germans produced 19.1 million tons of rubbish. It was 1.2 tons per capita; almost three times the rubbish disposed of in the West. The GDR was thrown on the rubbish heap (Ahbe).[8] Today, there are very few material witnesses of the GDR as a state. Even geographical points that once held a deep significance for East and West Germans, such as border crossings are virtually unrecognizable. The *Bahnhof Friedrichstrasse*, the point of entry into (and exit from) East Berlin does not even have a plaque that remembers the infamous door that once lead from one world into another.

It comes perhaps as no surprise that the first and only official enterprise to preserve the history of the GDR, the *Dokumentationszentrum Alltagskultur der DDR* (DoK) in Eisenhüttenstadt in its changing exhibitions focuses primarily on the material culture of the GDR. Acutely aware of the anxieties surrounding representations of GDR history, the *Dokumentationszentrum* attempted to provide a more balanced picture of the GDR, a picture that not only reflects its spectacular aspects, well publicised by the media, but also the quiet aspects of its public and private life with all its contradictions. And the material witnesses collected by the *Zentrum* are the medium of choice to accomplish this:

> No matter whether the objects appear as the results of planned, political acts, or as their opposite, what we are now used to calling the niche culture, political and social processes are reflected in the objects of everyday use and an intensive observation of the country. . . . This process did not stop with the events of 1989/90, but continued not solely restricted to the media favourites *Treuhand* and *Stasi*. The exhibition relies on the communication initiated by the displayed everyday objects to counter the narrowing of the debate surrounding the GDR. (Ludwig, Sensibilität 9)[9]

Ludwig's view indicates the still very problematic position of official institutions such as the *Dokumentationszentrum* whose approach in dealing with GDR history was commendable. Although the political dimension of the material culture of the GDR is definitely acknowledged, the personal dimension of social memory is still the main perspective of this enterprise. Despite the collections' reliance on individual experience and the spontaneous discussions the artefacts stimulate, Ludwig distances this enterprise from everything that could give it a nostalgic appeal; the publicly debated collective, romantic yearning for a supposedly better past, commonly described by the term *Ostalgie*, did not happen (9).[10] Despite this disclaimer, the official collection in Eisenhüttenstadt is a *lieu de mémoire* as described by Nora since its material witnesses are not merely collected, stored, and archived, but the *Zentrum*'s extremely successful emphasis on communication reinforces the role of the imagination of the viewer who imbues the material artifacts with significance. The task of remembering makes everyone his [*sic*] own historian (Nora 15).

III

To appreciate the significance of the otherness of the GDR's socialist material culture it is necessary to delineate its differences from capitalist consumer culture and its products. The history of marketing and branding under capitalism is a useful foil to illustrate these differences and the consequences of the different social and economic conditions on the actual products in terms of their appearance, quality, and perception. Western consumers, as a rule, tend to distinguish between various products of the same kind, such as breakfast cereals for instance, first and foremost by their brand name. This is apparent when one takes a closer look at the packaging of most Western products where the brand name usually dominates the layout. Differentiation of products based on content is usually secondary. Many of today's quality products can rely on a firm brand identity that strongly relies on intangible qualities such as reputation and image—the all important cool factor. To appreciate the significance of product identities, one has to be aware of the care that goes into engineering the appropriate brand identity of today's products.[11] Well-known household names such as Quaker Oats, Kraft Dinner, or Sunlight detergents may suffice to illustrate this point. One of the reasons that branding has become such a significant force in marketing is that established products can often trade on their high recognition value based on their history. Naomi Klein attributes the rise of the branded product identity to the rise of mechanization and the mass production of goods that has had a strong impact on the way in which they were sold to the customers. While shopkeepers had previously simply scooped bulk foods for their customers, the new industrially produced goods needed to be packaged to be shipped to stores and kept on their shelves. Apart from protecting the product, the package almost immediately took on a second function of displaying the manufacturer's name, lending the product an instant identity: what made early branding efforts different from more straightforward salesmanship was that the market was now being flooded with uniform, mass-produced products that were virtually indistinguishable from one another (6). Many of these early products are still around today and are the staples of today's consumer culture. In an early nostalgic attempt to hide the new, mass-produced nature of these products and to invoke the previous age of local production and direct sales, the labels on these packages were decidedly sentimental, harking back to an idyllic time and acting, as such, as the interface between the shopkeeper and the product in order to invoke the nostalgic notions of familiarity and folksiness in an effort to counteract the new and unsettling anonymity of packaged goods (6). For the capitalist consumer society this means that a network of knowledge about product identities has been in existence since the early days of mass-produced products.

In contrast to Western consumer capitalism, which could rely on the continuity of its product culture, the planned economy of the GDR did not have this history to build on. The earliest economic reforms in the Soviet Occupational Zone (SBZ) lead to the breaking up of large companies that had discredited themselves by supporting the Nazi regime (Kaminski 21). From this starting point one consequence of this change was that certain aspects of the material culture of the GDR faced its own zero hour. One can distinguish three distinct stages in the development of East Germany's material culture initiated by significant policy changes and reflected in the GDR's history of marketing and advertising. However, this process of transformation was far from consistent. Some products thus reflect the discontinuities of these various policy changes while others retained some very peculiar continuities since they were forgotten by these same changes, and continued to exist as fossilized remnants of previous ideological and historical conditions (Giersch 82–84). The first stage, starting with the foundation of the GDR in 1948 represents a random collection of more or less functional remnants of the industry of the German Reich, found within the boundaries of the new state. Goods produced by these companies that were still frequently under private ownership became the mainstay of the early East German economy, supplying a selection of goods from prewar times. In a parallel move, many of these companies relocated into the capitalist Western sectors and established themselves once more. Thus, until the building of the Wall, one could for a while purchase the same products made in the GDR, in the Federal Republic as well. However, problems with this divided status started early: many of the old owners who had moved their companies to the West won lawsuits that banned their Eastern counterparts from using the old established brands, which then had to be abandoned in the East. In addition, many companies that produced important goods simply did not exist in the East, which meant that these products had to be literally reinvented. Again, using the established brand-name was out of the question. Thus, practically overnight, entire brands and product identities had to be given up and substitutes had to be quickly invented. Many of these substitutes from the early days were to accompany the GDR until its end in 1990 (Giersch 76–77). To this era of improvisation much can be traced to what is typical about GDR products, such as their agricultural background, their lack of image, and their homeliness, in short, elements that demonstrate the classic features of their GDR origins: rough around the edges, hard to handle, somehow old fashioned [that] yet in a very personal, utterly inexplicable way engendered love–hate relationships (Ulbrich, *Lexikon* 105).[12] A typical example is the manufacturer of films and cameras. Agfa, for instance, had to rename its Eastern equivalent as ORWO, after the company owners moved to Munich in West Germany, taking the rights to the brand-name with them. ORWO, a well known Eastern brand of film—and later audiotapes—is typical of the *ad hoc* creations that characterized many of the new brands on the Eastern market. An abbreviation for Original Wolfen, the new name makes specific reference to the place of manufacture, the town of Wolfen near Halle (Ulbrich, *Lexikon* 75–76). However, these creations were not entirely randomly thought up, as the example of Bino illustrates. Bino was a substitute for Maggi, a well established liquid seasoning used mainly in soups and sauces and sold in the characteristic bottles that are still used today.[13] Other than the old Agfa works, the Maggi factory was located in Singen, West Germany, and thus Maggi was simply unavailable on the Eastern market. To make up for this lack in the product range, Bino was introduced to replace the Western product. The creation of Bino perhaps exemplifies the contradictions surrounding GDR brands. One the one hand, the name Bino, an abbreviation for Bitterfeld Nord, shows its ideological indebtedness by making a reference to the collective process involved in the creation of the new product (Tippach-Schneider, Bino 140), one the other hand, however, the new products had to compete against the brand recognition of its well-established predecessors and thus attempts were made to create alternatives that were phonetically similar to the lost brand-names. In addition, the package design was frequently similar to that of the original. The Bino bottle that incorporated the long neck design of the Maggi bottle is a case in point (140). Although many of the substitutes reached the quality standards of the originals, they had to fight an uphill battle to shed their image as substitutes or poor relations of the originals: many customers simply disqualified a product because it was manufactured in the East. The otherness of many of the products of the GDR, born out of political and economic necessity, as well as their attempts to establish their independent brand identities while at the same time trying to imitate their Western equivalent was to remain their most distinguishing characteristic during their production and was to become once again significant in their *ostalgic* reincarnations.

In the early 1960s the situation changed dramatically. With the building of the Wall, the market of the GDR became effectively sealed off from the West. With the new political focus now turned to the GDR and the other Eastern Block countries, implicit or explicit competition with the West ceased to be a priority. Products were supposed to lose their substitute character and new political and aesthetic guidelines were issued to underscore the significance of the product culture of the GDR as documented by the affected packaging and product advertising. Largely gone was the old, prewar design, to be replaced by new socialist requirements.[14] Product adverting was soon coupled with a political message that not only emphasized the product, but also drew attention to the working conditions of the workers who made its production possible in the first place:

> Our aim is to inform about the company collective, about production brigades, about the leading managers, the eminent scientists, engineers, and workers, about the position of the company within the national economy, about the developments of suggestions, about the company's social and cultural programmes. (Tippach-Schneider, *Messemännchen* 12–13)[15]

A second, perhaps more immediately visible, consequence was that the GDR products and their communication design were radically changed. Gone was the homely, Norman Rockwell–style of imagery that characterized so many ads and product labels in the 1950s. The new aesthetics drew on the formalist tradition that frequently dispensed images and reduced them to geometrical elements. It is this type of design that emphasized function over pure aesthetics that is today most well known as the typical GDR design. Guidelines published in 1964 emphasize that package designs which reflect the contents and advertise it, are possible. If the packaging reflects the laws of our socialist aesthetics, then they will be pleasing to the eye of the consumer (Giersch 84). However, as mentioned before, none of these changes in direction were applied consistently and many products sporting the new socialist aesthetics could be found side by side with remnants from the previous periods, such as the liquid seasoning Bino.

Examples that highlight this contradiction are the East German Coca-Cola substitutes—Club-Cola and Vita-Cola. At first glance, given the politically sensitive nature of product development and branding in the GDR, it seems slightly puzzling that the powers in charge even permitted the manufacture and marketing of a product that like no other is so symbolic for the cultural and political domination of US capitalism. As Miller points out, the signifying power of Coca-Cola is such that it becomes a meta-symbol. He claims the term Coca-Cola is one of three or four commodities that have obtained this status . . . The term Coca-Cola comes to stand, not just for a particular soft drink, but also for the problematic nature of commodities in general (Coca-Cola 170). However, for reasons unknown, when on October 14, 1954 the mineral water manufacturer and beer wholesaler Oskar Heinicke of Jena registered the name with the GDR patent office, his suggestion for a lemonade containing caffeine was warmly embraced.[16] Four years later, the Chemical Works Miltiz were able to supply the syrup base that, like Coca-Cola's ingenious system of franchising, could then be bottled locally by other independent manufacturers (Tweder, Stregel, Kurz 44–45). A particular ingredient was Ascorbic Acid (Vitamin C) that gave Vita-Cola its characteristic lemon taste. Vita-Cola, however, was not to remain the only Coke substitute in the GDR. After failed attempts to manufacture Coca-Cola as a joint venture in the GDR, another substitute for the original was needed, and in 1967 the brand Club-Cola was registered.[17] Again, reacting to the population's fondness of Coca-Cola, the new product attempted to overcome its substitute character by eliminating its lemon taste in an effort to emulate the quality of its American cousin while remaining entirely in East German hands. Again, the soft drink became a favourite with the consumers and its less sugary taste made it even more attractive to those who knew the original. In fact, the more palatable taste of Club-Cola was incidentally the direct result of scarce raw materials—its sugar content had been gradually reduced from 12 to 7 percent (47). An aftereffect of the popularity of Cola type drinks in the GDR was the proliferation of other smaller local brands that could bypass the cumbersome licencing process for the bigger brands, and names such as Quick-Cola, Disco-Cola, Inter-Cola, and the rather unfortunately named Prick-Cola started to appear (48–49). Although both Vita-Cola and Club-Cola became favourites, their widespread availability meant that they lacked the political associations with the West and were thus perceived as quite different from Coca-Cola that could only be purchased with hard, Western Currency. In Baudrillard's view of consumption as a communication system, the two colas, East and West, illustrate the fundamentally different significations of both products: although almost similar in taste, appearance, and packaging, Vita-Cola and Club-Cola had a radically different ideological and cultural valence as compared to the Western Coca-Cola. In fact, Coca-Cola was rarely consumed as a drink (only on special occasions) but was collected as a material witness of a world that was beyond the reach of most ordinary citizens of the GDR.

IV

With the monetary union of both German states, these status symbols of the other world suddenly became available to the ordinary citizen. A certain sales success was guaranteed simply because of their previously exclusive status. And predictably, among one of the first products to flood the Eastern market was the real Coca-Cola. While the soft drink's former status helped initial curiosity and ensured good sales in the East, its wide availability, obviously contrary to its perception, redefined its identity. In a radical resignification, it now became the everyday product as in the West, ceasing to be a symbol of unavailability. Predictably enough, lacking investment capital and distribution networks, the old *ersatz* colas that proliferated in the East did not stand a chance against the powerful competition form the West (Tweder, Stregel, Kurz 142). Who, after all, needs the substitute when s/he can get the original? And yet, in 1994, the East German company Thüringer Waldquell Mineralbrunnen reintroduced Vita-Cola. Some of the previously artificial ingredients were replaced by natural ones, but, most significantly, the characteristic lemon flavour, originally introduced to mask its lack of genuine ingredients, was retained, as was the design of its labels (Vita-Cola). In an almost complete reversal of events, the homegrown former substitute managed to replace the genuine Coca-Cola as a sales leader in Thuringia and held second place in the New Federal States (Vita-Cola).

Given the political significance of products from the West of being a metasymbol of Western consumer culture with all its ramifications may be part of the explanation why the product was rejected in a symbolic gesture when the residents of the New Federal States became disillusioned with their new economic system. And yet, I would claim that the continued success of genuine GDR brands such as Vita-Cola goes beyond a simple act of protest. The surprising success story of this product highlights Baudrillard notion of the sign exchange value (*Critique* 29) of products that are constantly under negotiation. In particular the radical resignification of Coca-Cola demonstrates the nature of this grammar of consumption. Ultimately devoid of a residual meaning, Coca-Cola and Vita-Cola have essentially changed places. This change in meaning is obviously symptomatic for the change in the morality system that surrounds both products. With the obvious social and economic upheaval in the New Federal States, an entire value system was lost and another, essentially that of the Federal Republic, had been substituted. The ensuing feelings of resentment when the price for the change had to be paid, with economic hardship of mass unemployment, are sufficiently well known. This new critical stance to everything that is highly symbolic is one of the reasons for the reinterpretation of the identities of many products. Interestingly, this critique of Coca-Cola is by no means an isolated issue; it rather reflects a global resistance to mega brands that by their sheer size are simply seen as domineering:

> Coca-Cola may . . . be suffering for its dominance and confidence. As with McDonald's and Microsoft, resentment against ubiquitous American products better known for their marketing than their quality, long simmering on the margins of consumer society, has begun to spread. (Beckett)

One aspect of *Ostalgie* is thus that the current preoccupation with multinational brands is not specifically an East German issue; it does signal, however, that the new Federal States are firmly a part of the new global economy and are thus reacting to some of its developments. As in other societies, one of the prevalent forms of resistance to economic domination by foreign or transnational companies is the focus on smaller, local companies and their products. Thus, within the global arena, the reintroduction of local soft drinks in the GDR reflects this move away from the brand bullies, to use Klein's words[18]

> In addition to taking a stance against corporations that with their uniform selection of goods attempt to eradicate regional differences, the significance of the products surrounding *Ostalgie* goes beyond a mere protest; they respond to a specific concern of the residents of the New Federal States. As part of the rapidly disappearing material culture of the GDR, as well as representatives of a history that is largely ignored by official historiography, they form very distinct lieux de mémoire in Pierre Nora's sense. The reason is that these products signify a very specific corpus of knowledge that was necessary to be a successful consumer under the conditions of the GDR's planned economy. As previously pointed out, consumers in the GDR lacked many of the conveniences, such as branded identities, that their Western cousins could take for granted. Since brands are (strategically manipulated) signifiers for desirable qualities, they reduce the act of shopping to the simple memorization of a few desirable names or acronyms. Since many pre-war brands migrated with their owners into the West, Eastern consumers rarely had this luxury.[19] In addition, advertising and package design was—depending on the respective cultural and political developments—more or less severely limited in the GDR, consumers were again barred from this shortcut. A continuously unpredictable supply of goods, as well as erratic quality standards, demanded from consumers a much more intimate knowledge of their products than just the simple remembering of the right brand name. Hence, consumers had to develop an entire network of knowledge surrounding the selection, availability and treatment of their products for themselves. In the case of the cola type drinks discussed previously, this knowledge includes things such as knowing which store would stock the desirable soft drink at which particular time, which soft drinks better to avoid,[20] or which bottles to reject due to frequent quality problems with the fit of the sealing caps; some even went so far as to identify individual bottlers, printed on the

product label, that seemed to have better quality standards than others. In short, the seemingly trivial act of purchasing soft drinks becomes a highly sophisticated task, involving intimate knowledge of the product, its packaging and distribution. The material product itself, then comes to stand for the knowledge that involves its purchase. As soft drinks discussed here are not an isolated case, but rather symptomatic for desirable goods in the GDR, one can conclude that a very specific form of social knowledge governed their consumption in the planned economy. Hence the former products come to embody a from of knowledge that was universally shared by everyone who consumed the GDR's products, which is its entire population, with perhaps the exception of the its highly privileged cadres. Since this knowledge is shared by almost every member of this society, the former residents of the GDR form a discourse community that defines itself by this knowledge— and distinguishes itself from the West Germans who are clearly outsiders to this discourse—thus validating its individual members by sharing these memories as a community. Our nostalgia for those aspects of our past that were . . . different becomes the basis for deepening our sentimental ties to others (Davis 43). Since the knowledge on how to be a successful consumer in a East Germany's planned economy is obsolete under the new consumer capitalism, it assumes a new currency as a *lieu de mémoire*. Now, a part of the communal memory, it facilitates the search for an East German identity. The objectives of this remembering are twofold: first, there is the desire to retain this knowledge, now that its factual usefulness has ceded; the moment of lieux de mémoire occurs at the same time that an immense and intimate fund of memory disappears (Nora 111–112). The second impetus behind the nostalgic recreation of the material culture of the past is political. Very much a personal response to discontinuities, it deliberately highlights the contradictions of the status quo by incorporating some of its elements in a synthesis of sorts into the present. As such we can understand the renaissance of products and brands of the GDR. Although they may retain their names, labels, some desirable characteristics, and frequently the communication design from the days of the GDR, these products are anything but GDR products. Their success would be more than doubtful without their adoption of Western quality standards. They do, however, by their sheer otherness and simply by beating the odds propose an alternative to the pervasiveness and slickness of Western consumerism. Their continued existence and rising popularity are not only testimony to their previous importance but also challenge views held by conservative business theoreticians, like Francis Fukuyama, who, in a strange reversal of the Marxist view of history, pronounced in 1989 the end of history as such: that is, the end point of mankind's ideological evolution (4) supposedly brought about by the material blessings of neo liberalism. The way the material culture of East Germany has persisted and developed in the following decade has done little to validate Fukuyama's thesis. In retrospect, the resurgence of the material culture of this loser of history not only proves the existence of the contested GDR identity but also demonstrates the validity of experience and memory for the social and material construction of identities as underscored by Teresa de Lauretis's definition: Experience is the process by which, for all social beings, subjectivity is constructed. Through that process one places oneself or is placed in social reality and so perceives and comprehends as subjective (referring to, even originating in oneself) those relations material economic, and interpersonal which are in fact social, and, in a larger perspective, historical. (159)

If *Ostalgie* and its material culture are recognized and understood as remembered experience, as a part of German history, if they are viewed without the prejudices surrounding nostalgia, they can contribute to a more differentiated view of the German past and add some diversity to an increasingly uniform and branded landscape of material culture.

Notes

1. Nostalgie beflügelt Absatz von Ost-Produkten. All translations are my own.
2. For commercially available reproductions of GDR items, see, e.g., the following websites: http://www.mondosarts.de and http://kost-the-ost.de.
3. See in particular the collection of articles in Härtel and Kabus's *Das Westpaket*.
4. That this practice of displaying Western packages has been the object of Western satire demonstrates the large cultural gaps that existed between Eastern and Western consumer culture. See, e.g., Max Gold's column Quitten für die Menschen zwischen Emden und Zittau (160), originally published in February 1991 in the satirical magazine *Titanic*.
5. On the history of nostalgia see in particular Starobinski.
6. Da nimmt es auch nicht weiter Wunder, dass es einen manifesten Stigmatisierungsdiskurs gegenüber der anders gearteten Ostkultur und-erfahrung und natürlich deren Trägern, den Ostdeutschen, gibt. So verlor das Ostvolk nicht nur seine Illusionen. Es verlor auch sein Prestige als Volk, das . . . von sich sagen konnte, dass es das Volk sei . . . Aus dem Volk der Revolutionäre wurde ein Haufen undankbarer Nostalgiker.
7. Ostalgie ist eine Praxis von Laien.
8. 1990, im Jahr der Währungsunion, produzierten die Ostdeutschen 19.1 Millionen Tonnen Müll. Pro Kopf warem das 1.2 Tonnen, fast das Dreifache dessen, was im gleichen Jahr im Westen anfiel. Die DDR wurde in den Müll geschmissen.
9. Gleich, ob die Objekte als Ergebnisse planvollen politischen Handels erscheinen oder als ihr Gegenbild, das wir Nischenkultur zu nennen uns gewöhnt haben, politische und gesellschaftliche Prozesse schlagen sich in den Alltagsobjekten und in einer intensiven Beobachtung des Landes nieder . . . . Dieser Prozess fand mit den Ereignissen von 1989/90 nicht sein Ende, sondern setzte sich fort, wenn auch nicht beschränkt auf die mediengerechten Themen Treuhand und Stasi, fort. Die Ausstellung baut, gerade um der Verengung der Debatte um die DDR zu begegnen, auf Kommunikation, auf das durch die alltäglichen Objekte angeregte Gespräch.
10. Die in der öffentlichen Debatte durch den Begriff Ostalgie nahegelegte kollektive verklärende Rückbesinnung auf ein vorgeblich besseres Vorher fand in der Ausstellung keine Bestätigung.
11. On branding in consumer capitalism see esp. the first chapter of Klein's study.

12. ... warteten mit den klassischen Merkmalen ihrer DDR-Heimat auf: grobschlächting, schwer zu handhaben, irgendwie altmodisch und auf eine sehr persönliche Weise gehaßliebt.

13. For a history of early food extracts and seasonings, such as Maggi see Grimm, pp. 50–52, who quotes a jingle for Maggi written by Frank Wedekind.

14. These guidelines were notoriously vague, but stipulated that all newly designed packages had to be submitted to the committee for packaging of the GDR. This committee then approved the design if the appearance of the product reflects the regulations of our socialist aesthetics, it will give the customer aesthetic pleasure and enjoyment (Giersch 84).

15. Es wird informiert über das betriebliche Kollektiv, über die Produktionsbrigaden, über die die Leitungskräfte, über hervorragende Wissenschaftler, Konstrukteure und Arbeiter, über die Stellung des Betriebes in der Volkswirtschaft und in der internationalen Wirtschaft, über den Entwicklungsstand der Neuererbewegung, über betriebliche und kulturelle Einrichtungen.

16. This is all the more puzzling when seen in the light of the lasting official resistance to another American icon, the Levis Jeans. For one of the best descriptions of the sigificance of jeans in the early 1970s see Ulrich Plenzdorf's *Die Neuen Leiden des Jungen Werthers*.

17. Following the lead of the Soviet Union, Coke's main competitor, Pepsi-Cola was manufactured under license in the GDR from between 1977 and 1980. Due to the high price, of 1 M, twice the price of Club-Cola, the joint venture was abandoned (Stregel, Tweder, pp. 54–55).

18. The same phenomenon can also be observed in Russia where Coca-Cola has to face a massive loss of its market share and attempts to jump on the bandwagon by manufacturing soft drink concoctions known from the Soviet period: In a reverse of the cultural imperialism of Coca-Cola's aggressive invasion of Russia in the early 1990s, the firm has been forced to make concessions to local demand ... Last month's announcement of a move into nostalgic Soviet era drinks marks the business's latest attempt to squeeze a profit out of Russian consumers who are increasingly apathetic toward coke itself (Gentleman).

19. A notable exception here is the Florena brand of cosmetics that was well respected in the GDR and continues its success today (Florena).

20. Here the example of the rather unfortunate apple-peppermint juice mix comes to mind: an emergency development in 1977 when the manufacturer did not receive its allotment of lemons that had to be bought with hard currency (Tweder, Stregel, Kurz 51).

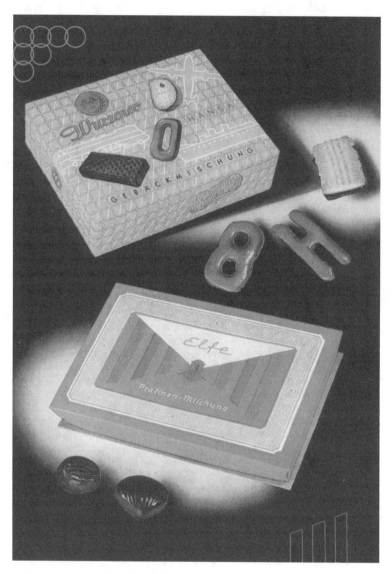

Figure 1 HANSA Gebackmischung & ELFE Pralinen Milchung

Figure 2   KONSÜ Waffeln & Capri Orangen–Geback

152

Figure 3　Vita Cola VEB Edelstahlwweerk, 8. Mai 1945, Freital (single) enlarged

153

Figure 4   Vita Cola (a collection of 10 Vita Cola cards)

Figure 5 Coffeinhaltiges Colagetrank Prick Cola

Figure 6 Vita Cola Coffeinhaltige Limonade Mit Zusatz von Vitamin C 0, 71 (single enlarged)

Part III
Germany and Its Minorities

CHAPTER EIGHT

AUSSIEDLER AND AUSLÄNDER:* TRANSFORMING GERMAN NATIONAL IDENTITY

Nora Räthzel

In order to understand the nature of present contradictions within the German national identity it is necessary to outline certain historical specificities that have proved crucial to its development.

Concept of Nation

Rather than attempting yet another definition of the nation[1] I propose to examine how its concept is used to organize consent to state institutions or to resist them. The nation as a concept is used to bridge the contradictions between the rulers and the ruled, and, in the economic field, between labor and capital. This may be called the "homogenization of vertical contradictions." The second aspect of its function is the homogenization of horizontal differences because in almost all cases no nation-state is based on one single ethnic group. Ethnicity tends to be constructed in constructing a nation (see Balibar, 1988, p. 70).

My interest in looking at the conceptions of the nation is thus to find out how they tend to organize the people for and against the state and how they tend to define the characteristics which allow for the perception of heterogeneous groups living within the boundaries of a nation-state.

---

* Ethnic Germans coming back to Germany after their ancestors have emigrated, two to seven hundred years earlier, and foreigners living in Germany.

Some Historical Observations

Ideas of a united centralized German state were articulated rather late, the first attempt occurring just after the French Revolution, having been inspired by it, drawing upon the values of Liberty, Equality, Fraternity.

Such ideas, however, soon lost their positive meaning for many German intellectuals because they were not accompanied by the occupation of Germany. This was not necessarily true for the whole population, though, because some experienced this occupation as a liberation from their feudal rulers and voluntarily united with the French.[2]

Universalism and Particularism

It is often said that the German construction of the nation, as opposed in particular to that of France, is based on a romantic notion of an ethnic unity or a unity of blood rather than the political will of the people and universalistic human rights.[3] This view has some limitations, however, first, because it underestimates the struggle between universalist and particularistic notions of the nation, and second, because it ignores differences within the so-called particularistic as well as within the so-called universalistic concepts of a nation.

Universalistic Concepts and Their Contradictions

Goethe, in his later years, Schiller, and then Heinrich Heine exemplified a universalistic notion of the nation. They combined universalistic ideas about a humanity that transcends the nation together with a patriotism conceived as nonexclusive. To sum up their position in this way means ignoring their personal developments and contradictions, but for reasons of space I shall concentrate in particular on Schiller:[4] "No writer, however strong his indication to be a citizen of the world, can escape his fatherland in his modes of representation. Even if it is only his language that leaves its mark, that alone is enough to restrict him within the limits of a certain form, so as to give a national characteristic to his work . . . It is poor and narrow-minded to write for a nation. This limitation is unbearable for or a philosophic mind."

In the same spirit Goethe says, "As a person and as a citizen, the poet will love his fatherland. But the fatherland of his poetic power and action are the Good, the Noble, and the Beautiful. It does not depend on a certain location; he takes it from where he finds it." (See Eckerman, 1986.) Heine more lyrically thought that:[5]

> Patriotism for the Frenchman is such that it warms his heart dilating and expanding it, so he embraces in his love not only those closest to him but the

whole of France, the entire country of his civilization. The patriotism of the German on the contrary is such that his heart becomes narrower and shrinks like leather in the cold. He hates foreigners and no longer wishes to be a citizen of the world, but a mere German. This is the idealistic loutishness that Herr Jahn erected into a system as pernicious opposition against an attitude that has created all that is lost and most sacred in Germany: the cosmopolitanism of our great intellectuals: Lessing, Herder, Schiller, Goethe, Jean Paul, which has been embraced by all educated people in Germany.

The last quotation especially shows that the humanism and universalism of these intellectuals was one for the "educated people." It was not intended to organize the people for their liberation. This universalism was that of the international community, one that was remote from the "ordinary people"— it could not and was not intended to become hegemonic.

The Particularist Concepts and Their Contradictions

It has often been said of Herder that his ideas concerning peoples and their different cultures was the first articulation of the particular concept of the nation, since it laid stress on the differences between peoples. At the same time, however, this conceptualization drew upon the ideas of self-determination.

[The happiness of a people cannot be imposed by others. The roses of the garland of freedom have to be picked by their own hands, from their own desires, their own pleasures, and their own love. . . . The people are the active factor in national life, the source of beauty and strength.]

Even in this particularist vision a universalist element can be detected.

[Like Herodotus we must look at peoples without prejudices and describe each one in its own context taking account of its morals and customs. Then we will realize that all nations, though different, follow the same law: only the right balance brings happiness, arrogance always bears its own revenge . . . No people is the only chosen people by God, all have to strive for truth and all must cultivate the garden of the common good.]

All the same, the way in which Herder perceived differences was at times rather narrow-minded. He rejected the idea of learning foreign languages because, he thought, the only language one could ever speak was one's own "mother tongue." As Kohn (1950) points out, Herder's perspective was that of peace between nations and fatherlands.—"Princes and states can think of wars, politics, and domination: nations and fatherlands for their part aim at the peaceful co-existence of mankind."

Like Goethe and Schiller, though, Herder was not concerned with political organization, leaving this to *Fürsten* and *Staaten*. He tried rather to articulate a sense of cultural belonging or, as one would say today, cultural identity that was neither with the state nor identified as opposed to it, but was outside political concepts of the nation-state. This was not true of Fichte and Arndt who saw their mission as consisting in the construction of a united German nation willing to fight against French occupation. Their concepts of the nation, therefore, tried to link identity with a political program of liberation. The key term for the young Fichte was culture: "[T]he concentration of all our forces on the aim of total liberty, of total independence from everything which is not our self, which is not our pure ego" (Fichte, 1845–46, p. 86).

Fichte defined Germans by their language. He rejected the notion of a "pure race" as Germans were, like any other people, of mixed race." (One should not emphasize the fact that people of Germanic origin mixed with the inhabitants of the countries they conquered. The result of this mixture was a Germanic people. The same happened in the homeland, where they mixed with Slavs. None of these peoples coming from Germania would be able to prove pure descent) (Fichte, 1978).

Arndt took an opposite view:

> The Germans are not bastardized by alien people, they have not become mongrels. They have preserved their original purity more than many other peoples and have been able to develop slowly and quietly from this purity according to the lasting laws of time; the fortunate Germans are an original people.

Arndt and Fichte addressed the people and developed programs of education for all (*Nationalerziechung*), however, this was not meant, as Fichte wrote in *Reden an die deutsche Nation*, to make all individuals equal. As a young man Fichte was opposed not only to foreign oppression but also to all kinds of state power orientated toward the oppression of the individual. He addressed the monarchy of his time:

> You are afraid for us, that we might be oppressed by a foreign power, and in order to rescue us do you prefer to oppress yourself? We believe, that you do prefer to oppress us yourself instead of having others doing it. But we don't know why we should prefer it.

But later, especially for Ernst Moritz Arndt and, under the influence of the minister of the Prussian State, Freiherr vom Stein, their concept of liberation was articulated *within*, not against, a concept of state power. Their revolutionary intent was to get rid of the "foreign power," but they did not oppose state power as such. On the contrary to be German was bound up with being faithful (*treu*), disciplined, and obeying God defined in opposition to the foreign foe, the French. In the poem, *Was ist des Deutschen Vaterland?* (What is the German fatherland?), Arndt (1860) wrote: "Where anger destroys the Latin trinkets / where every Frenchman is a foe / where every German is a friend."

The same hatred against the French appears in many works of those who attempted to formulate the concept of the German nation at that time. It seems that there is a connection between the fact that the nation is not linked with political self-determination, with a democratic project, and the fact that its definition becomes increasingly revitalized. The opponents, when defining the nation, are not "people" and "state" but "Germans" and "foreigners." This is obvious in Arndt's quotation. But the racist sense is even worse in "*Turnvater* Jahn," the organizer of large groups of young people in national mass-sport events. They understood themselves as fighting for liberation and equality. Jahn (1887), for instance; writes,

> It goes without saying that a real man must give try to give his children a mother who comes from his own people. Every other marriage is like a mating of animals without a true spouse. Anyone who has children from a foreign woman degrades his country and paternity.

This is not the place to analyze why the political projects of liberation developed a racialized concept of nation. One reason might be that there was no territorially united "Germany" comparable, for instance, with that of France under the monarchy. Therefore, "German-ness could only be defined by ancestry or language. This is the explanation offered by Kohn (1967).

So, on the one hand, we find a universalistic conception of nation and humanity that is formulated for an educated elite and does not address ordinary people, on the other hand, we find a cultural particularistic concept of the nation, stressing cultural differences, but, at the same time, at the base is to be found the equal value of peoples as well as the strength of the people. But this concept, though emphasizing self-determination, is not articulated within a political project either. The only concept of nation that addresses the people and is formulated as a political project of liberation defines it mainly in opposition to a *foreign* oppressor. At the same time it is influenced by forces within Prussian state power and fails to formulate a democratic perspective originating from its base against its "own" state-power.[6] Even the members of the Parliament (*Frankfurter Paulskirche*), who, after the revolution of 1848, tried to construct a united Germany under a democratic definition offering the crown to the king of Prussia who refused it. Instead, the German state was built "from above" by Bismarck, by means of "steel and blood" as a result of several wars. It did not include all territories that constitute the Deutsche Bund (e.g., Austria), and so it was called the "*kleindeutsche Lösung.*"

I now want to take a brief look at the way in which citizenship was defined in the new German Reich and later. For this purpose I take legislation as an example.

Who is a Citizen of the German Reich?

The first thing to note is that, in spite of the unification of the Reich under the aegis of Prussia, the states still had a great deal of autonomy. For instance, there was no central German citizenship. Citizenship of the Reich could only be obtained by possessing the citizenship of a state, and the regulations differed from state to state. It was policy of the Reich, therefore, to unify those regulations as a means of centralizing its power. The only ones who could ask for direct citizenship of the Reich (*reichsunmittelbare Staatsangehörigkeit*) were the inhabitants of the colonies. Citizenship in the state could be obtained through being in the civil service, through marriage, settlement, or birth. Although there was a strong emphasis on *ius sanguinis* it was not the only criterion to become a member of a state or of the Reich. One could be Polish or Danish and still be a member of the state with full rights.

Later, in the legislation of the Weimar Republic, we do not find any equation between ethnic German-ness, however defined, and German citizenship. One clear example for this is a paragraph in the constitution of 1919 (Art. 113) that speaks about the non-German parts of the *Volk* and their right to use their mother-tongue language in schools and state institutions. This does not mean, in fact, that reality corresponded with the article in the constitution. For instance, such rights were not really granted to the Polish minorities. Certain political groups wanted to homogenize the nation by including territories occupied by German-speaking peoples into the Reich and by inviting "Germans" from all over to "come home" (*Der Alldeutsche Verband*). But there was also strong opposition against a racialized conception of the German nation. In the parliamentary debate about the nationality law in 1912, the Social Democrats attempted to grant the right of citizenship to all immigrants who had lived in Germany for at least two years. Such contradictions in defining German nationality were only "resolved" under Nazism.

Construction of the German Nation in Nazi Legislation

Here the racialized conception of the nation not only gained political and cultural hegemony, but became dominant in the theories of "races," especially concerning the domination of the Aryan race. The Nazis were the first to institutionalize legally a central German nationality in the Nürnberger *Reichsgesetze*:

> The nationality of the German state ceases to exist. There only exists one German nationality.
>
> Only the national of a German or a kindred blood who proves by his behavior that he is willing and able to serve the German people and the Reich truly is a *Reichtsbürger*. (This term meant that those were the only ones to whom rights of citizenship were granted—the few that were left).

The loose ends are thus tied together. German-ness is defined by blood and this definition becomes the determining definition for the first centralized German nationality law. At the same time, state and the definition of who belongs to the German nation are linked and "Volk" and state are defined as a unity. The Nazis use Hegel as one basis for this identification:

> All those who are of the same blood are *Volksgenossen*. This idea was self-evident when our people entered history. There was a Germanic people before there was a Germanic state. "But the people aspire to statehood. Only in the state does a people knows what it wants" (Hegel). A state that has grown out of a people of the same blood has no legal directives other than those serving the life of the people. A true state is not just some form of organization that can be changed by the people like a dress. On the contrary, it is the external expression of the people corresponding to the state of its development. The state is not a dress, but the body, and therefore a specific people can only have one specific state according to its only real form. *(Gestalt)*

According to the Nazi conception, the state grows out of the "Volk," whose unity is based on the sameness of blood. Biology, therefore, defines not only the Volk, but its "expression," the state itself, thus naturalizing both. This is to be understood as a means of reorganizing the populist energy the Nazi had created against the former state. Now that they themselves were the state, they had to define it as expressing the will of the people. The populist energy was directed against another enemy, the "counter-Volk," the Jews (see Laclau, 1977, 1979 and *Projekt Ideologie-Theorie*, 1979). But one must not take this reference to "blood" too literally. First, Hitler himself thought that notion of "race" was nonsense, but that it was nonetheless the only concept which could unite contradictory political and economic forces:

> I knew perfectly well, just as well as those tremendously clever intellectuals, that in the scientific sense, there is no such thing as race. [But] I have to fuse

those nations into a higher order if I want to get rid of the chaos of an historic past that has become an absurdity. And for this purpose the conception of race serves me well. (Quoted in Snyder, 1978, p. 215)

Moreover, one can see by reading the first paragraph of the *Reichsgesetze* that those who have the "right blood" must also prove by their *behavior* that they are true Germans. It is important to stress this because it explains the way in which the construction of a *Volk* and a *Gegenvolk* served the purpose of domination. "Wrong Behavior" could prove that the person was not a "real German" which meant that he or she could be assigned to the *Gegenvolk* and thus assigned to extermination. This fear of becoming *ungerman (undeutsch)* with all of its consequences is one (though by no means a sufficient) explanation for the subordination of the majority of the people during the Third Reich.

The German Nation Today

West German Law and the Construction of the Nation in the West German State

Definitions of the nation and nation-state under Nazism enable hegemonic consensus to be achieved, although not exclusively by force and through the genocide and extermination of those who were deprived of German nationality, mainly Jews and Gypsies. Additionally, however, Eastern European populations, homosexuals, disabled people, and political opponents were sent to the concentration camps and killed.

What is important to see here is the flexibility of the construction of "blood" and "behavior" which facilitated the organization of consent and submission. Surprisingly, regarding legislation, the West German definition of who is to be regarded as German did not differ much from the Nazi legislation. A German according to the Basic Law (para 116 of the German Constitution) is somebody who possesses German nationality or is a refugee or displaced person of German *Volkszugehörigkeit*. Who then is a *deutscher Volkszugehörigkeit* (a member of the German people)? Let us compare the formulation of the Nazis in 1939 and the West German state in 1953 (quoted in Rasche, 1962).

Both formulations state that a German *Volkszugehöriger* is somebody who lays claim to German-ness and who has certain German characteristics such as language, education, or culture. While the West German formulation, of course, does not include the sentence that those of foreign blood, such as Jews, cannot be German, it adds the word *Abstammung* (descent) to the formulation of 1939.

This is the basis on which so-called Aussiedler, whose ancestors emigrated 700, 400, or 200 years ago from parts of a territory that at the time was not "Germany" but rather Hessen, Pfalz, etc., are accepted as Germans, as long as they can prove having their German-ness and providing they possess one or two "objective" characteristics.[7]

To say that Aussiedler emigrated from "Germany" is another way in which an eternal German-ness and a homogeneous German history are constructed. Without wanting to say that the West German state was similar to the Nazi state, one has to admit that as far as the definition of German nationality is concerned, its legislation was closer to that of the Nazi-state than to that of the *Kaiserreich* where one had the right to be nationalized after having served five years in public service. Today one can only become a civil servant after having proved one's German-ness. In Hamburg, for instance, until 1994 any one who wanted to enter the civic service had to fill in a form declaring that his or her grandparents were German by birth and had not lived abroad for an extended period.

The explanation justifying this declaration was as follows: "In order to avoid your appointment being legally invalid, we have to check whether you fulfill the requirement of being German. There can be doubts about this, when ancestors from the generation of parents and grandparents were born abroad or have been living abroad for an extended period. For these purposes, 'abroad' means outside the borders of the German Reich of December 31, 1937."

The Construction of German Identity before Unification

So much for legislative matters. Another way to examines the way in which the German nation was constructed after 1948 is to look at different forms of public discourse. I shall give you a brief summary of some findings from a project I am still dealing with, looking at four different national newspapers during the last forty years (Raethzel, 1992).

The construction of the German nation in public discourse has evolved over time, but as there were two German nation-states, it has always dealt with one main question: is there a united German nation in spite of the existence of two states? The question is always answered affirmatively. Differences are then to be sought in the reason given for the existence of the single nation. The discourse dominant during the 1980s was the liberal one according to which unity lies in a common culture—is defined extremely variably. It means here either art, literature, or the everyday experience and behavior of people. Some try to define the unity of the nation by its language. All these definitions, however, have problems: the German language is spoken not only in the nation states defining themselves as German.

On the other hand, the cultures of the two German nations could also be described as differing from one another. On solution to this contradiction is to separate the definition of the nation from that of the state, thus saying that all people speaking the German language are members of the German nation and that there is no need to link nation and state. This definition has links with the historical split between cultural and political definitions of the nation. The opposite solution is to demand political unification in the long run as a means to avoid the separation of the peoples in the two German nation states resulting from different everyday experiences, different values, and different ways of living.

But while the unity of the German nation is described as using abstract concepts of culture only, things became more complicated when describing the reality of the German nation during the 1980s. As far as political orientation, political and cultural values are concerned we find the irritating fact that the two German nations are described as being different and opposed to each other (e.g., democracy versus dictatorship, modernity versus old values, western orientation versus eastern, consumerism versus productivism). In the dominant liberal discourse of the 1980s the East German nation provides both the Self, with which it is united, and the Other against which the West German nation can formulate it own identity. (The difficulties of present-day unification have one of their roots in this relationship between West and East Germany.)

The second Self providing at the same time a Counter-Self, the negative Other, is the Nazi past. It is seen at least in one of two ways. It is sometimes conceived as having been overcome completely (one must remember that the founding of the Federal Republic of Germany is conceptualized as the zero hour, reminding one of the year zero, of Christ's birth, symbolizing the rebirth of humankind without sin). Alternatively, and this is true for critical intellectuals mainly, the Nazi, past is seen as still having influence in today's Germany and, therefore, the only way of distancing oneself from it is to deny one's own belonging to the German nation and to deny the necessity of belonging to any nation however defined. Any attempt to formulate a certain mode of belonging to a German nation is thus seen as a nationalist, right-wing position.

What is especially striking in the liberal discourse of the Germans is the complete absence of any notion of *Ausländer* (foreigners). They simply do not exist. This indicates to my view, that even in the liberal discourse there is a subconscious self-evident "knowledge" that only Germans by birth belong to the nation. This in spite of the fact that it is never articulated but on the contrary explicitly rejected (See Raethzel, 1992a).

But the discourse of the Other does have a function in the discourse of the nation, a function that derives precisely from the fact of being absent from it. Whenever migrants are discussed, problems are discussed: school problems, housing problems, the problems of social security, the problem of unemployment. On the other hand, in discussions concerning the nation we never find such prosaic problems at all. Whereas the nation is the realm of sweetness and light, migration is the real of problems, contradictions, and fear. In this way it provides the space for discussing everything people are suffering from. By securing the borders between the discourse of the nation and the discourse of *Ausländer*, the latter serves as a means to construct the inner contradictions of the nation, of the society as contradictions between "the interior" (that is thus homogenized and idealized) and "the exterior" (that which is similarly homogenized but demonized). This serves to organize consensus (within certain limits) and provides an imaginary solution to almost all problems of society and of the nation: a control of immigrants. In this context, control and planning themselves lose their negative connotations with bureaucratic socialism and allow people to imagine themselves as active and problem-solving.

National Identity and Aussiedler and Übersiedler

The complication of the German nation in which East Germany and Nazi Germany serve as "the Other" in different ways, that is, the balance between racialized and political constructions of the German nation, comes into crisis firstly with the arrival of large numbers of *Aussiedler* and *Übersielder*, and secondly with unification.

The problem from this point of view of the unified government was as follows: on the one hand West Germany had always criticized governments of the Eastern block for not letting ethnic Germans leave their countries. In legislation, Germans were defined as such by descent, culture, language, and because they were oppressed by the communist regimes. Their German ethnicity thus gave them the right to enter the country and to acquire citizenship, once they proved their German descent. There was no way for the government to deny them entry except by altering the constitutional law.

On the other hand, it has been a tenet of the dominant discourse since 1973 that West Germany is overcrowded, that "the boat is full," and that consequently immigration must be stopped.

With the arrival of 300,000 immigrants a year, due to the loosening of emigration regulations in Eastern countries, arguments had to be found why this full boat was suddenly able to carry a much larger number of people than what had previously been considered unsupportable: around 100,000 refugees a year.

The arguments invoked are of two kinds:

1. The newcomers were *Germans*, it was stressed. Therefore, it was not only an act of humanism to welcome them, but an act of patriotism (as the late Franz Joseph Straub put it).
2. These immigrants would solve the demographic problems of the German economy: lack of a qualified workforce, and the problem that too many old people had to be supported by too few younger, working people.

All these arguments boil down to the innate German-ness of the immigrants, because otherwise they would also be true *Ausländer*. Of course, there was a problem in defining such groups as German because it meant getting very close—in public—to the Nazi definition (or the definition connected with Nazism) of "German by blood." The government was well aware of this, as we can see in the regulations for the application of the *Bundesvertriebenengesetz* released in 1980, when the Social Democrats and the Liberals were still in power. These regulations say that belonging is a juridical term, not an "ethnological" one: belonging can only be derived from open declaration of German-ness in the country of origin and/or objective cultural traits. But at the end of the day the ethnological definition, as it was called, becomes the only "valid" one. The others, such as language, culture, and education (the so-called objective traits) as well as declaration are highly problematic:

Language: most of the *Aussiedler* do not speak German.
Declaration: it was argued that in the face of oppression one could not expect declaration because this would amount to expecting heroism,
Education and Culture: if German culture and a German education were forbidden in the countries people came from, this could hardly be expected of them.

The bureaucrats ended up looking at the membership cards of SS and SA and the German Army in order to check up on the German-ness as it was assumed that one could be a member of the organizations only if one were in fact a true German.[8]

The myth of a "German origin" became real through the incredible bureaucratic activity of checking documents, going back to the places people lived to find out, through the interrogation of neighbors, whether a person holding an army book really did have children and grandchildren and how many.

The assumption that the people coming in were German not only led to a marked increase in the flow of money from all kinds of sources for the different tasks necessary to integrate them—construction of buildings to provide homes, provision of additional training, language courses, and so on—but also revised the discourses of immigration, integration, the clash between different cultures (culture conflict), numbers, and overpopulation. I want to give a few examples. The source for the argument of *Aussiedler* is material provided by the government or governmental organizations for political education. For *Ausländer*, quotations derive from the conservative and liberal press, sometimes quoting members of the government (see Box 8.1).

Box 8.1

Regarding Aussiedler

Minority Rights
"Until now all members of the Warsaw Pact have denied their minorities, including Germans, basic rights and freedoms. The policies of these states aim at the assimilation of Germans living in their region. The Poles are guilty of cultural genocide by denying the existence of the German minority and by ruthless Polonization, which has lead to the fact that the Germans in the Polish region do not even speak their mother tongue any more" (from *Das Parlament*, 39 Jahrgang, Nr. 35, August 25, 1989, p. 3 a journal funded by the Ministry for Political Education).

Integration of Minorities
"If *Aussiedler* and *Übersiedler* realize that what they have to offer is needed, that we want them as fellow human beings, but also as citizens who are ready to take up responsibilities for society, then this is the best presupposition we can offer them for good integration" (*Information zur politischen Bildung*, Nr. 222 1989, p. 9, the magazine from the Ministry for Political Education.)

Cultural characteristics and their relation to the "German Culture" in West Germany
"They are more orientated towards the family. They see if as a community of solidarity that supports them . . . this is shown by the fact that they marry at an earlier age and have more children while

Regarding Ausländer

"Integration means offering to foreigner who live in Germany, an opportunity to live in our society the way we live, by participating in professional and social life" (Liselotte Funcke, former Ombudswoman for "foreigners" in *Die Welt*, November 27, 1981). A newspaper article criticizes, "Many foreigners, especially the Turks in Frankfurt don't want to integrate. They want to go on speaking their language, practicing their religion and above all, they want to keep their nationality" (*Die Welt*, November 11, 1981).

"Integration—for foreigners who have been living here for a long time—is desirable as far as they want it themselves . . . But first they have to insert themselves into our social relations and when they have done this properly then they may ask for citizenship" *Frankfurter Allgemeine Zeitung*, June 28, 1990, quoting a member of the CDU).

"In our country we have only space for those views of human dignity, tolerance, honor family and the dignity of women, which are written down in our constitution" (*Die Welt*, December 13, 1981).

young" (*Information zur politischen Bildung*, Nr. 222 1989, p. 9, Magazine from the Ministry for Political Education). "The Russian Germans will experience the greatest difficulties. They are not allowed to drink alcohol, smoke or go to places of pleasure . . . Such families will experience problems. But perhaps their more traditional views can also have a positive influence on their neighborhood and they can bring back some useful old values to their friends" (*Das Parlament*, 39, Jahrgang, Nr. 35, August 25, 1989, p. 11).

"Arranged marriages have nothing to do with the marriages mentioned in our constitution" (*Die Welt*, February 5, 1982).

Reasons for Migration
"Aussiedler emigrated because they no longer felt at home. Their basic human rights were violated, they could not practice their religion, work and access to goods was a problem in a society of scarce resources. (*Information zur politischen Bildung*, Nr. 222, 1989, p. 48).

"The right to asylum does not protect against all kinds of violation of basic human rights. It protects only against violations due to race, religion and nationality. It does not protect against general bad conditions of living, famine, natural catastrophes, war or civil wars" (*Die Welt*, June 24, 1985, quoting the official view of the government).

"It is only natural, that financial reasons play a role as well . . . Anyway, you cannot separate economy and politics in modern states" *Das Parlament*, 39 Jahrgang, Nr. 35, August 25, 1989, p. 7).

Numbers
"There has always been a lack of housing. The arrival of *Aussiedler* is not its cause, it only makes this lack visible. Many people think that our country is over-populated and is unable to host hundred and thousands of *Aussiedler*. The facts are: the German population has decreased between 1970 and 1987 by 1.3 million. Even if the number of *Aussiedler* and *Übersiedler* amounted to 300,000–400,000 every years, this would not pose a problem" (*Ihre Heimat sind WIR*, Aktion Gemeinsinn 1989, p. 27).

"It is obvious that in a country as densely populated as the Federal Republic of Germany all efforts towards integration are destined to fail if incoming numbers stay as high as they are today (650,000 during the last three years). The main problem is not even the labor market, but the rejection of foreigners by the population. It occurs inevitably, when the threshold of tolerance is transgressed" (*Die Zeit*, January 1, 1982).

"The threshold of tolerance as perceived by our French and English neighbors lies at about 10 percent and has not yet been reached in our country—if we do not count the Austrians (*Die Zeit*, October 18,1985).

This is from the official form given to those who apply for a position (for instance as lawyers or teachers) in the civil service by the Hamburg Administration.

Comparison of these quotations highlights a number of elements crucial in constructing the nation and organizing consensus.

a) Immigration does not seem to be an objective problem. It is construed either as a problem or a benefit, depending on political will and interest. The description of almost the same cultural features can result in warnings to the "foreigners" to integrate or else lead with the hope that the natives might learn something from the newcomers.

b) The way in which universal civil rights such as the right to use one's mother tongue, the right to religion, the right to immigrate, and to emigrate, and so on, are linked with nationality shows clearly that those universal rights are interpreted in a particular way. They are only meant for those defined as nationals, who alone seem to belong to the human race for which universal rights are valid.

c) German-ness is seen purely as a matter of descent. This can be concluded from the way in which language, as well as culture, education, values, and family-life are described as different and likely to produce problems (though in this case not for West Germans, but for the *Ausslieder* if they have to assimilate). Nevertheless, the people possessing such different cultural traits are portrayed as being German. The argument according to which the cultures of *Aussiedler* express "Old German values," that disappeared in the West (whether you accept this or not) is a contradiction in itself, because it shows that there is no such thing as an eternal national culture, but that cultures and behaviors change over time.

Reactions in the Aussiedler and Ubersiedler by the West German Population

Initially the strategy of integrating the *Aussiedler* worked. It was assisted by the press describing the newcomers as young, qualified, healthy, willing, and able to work, paying into the German pension system. But within a couple of months perception changed, again assisted by the press, which—from Right to Left—suddenly found out that the *Aussiedler*, and especially the *Übersiedler* (people coming from GDR), were lazy, had social problems, were not accustomed to work, did not show any responsibility either for work or for material, were antisocial, and in fact, alcoholics.

The argument against the policy of the government, voiced partly by Lafontaine, the then show-chancellor of the Social Democrats, who repeated the findings of the opinion polls, was that the *Aussiedler* were not "real Germans." On what grounds was this stated? Well, precisely taking seriously the definitions given by others for their belonging to the nation: that they did *not* speak the German language, they *had* different ways of living, did *not* fit into the market, company, believed in traditional values, and other such reasons.

The racialized definition of the nation which included *Aussiedler* by virtue of descent (*Abstammung*) was challenged from below by using social definitions of the nation, such as language, culture, and behavior. But those characteristics were used precisely to exclude a group of people, to prove the incompatibility of the natives and the newcomers. As a result those traits were transformed into quasi-natural categories. They became static features which one could either possess or not.

In other words, what could be observed was a struggle between an old genetic racism and a new so-called cultural racisim, and the latter was more exclusionary than the first.

One result of these debates has been that the notion of German-ness has become more popular in public life. German nationalism, at least when articulated in a certain way, became more respectable—without the consequence, though, of accepting the *Aussiedler* as a new group belonging to the nation. As a result of this (of course, this was not the only reason, but I believed it helped a lot), a new German extremist right-wing party could gain a high percentage of votes in local and European elections: the so-called Republican Party (*Das Parlament*, 1989).

The second result appeared without much publicity: access of ethnic Germans to the country was made more difficult; less money was given to them, and they could only come if they had already been able to prove their German-ness in the country in which they lived.

Unification and the Reorganization of National Identity

Unification does not only pose economic problems. If what I have said above about the construction of the German nation during the last fifty years is true, unification also poses a problem for "national identity." The relation between West Germany and East Germany, where East Germans provided at the same time for West Germans the image of Self and Other, does not hold any longer. The Other has invaded the Self and is reclaiming its identity in terms of equality with West Germany. But it is denied its "birthright" and marginalized as "not yet civilized." In this situation the "foreigner," previously necessary only as a means to construct social conflicts as problems "imported from outside," seems to become the necessary "counter-self" for the construction of the new German Self.

Although I do not want to reduce the reinforcement of racism in East and West Germany to problems of reorganizing a national identity, I do suggest considering it as one of the factors leading to it. It is telling that the political groups which were the quickest to unify and to establish stable contacts between East and West were the right-wing extremist groups. It must be borne in mind that much of the "spontaneous" actions of extremist youth in East Germany are organized by West German fascist groups. Certainly, their mere presence does not explain why East German young people answer positively to the attempts of extremists to organize them, and certainly there is much right-extremist activity that is not organized by anybody from the West. Another myth concerning neofascist activities against migrants is that those perpetrating them are poor, homeless, unemployed, and without prospects. As far as empirical studies show, this is not the case: the majority are young working people who are often the sons of the former members of the Nomeclatura in the former GDR.

The left (if I may use this generalizing term) has split into countless factions as a result of unification, some leaving the Green party, some trying to form a new party, attempting to push the Green party to unite with the civil movement in East Germany—or what is left of it. Some of those who left the Green party together with other left groups fear the emergence of a "Fourth Reich." Others enter the national discourse by stating their fear of the loss of West German "civil society" that they, like the "sixty-eighter generation," participated in constructing. Now they see all their efforts put at by those "uncultivated" Germans from the East who have no idea of "civil society" because they are used to nothing but obeying the authorities (see Raethzel, 1992b, for a more detailed analysis).

My concern in this context is not whether those fears are legitimate or not. Neither do I see a problem in identifying with the democratic achievements in West German society. What I find interesting and problematic today is the way in which this discourse fits into the dominant hegemonic discourse of German politics. In modern societies consent is not organized by a unifying agreement on crucial political questions but by providing the framework within which questions are discussed. In this case, the framework would consist in the notion of the West, of West Germany as the modern civilized state and the East as the barbarian state where authoritarianism and particularism rule. (One wonders, then, how these barbarians managed to get rid of their regimes, and how the Russian people were able to challenge "The Putsch"). To argue that civil society is in danger from Eastern peoples or from Turkish Muslims and to conclude that they should either be kept out or assimilated as fast as possible is a way of trying to protect civil society by denying it. If anything, civil society (if we understand it in the way Gramsci conceptualized it) is a concept based on how conflicts of values, ways of living, and so on, are carried out. To propose assimilation and, in doing so, to assume that the other, the majority, is not only a homogenous group but also right, undermines the very concept of civil society. It cuts off the process of winning hegemony, whereby groups (ideally) learn from each other and try to win each other over to their views by imposing the views of a minority. It is precisely this concerning which the East Germans are complaining. They see their views as totally rejected by West Germans, from the political right to the political left. To state that a whole population is not able to act in a civil society comes very close to treating this ability as a kind of natural feature that either one possesses or not.

But these concepts of who belongs to the nation or who is able to participate and take responsibility within the society, are the notions on which a nation is (re)constructed. In this context it is less important that dissident groups disagree with the government about the prospects of unification. It is more important that they take part in constructing a static concept of the nation that implies inflexibility and thereby "correctness" of certain values and certain forms of living. From this point of view the question of who is allowed to join the closed shop and who must be kept outside may be answered in different ways, but it stays/becomes a legitimate question.

"Foreigners" and other aliens are thus not a threat to the stability of a nation, instead, they are a means by which it is constructed. The definition of who does not belong defines those who belong and provides security for them. If "foreigners" did not exist, they would have to be invented. A good example of this is the opinion poll in East Germany, where the population was asked w hom they saw as the biggest threat to their stability. The answer was the Turks, though at that time, 1989, only about 90 Turks were living in the whole of the GDR.

Another strand within the left, which also finds adherents among liberal intellectuals, artists, people in the media, in advertising, and other such professions, and those who started campaigning against the new virulent forms of racism, argues in a different way. This group distances itself from racism and nationalism by stressing multiculturalism, and the pleasure experienced through contact with different cultures. What is denied (and this reminds us of the statements made under very different conditions by Goethe and Schiller, who are quoted quite often in this context) is the necessity for a sense of cultural belonging. Some groups tend to idealize what they see as the cultures of migrants, thus reducing them to certain folkloric expressions of culture. This exoticism goes so far as to carry banners at demonstrations against racism saying. "Germany not to the Germans" or "Never Again Germany." While proclaiming that wanting to belong to a nation is exclusionary and racist they assume that they themselves do not need a sense of belonging and are therefore not exclusionary. But their discourse is merely a reversed exclusion. They belong to a specific intellectual German culture which articulates their specific form of belonging as not belonging to any group. But in fact they exclude on moral grounds those whom they see as not being as open-minded a they understand themselves to be. If one attempts to analyze their discourse more closely it seems that they tend to formulate the contradiction between the open-minded universalists and the narrow-minded nationalists in class terms, depicting nationalists as being poor and less educated.

Political Prospectives

It is likely that the German constitution will be changed to include elements of *ius soli* into the legislation? Many people think so, arguing that as Germany has become a country of imagination the *ius sanguinis* legislation is obsolete. But to my mind politics operate with another logic than that of the mere rationality of "facts." Otherwise, it would be difficult to understand why the German government is still wedded to the declaration that Germany is not "a country of immigration."

Political strategies are concerned with maintaining power. This includes, among other things, constructing a sense of belonging. To serve this purpose the *ius sanguinis* legislation is extremely useful and not obsolete at all. As we have seen, there is no need for purity. That is, "blood" can and has always been defined in political and cultural terms and vice versa. But if necessary, it provides the ruling classes with a rather useful argument for excluding (or including) the groups they want according to economic and/or political situations. I would foresee some additional legislation to make it easier for migrants born in Germany to achieve nationality and to give members of the European Community voting rights in local elections. But generally, I am afraid, it is more likely than not other European countries will include more elements of *ius sanguinis* (as Britain has done already).

Though I would consider it progressive to define nationality in terms of *ius soli* only, I do not see it as a means by which to escape racism and exclusion. State institutions will always find ways to exclude/include, and as racism and exclusion are tools in the struggle for hegemony they do not derive from a particular legislation. The latter only "freezes" the self-definition of the nation-state at a given time. At the same time, those wishing to define themselves as belonging to the nation will tend to do so against reversed mirror images of the Other, and not be defining themselves against power structures.

To me the problems seems to be that those who emphasize human rights and universalism fail to integrate them with the right to difference, and thus apply universal rights only to nationals, thus transforming them into particularistic rights; or else, and this would be true for much of the left and of liberals, they disconnect universalism and the right to difference from any notion of cultural belonging.

The struggle between "nationalists" and "non-nationalists" is not so much a struggle between romantic and rational forces as between forces who seek to win the support of people in a populist manner, that is, by subordinating them to the structure of domination, and those who stress democracy and civil liberties but stay remote from the needs of large parts of the population. As there is no attempt to formulate a popular democratic discourse that would be able to bridge the deep gulf that separates East German from West German workers, East German from West German women, and similar binaries, people nationalize themselves by identifying with an authoritarian nation against "foreigners." Considering the acute new contradictions resulting from unification and the break up of the "real socialist" regimes, only in not being "foreigners" can people see themselves as being something, that is German. In order words, there is a populist discourse and a democratic discourse but not a popular democratic discourse of belonging.[9]

Any prospect for change lies, as far as I can see, in a process of democratization in which the development of a capacity for action from below provides enough collective and individual strength to allow for the flexibility of a sense of belonging. This would be something like a conception of the nation that combines a sense of belonging to a certain local space with its ways of living, cultural expressions, and so forth, with a sense of belonging to the world as a whole. There is a need for a new internationalism. "New" means that it should not be formulated in opposition to national/local feelings of belonging and that it should not be grounded in abstract moral values but based on everyday experiences. There is hardly a workplace without connections to the "outside" of the nation state. The things we use are constructed throughout the world as is the material out of which we build our local cultural identities.

The dependence of every individual on international developments may be experienced as a threat, for instance, to ecological matters. On a political level the practical conditions necessary for the articulation of identities that are at the same time global and local do exist. But it is precisely the existence of these conditions which lead people to retreat into local identities as worldwide relations and dependencies seem impossible to deal with from below. The more this happens, and the more democratic processes are concealed (for instance in construction of a united Europe), the more racism will be used as a means from below and from above to secure a sense of belonging and also a sense of "capacity for action." In controlling "foreigners" and their numbers (or in trying to do so) people as well as politicians create the illusion that they are in control of social developments. A process of democratization which seeks to strengthen capacity for action from below in relation to local and global developments might be a way out of a narrow, exclusionary construction of the nation. But at the moment no political force able and willing to take up this challenge has appeared in Germany.

Notes

Ausländers: Ethnic Germans coming back to Germany after their ancestors have emigrated, two to seven hundred years earlier, and foreigners living in Germany. This essay originally appeared in Social Identities 1/2 1995.

1. One of the most quoted definitions of the nation is the one by Renan, defining the nation as a daily plebescite. For a critique of such subjective and also of objective definitions of the nation see Hobsbawm (1990). Anderson's suggestion to define the nation as a sovereign "imagined community" within territorial boundaries is widely accepted nowadays, although it is interpreted in many different ways (see Anderson, 1983). Gellner wants to combine the subjective and the objective definition, thus stating that people belong to the same nation if they have the same culture and if they accept themselves as members of the same nation (Gellner, 1983). The vagueness and incompleteness of these definitions are seen by the respective authors themselves. Instead of looking at the contents (culture, language, territory, etc.) by which nations can be and are often defined, it seems to me more useful to analyse the nation and the nation-state as a specific historic form of social organization, that is, as a specific relationship of domination and self-determination.

2. For the influence of the French Revolution on German-ness see James (1991) and Grab (1991).

3. The dichotomy was originally developed by Kohn (1945), chapter VII. For a recent articulation of this position see, e.g., Brubaker (1991). For a critique of its methodology see Winkler (1985).

4. *Schillers sämtliche Werke* (undated), p. 429. But the writer was not reduced to his national belonging, see his letter of October 13, 1789, Stuttgart: Cotta: v. i, p. 90.

5. See Heinrich Heine's *Sämtliche Werke*, p. 237. In earlier editions the paragraph was censored.

6. For a detailed analysis of the relations between the nationalist intellectuals and the political forces within the Prussian state see Johnston (1990).

7. For an analysis of the immigration of *Volkdeutsche* (ethnic Germans) into West Germany that shows that the country of origin was not "Germany," but rather from a variety of different states, see Otto (1990).

8. Which is not even true, because of a scarcity of manpower, especially toward the end of the war, "foreigners" were allowed into the army and the SS and were granted the right to German nationality after five years as a reward.

9. For the difference between "popular" and "populist" see Hall (1980).

References

Anderson, B. (1983) *Imagined Communities*. London: Verso.

Arndt, E. M. (1860) *Gedichte. Vollstundige Sammlung*, Berlin: Weidmannsche Burchhandlung.

Balibar, E. (1988) "Racisme et nationalisme," in E. Balibar and I. Wallerstein (eds.) *Race, Classe, Nation*, Paris. La Decouverte.

Brubaker, W. R. (1991) "Immigration, Citoyennete et Etat-nation en France et Allemagne: Une Analyse historique comparative," *Les Temps Modernes*, August: pp. 293–332.

Eckermann, J. P. (1986) "Gesprache mit Goethe," in Johann Wolfgan Goethe, Sämtliche Werke, München, 19.

Fichte, J. G. (ed.) "Sämtlich Werke," Berlin: Veit und Comp. 6, Beiträge zur Berichtigung der Urtheile uber die französische Revolution.

—— (1978) *Reden an die Deutsche Nation*, Hamburg: Felix Meiner Verlag.

Gellner, E. (1983) *Nations and Nationalism*, Oxford.

Grab, W. (1991) "*Deutsher Jakobinismus und jüdische Emanzipation,*" in W. Grab, ed., Der deutsche Weg der Judenemanzipation. 1789–1938, München.

Hall, S. (1989) "Popular-democratic vs. Authoritarian Populism: Two Ways of Taking Democracy Seriously," in A. Hunt, ed., Marxism and Democracy, London: pp. 157–185.

Heine, H. (1887–1890) "Die romantische Schule," *Henrich Heine's Sämtliche Werke*, Leipzig: Ernest Elster (Hrg.) v.237.

Hobsbawm, E. J. (1990) Cambridge: Cambridge University Press.

Hoffmann, L. (1990) *Die unvollendete Republik*, Köln. PapyRossa Verlag.

Jahn (1887) Werke, 2 Teil 2.

James, H. (1991) *Deutsche Identität*. 1770–1990, Frankfurt/Main, New York Campus.

Johnston, O. W. (1990) *Der Deutsche Nationalmythos. Ursprung eines politischen, Programms*, Stuttgart: J. D. Metzlersche Verlagbuchhandlung.

Kohn, H. (1945) *The Idea of Nationalism*, New York: Macmillan.

—— (1950) *Die Idee des Nationalismus*, Heidelberg: Lambert Schneider.

—— (1967) Prelude to Nation-States: the French and German Experience, 1789–1815. Princeton, New Jersey: D. Van Nostrand Company.

Kühnemann, E., ed., *Herder, Werke*, XVIII: Briefe zur Befürderung der Humanität.

Laclau, E. (1977) *Politics and Ideology in Marxist Theory*, London: Verso.

—— (1979) *Projekt Ideologie-Theorie: Theorien uber Ideologie*, Berlin: Argument-Verlag.

Otto, K. A. (1990) "Aussiedler un Aussiedler-Politik im Spannungfeld von Menschenrechten und Kaltem Krieg. Historische, politisch-moralische und rechtliche Aspekte der Aussiedler-Politik," in K. A. Otto, ed., *Westwärts— Heimwärts?*, Bielefeld: AJZ Verlag.

Rasche, G. (1962) "Das Deutsche Staatsangehörigkeitsrecht. Eine Zusammenstellung."

Räthzel, N. (1991) "Germany: One Race, One Nation?" in *Europe: Variations on a theme of Racism, Race and Class*, 32 (January–March).

—— (1992) "Deutsche Nation und Bilder von 'Ausländern' in der westdeutschen Presse," in *Osnabrücker Beiträge zur Sprachtheorie* Nr. 46 März.

Räthzel, N. (1992) "Die Widersprüche bei der Reorganisierung der nationalen Identität im vereinigten Deutschland: Die Bedeutung von Asylpolitik und neuem Rassissmus" in S. Jäger and C. Butterwegge (eds.) *Rassismus in Europa.*

Schiller (undated) *Schillers sämtliche Werke*, München, George Muller, II.

Siegler, B. (1991) *Auferstanden and Runinen*, Berlin: Edition Tiamat.

Snyder, L. (1978) *Roots of German Nationalism*, Bloomington/London: Indiana University Press, originally in H. Rauschnin (1939) *Hitler Speaks*, London.

Winkler, H. A. (1985) "Der Nationalismus und seine Funktion," in H. A. Winkler, ed., *Nationalismus*, Konigstein/Ts. Athenaeum.

CHAPTER NINE

GERMANY'S COMING OUT: CITIZENSHIP AND IMMIGRATION REFORM SINCE UNIFICATION

Hermann Kurthen

Nations are defined as populations endowed by specific citizenship rights within a bounded territory under the control of a political regime. The degree of existing rules of inclusion and exclusion, the shared collective self-definitions, and popular practices determine the easiness of how boundaries can be crossed by insiders and outsiders.

Most populations and countries that originate from historic roots grounded in ethnic, religious, linguistic, or other cultural particularities assert their national identity and right to self-determination and sovereignty by claiming a territorial, legal, and political identity between ethnocultural "nation" and "state" (Staatsvolk). Naturally, such countries made the incorporation of minorities and of immigrants more difficult than more recent settler or immigrant nations (such as the U.S.), which derive their unity, identity, and laws primarily from shared civic principles and universalistic liberties; or states like France, which superimposed a secular political culture won in a revolution against older feudal-aristocratic orders on top of an ethnic nation.

Germany belongs to the group of nonsettler and nonrevolutionary countries that arose out of territorial feudal regimes that pre-date its modern existence as a nation. Germany's particular historical fragmentation during centuries of the Holy Roman Empire, the specifics of her comparatively belated national unification, and attempts to legitimate her late nineteenth century rulers' imperial claim as a rising world power encouraged a more stringent "voelkisch" ethnocultural nation-building project.

Then, in the twentieth century, for many reasons, Germany as a large, powerful, and envied country in the center of Europe, experienced extraordinary historical ruptures and regime changes. It started with Germany's defeat in World War I, continued with the political and economic failure of the liberal democratic experiment of the Weimar Republic (1919–1933), the extremely racist period of the Third Reich (1933–1945), and ended with the country's almost total destruction in World War II, followed by foreign occupation, dismemberment, and division into hostile camps during the Cold War.

In 1948/1949, the newly created semi-sovereign West German Federal Republic maintained references to its ethno-cultural origins (ironically reinforced by the imposed stigmatization of all things German by the victims of National Socialism and the victors alike) AND created a democratic polity based on universal principles and a liberal constitution (Basic Law).

The decision to retain elements of "ius sanguinis," or more specific, parentage-based citizenship law (1913) of the Imperial period for persons born in prewar and postwar Germany and expellees/refugees/resettlers from the East was supported for various reasons: the need to integrate post–World War II ethnic German expellees mostly from Eastern Europe and the Soviet Union; the rising number of refugees from Stalinist East Germany; and the wish to re-naturalize forcefully expatriated Nazi victims. On the other hand, the wish to compensate for the digressions of the Nazi regime motivated the conception of one of the most generous and liberal asylum laws in the world and a constitution that enshrined elementary principles of the U.S. bill of rights. Moreover, to avoid the impression of forced ethno-cultural assimilation, naturalization required a voluntary and permanent desire to remain in Germany, basic knowledge of the polity and a pledge to the newly democratic foundations of the Federal Republic. It also demanded active command of the German language, fifteen years residency in Germany, a secure job, legal competence and no criminal record. But it did in no way prescribe an applicants, genealogical, ethnic, national, racial, religious, or other ascriptive characteristics or origins.

Then, at the turn of the twenty-first century after fifty years of a slow evolutionary process, Germany's ethno-national foundations gave way to a more civic and inclusive self-definition of the German nation guided by universalistic principles of an open and pluralist society. This shift was advanced by the dynamics of the postwar decades, in particular, prudent leadership, reeducation of the population, a broadened democratic political culture, and economic growth. But the shift also was forced by the long-term and unintended consequences of guestworker immigration, of raising global refugee flows, of the logic of European integration, and of the worldwide groundswell of post-national and universalistic human and citizenship rights. Finally, German unification and decisive political events in the 1990s helped to advance the decoupling of nation and state and led to reforms of immigration and naturalization policies. With it a new valuation of diversity and multiculturalism is developing also unearthing Germany's previously suppressed history and experience of religious, ethnic, and cultural pluralism in central Europe as a result of manifold inward and outward migration movements and mixing of populations since the beginning of history (Kurthen, 1997).

Germany's Postwar Immigration Experience

Over the past fifty years Germany has experienced several phases of large migrations, among them the movement of over twenty million ethnic Germans and the immigration of about 8 million foreigners (Bade and Muenz, 2000, Motte et al., 1999).

The World War II and Cold War movement of Germans meant

- the successful integrating of an estimated 12.5 million persecuted and expelled ethnic Germans (Vertriebene) from lost pre–World War II Eastern German territories and from Eastern European German enclaves between 1945 and 1949. About 8 million settled in the territory that became the Federal Republic of (West) Germany and West Berlin in 1948.
- providing safe haven for an estimated 4 million refugees from the communist East German Democratic Republic (GDR), most of which arrived between 1949 and the building of the Berlin Wall in August 1961.
- aiding 4.1 million ethnic German resettlers (Aussiedler) from Eastern Europe and the former Soviet Union to become (West) German citizens between 1950 and 2000. Half of all resettlers arrived after German unification until their overwhelming influx was limited in the mid-1990s (see table 9.1).

Upon arrival in West Germany, expellees, GDR refugees, and resettlers all had a constitutional claim to German citizenship plus access to social benefits, ranging from language and job training to subsidized housing, pensions, and health care.

Non-German immigrants ("Ausländer" or foreigners) also were made up of distinct groups arriving at different periods.

The first group is comprised of the original "guestworkers" from southern Europe. Italians arrived first in the mid-1950s to satisfy the growing demand for labor, followed by Spaniards, Greeks, Portuguese, Yugoslavs, and Turks. After the worker rotation and recruitment stopped in 1973, West Germany's family reunification laws allowed for large and continuous

Table 9.1 Selected characteristics about immigrants and immigration in Germany 1990–2000

	1990[a]	1991	1992	1993	1994	1995	1996	1997	1998	1999	2000
Immigrant population in Germany in 1,000	5.343	5.882	6.496	6.878	6.991	7.174	7.314	7.366	7.320	7.344	7.297
Immigrant as % of total population	8.4	7.3	8	8.5	8.6	8.8	8.9	9	8.9	8.9	8.9
"Guestworker" immigrants in 1,000	3.452	3.680	3.989	4.154	4.158	4.333	4.370	4.414	4.425	4.527	4.277
Turkish immigrants in 1,000	1.695	1.780	1.855	1.918	1.966	2.014	2.049	2.107	2.110	2.054	1.999
Net immigration of Turks in 1,000	+49	+46	+40	+22	+18	+30	+30	+10	+3	+6	N/A
Unemployment ratios of foreigners (Germans)	10.1	10.6	12.3	15.3	15.5	16.2	18.6	19.7	18.3	19.7	18.0
	(6.6)	(6.0)	(6.5)	(8.3)	(8.8)	(9.0)	(10.0)	(10.7)	(9.8)	(11.2)	(10.0)
Persons employed in foreigner owned businesses in 1,000	N/A	169	N/A	213	246	239	251	248	250	263	258
Discretionary naturalizations of foreign born in 1,000	20	27	37	45	62	72	86	83	107	143	187
Criminal acts w. anti-foreigner background	389	2426	6336	6721	3491	2468	2232	2953	2644	2283	3594
Net influx of family/labor migrants in 1,000	+376	+423	+593	+277	+153	+225	+149	−22	−33	+118	+86
Immigrant children born in Germany in 1,000	86	90	101	103	101	100	106	107	100	95	95[b]
Immigration of German resettlers in 1,000	397	222	231	219	223	218	178	134	103	105	96
Immigration of asylum seekers in 1,000	193	256	438	323	127	128	116	104	99	95	79
Refugees with temporary protected status from former Yugoslavia in 1,000	0	0	0	97	287	350	345	243	92	76	40
Jews from the former Soviet Union admitted for humanitarian reasons in 1,000	3	6	8	9	9	15	16	19	18	18	17
Non-EU seasonal labor migrants in 1,000	100[b]	129	212	181	138	177	198	206	208	119	100[b]
Non-EU temporary contract labor migrants in 1,000	27	74	95	70	41	49	46	38	33	30[b]	30[b]
Sum of annual net immigration, births, resettlers, asylum-seekers, Kontingenz/temporary refugees, seasonal/contract laborers	806	777	1085	1002	926	1037	1005	829	620	538	457

Notes
[a] 1990 data for West Germany, 1991–2000 data for united Germany
[b] author's estimates.

Source: Bundesanstalt für Statistik; Bericht der Beauftragten der Bundesregierung für Ausländerfragen über die Lage der Ausländer in der Bundesrepublik Deutschland. Berlin und Bonn 1999ff; Harald W. Lederer. 1997. Migration und Integration in Zahlen. Bamberg: Europaeisches Forum für Migrationsstudien (efms).

family migration and the long-term settlement of former guestworker migrants and their families (see table 9.1). Attempts to promote the return of guestworkers in the mid-1980s failed. Overall an estimated 26 million foreigners moved into West Germany and about 19 million foreigners left the country in the last 45 years.

The second group was asylum-seekers and refugees. Originally their numbers were small but applications skyrocketed particularly between 1988 and 1993 and created a huge backlog of unresolved cases and those permitted to stay on welfare. Because these unexpected developments and a parallel huge influx of resettlers and other migrants (see table 9.1) immediately after the costly unification created resentment and hostility in the early 1990s, all political parties agreed to an overhaul of the asylum law in 1993. After that, asylum numbers declined significantly. Since 1950 about 260,000 asylum requests were positively decided, and of those 120,000 between the years 1990 and 2000. In the 1990s some new categories were created, such as persons admitted out of humanitarian considerations (Jews from the former Soviet Union) and persons receiving a temporary protected status (mostly civil war refugees from former Yugoslavia).

The third group results from the expansion of the European Union and the subsumption of national sovereignty rights under European law. This meant that citizens from EU member states, including former guestworkers from Italy, Spain, and Portugal, became denizens of Germany, with privileged residency, employment, trade, and voting rights at local and European Parliament level elections. Similar rights were granted to citizens of other non-EU countries of the European Economic Area and to Switzerland. Turkish citizens also had an easier entry to the German labor market and permanent resident status because of a 1963 Association Agreement between the EU and Turkey. Currently about 25 percent of all foreigners in Germany are EU citizens and have almost the same rights as native-born German citizens.

A fourth group arrived after the painful lesson of the early post-unification years, when the old asylum law had become a loophole for "economically driven" immigration. In the early 1990s, the conservative Kohl government devised four new foreign workers programs to recruit laborers, primarily from Poland and the Czech Republic. These programs were as follows: temporary contract or project-tied workers for up to three years; seasonal workers for agriculture, construction, and service jobs for up to three months; cross-border commuters in jobs for which no local workers were available for up to two nights weekly; and training programs for up to eighteen months (see table 9.1). All four programs were considered beneficial because they addressed micro labor shortages and provided needed income/remittances and skill training to neighboring Eastern European countries. At the same time they avoided costly long-term integration measures.

The final, more heterogeneous group, consists of temporary migrants, such as students, trainees, managers, and employees of transnational companies, au-pairs, and persons working in entertainment or service industries.

Currently the country hosts 5.6 million legal first generation immigrants with foreign citizenship (about 9 percent of the total population) plus an unknown number of undocumented persons (see table 9.1). If one adds asylum seekers, naturalized foreign born immigrants, and ethnic German expellees/resettlers (but excluding German refugees from the former communist GDR), the total number of foreign-born first generation immigrants living in united Germany in the year 2000 adds up to more than 12 million or 15 percent of the population, clearly refuting the notion that Germany is NOT an immigration society. The reality of immigration becomes even more visible when one considers persons with foreign citizenship who were born and educated in Germany. In 2000 about 1.66 million (750,000) or 23 percent (37 percent) of 7.4 million (2 million) registered immigrants with foreign citizenship (immigrants with Turkish citizenship) were born in Germany and would be considered the second or even third generation of immigrants if they had received citizenship upon birth ("ius soli"). Among foreigners under age 18, estimated at 1.64 million persons, two out of three were born in Germany.

Germany at the Crossroads in the 1990s

To domestic and foreign observers, the first years after unification did not bode well for immigrants. Many commentators evoked the ghosts of the past to predict a return to ugly nationalism, ethnocentrism, and xenophobia. The economic downturn in the early 1990s in combination with the raising costs of integrating East Germany and a continuous influx of resettlers, civil war refugees and asylum seekers mostly from the Balkans, Turkey/Kurdistan, Iraq, Iran, Afghanistan, Vietnam, Sri Lanka, and other areas helped to stoke a wave of resentment. Particularly in economically deprived smaller communities in East Germany confronted with the sudden relocation of asylum seekers, violent clashes, arson, and murder were the order of the day (Kurthen, Bergmann and Erb, 1997). Initial clumsy, populist and ambiguous reactions of the Kohl government, media sensationalism inside and outside of Germany, bureaucratic inertia, and legal tinkering did not help to break the fire early on.

Only after strong domestic public protests and pressure from world opinion did the conservative government take measures to curb the violence more effectively. Extremist groups and propaganda was prohibited and severely punished, a discussion was set in motion to streamline the asylum law, and asylum requests were processed more effectively. But the conservatives were still hesitant to begin a serious political debate about needed changes in the citizenship law, immigration policies, and public attitudes.

The controversial four-party compromise on asylum in 1993, which required a change of the German constitution, revoked unconditional access to formal asylum by turning aliens back at the borders and airports or by returning them to previous "safe" third transit states. In addition, a list of states "free of persecution" was drawn up. Requests for asylum were not accepted from applicants of these states unless additional proof was given. The reform also brought Germany's policy more in line with the less generous policies of its European neighbors, and with the EU and International Law (Meier-Braun, 2001).

But the immediate effects of the new asylum policy in curbing the influx of refugees and asylum seekers to pre-unification levels were somewhat blurred by the conflict in the Balkans, which not only led to the exodus of up to 350,000 Bosnians seeking temporary refugee status in Germany, but also prompted legal migrants already residing in the country to bring their family members to Germany. Therefore the net numbers of persons moving into Germany did not significantly abate until 1997 (see table 9.1).

Because the influx of ethnic resettlers and their entitled family members (since 1993 called "Spät-Aussiedler" or late resettlers) also skyrocketed in the early 1990s, the German government also streamlined admission criteria, set quotas (1993), and required a language test abroad before resettler applicants would receive entry permits (1996). These measures reduced the numbers of admitted resettlers to about 100,000 at the end of the decade (see table 9.1).

Looking back ten years later, the xenophobic wave and heinous acts of violence and arson in the early 1990s not only darkened the bright image of the peaceful reunification of Germany, but also helped to hasten necessary changes in Germany's national self-identity as well as its citizenship and immigration policy and law.

The sheer numbers of new immigrants and the integration challenges posed by these developments, made the German public in general, and businesses, churches, unions, civic associations, and democratic political parties in particular, recognize that Germany's immigrants and their offspring were here for good. It also became clearer that a continuous influx of qualified and motivated immigrants for the foreseeable future was necessary and beneficial to maintain Germany's social security system, provide the economy with sufficient labor, and maintain a healthy demographic balance. In Germany, without future immigration, the population is projected to fall from 82 million today to 58 million in 2050. This process will mainly affect the younger members of the population leading to a sharp decrease in the working age population. At the same time the proportion of people older than 60 would rise from today's level of 23 percent to 40 percent in 2050.

A first attempt to address the integration of rising numbers of second and third generation foreigners born in Germany (and also a departure from ethnonational principles) was the 1991 reform of the Alien Law. It offered easy naturalization to offspring of labor migrants in Germany if they were under the age of 23, had lived at least for 8 years in Germany and had been educated in Germany. The naturalization fee was reduced to a symbolic US$50. Neither fifteen years residence, nor the proof of German language knowledge, a secure job, or identification with the polity was any more a necessary prerequisite. Only for foreigners older than age twenty-three the fifteen years residence requirement remained and proof of a guaranteed subsistence (employment, pension) in Germany.

Then in 1993, parallel with the asylum reform, naturalization requirements were relaxed even further for long-term foreign residents and their children. Foreigners between the ages of sixteen and twenty-three could apply for naturalization if they had resided legally in Germany for eight years, had attended a school in Germany for six years, had given up their previous citizenship, and had not been convicted of a major felony. Foreigners legally residing for fifteen years had a claim to naturalization if they gave up their previous citizenship, had not been convicted of a major felony, and were able to support themselves and their family or received public assistance for obvious reasons not in their responsibility. Spouses and underage children could be naturalized together with the original applicant without having to fulfill the fifteen-year residency requirement.

After the departure of the conservative Kohl government in 1998, the newly appointed Red-Green coalition who had campaigned on a recognition of immigration, ended the piecemeal approach of their predecessors and began to more boldly implement a reform of immigration and integration (citizenship) that would stand its time.

The first step was a complete overhaul of the naturalization law in 1999. It accepted de facto what had already been in the making for quite some time, namely that Germany was becoming a multicultural "immigration society" and that the only effective solution to integrate the large and still growing second and third generation of German born immigrants was to institutionalize the territorial "ius soli" (birth right) principle, thereby paving the way for a new, republican understanding of nation and citizenship independent of parentage or ethnocultural belonging.

The original proposal to automatically grant dual citizenship was modified after pressure of a voter mobilization by the Christian Democrats and electoral setbacks. Now children born in Germany to legal immigrants with eight years residence and underage children residing five years with at least one parent holding unlimited residence receive German citizenship but have to decide between age 18 and 23 if they want to continue it. Naturalization of foreign born also has been relaxed to a minimum of 8 years of residence instead of 15 years. Multiple nationality is only permitted if the country of origin poses unreasonable conditions or does not release an applicants petition in time. Prerequisites to naturalization are a German language proficiency test and the ability to sustain oneself (German Citizenship and Naturalization, 1997).

The significance of this new integration policy cannot be underestimated. About 100,000 migrant children born annually in Germany and about 4 million foreigners (1.2 million Turks) who have lived in Germany for more than ten years are now eligible for citizenship. The steady rise of naturalizations after the 1991/1993 relaxation of discretionary naturalizations, and the acceptance of dual or multiple citizenship in particular, indicate that immigrants are increasingly identifying with Germany and are willing to make a long-term commitment. Naturalizations of non-ethnic German immigrants increased more than 13-fold from about 20,000 in 1990 (0.4 percent of all foreigners) to 187,000 (including 83,000 or 44 percent dual or multiple citizenship) cases in 2000 (2.6 percent of all foreigners, see table 9.1). Between 1980 and 1999 an estimated 800,000 persons, of which 340,000 were Turks, received German citizenship. And an additional half million naturalizations (including 100,000 children) occurred in the past two and a half years after the birthright was put into law (Beauftragte der Bundesregierung für Ausländerfragen, 2002).

The second reform step focused on immigration and led to the establishment of a Green Card Program (2001) which provides temporary and limited residence permits for up to five years to 20,000 computer specialists and other highly skilled experts—primarily recruited from Eastern Europe/Russia and Asia/India annually. This program resembles efforts of other Western nations, namely the United States and Canada, to make up for a deficit in hi-tech workers and to gain a competitive edge in global markets. Although the program encountered resistance from the unions and conservatives for reasons of unwelcome job competition and perhaps some ethnocultural fears, particularly against Asians, by Spring 2002 about 12,000 German green cards had been issued.

Finally, the third reform step planned to combine immigration and integration and to develop a comprehensive policy. It began with the establishment of an independent federal commission on immigration reform in July 2000, headed by Rita Süssmuth, former speaker of the German lower parliament and prominent member of the Christian Democratic Party (CDU). The commission was set up to make proposals for a comprehensive law, administrative institutions, and research facilities as well as to garner public and multi-partisan input and support. In its report published in July 2001, the so-called Süssmuth commission argued that Germany will need immigrants throughout the twenty-first century and therefore should embrace its status as an immigration country. The most important recommendations of the report were (Muenz and Ulrich, 1999ff.):

- a program allowing migrants to apply for immigration to Germany and their subsequent selection based on criteria such as qualification, professional skills, age, German proficiency, etc. Successful applicants would be granted a permanent residence permit.
- a program allowing German employers to recruit a limited number of foreign laborers for up to five years if jobs cannot be filled with Germans or immigrants already in Germany. During their stay the labor migrants would be entitled to apply for a permanent resident status and selected according to criteria mentioned above.
- active recruitment of foreign students and trainees with a later choice to apply for permanent residence status.
- an immigrant entrepreneur and investor program based on the quality of their business plans.
- a comprehensive integration policy including 600 hours language and civics courses for newly arriving immigrants and some foreigners already residing in Germany. Easier access to German citizenship would be granted to those who successfully finish courses.
- easy access to employment and jobs for immigrants age 16+.
- more liberal family reunification policies for children of immigrants below age eighteen.
- more efficient processing of asylum requests and extradition of those denied asylum.
- the establishment of federal agencies responsible for the administration and research on migration, asylum, and immigrant integration.

The report created a lively debate and all major political parties, trade unions, employers' associations, and religious organizations came up with comments and alternative proposals in 2001. What was most important was the participation of the conservatives. The so-called Müller commission, headed by the CDU prime minister of the state of Saarland, made suggestions that came close to those of the Süssmuth commission report.

After some modifications to his original proposal, Otto Schily, Germany's federal minister of the interior, published a draft for a new law regulating immigration, asylum, and integration in August 2001. The bill included most of Süssmuth's original proposals; including the recruitment of permanent and temporary migrants (Muenz, 2002). Schily's bill was, however, more restrictive on family unification, reducing the children's immigration age to twelve years in order to facilitate their integration, except for new immigrants, who would be entitled to bring their children up to age eighteen. Similarly, asylum seekers would be up for review after a three-year period and public subsidies would be reduced for undecided cases after two years though allowing third party sponsors (churches) to sponsor and support non-recognized asylum seekers until they found employment. On the other hand, the bill allowed certain unsuccessful asylum seekers for humanitarian reasons to improve their status if they could not be sent back to their country.

The proposal, oriented to a large part at the Canadian model, was criticized both by the Christian Democrats (CDU/CSU) and parts of the Green party for opposite reasons. The conservatives argued that the proposal would not reduce and control immigration but eventually increase it. The Greens, on the other hand, were unwilling to accept restrictions for asylum seekers and for children.

Originally the coalition government had planned to discuss Schily's proposal on September 26, 2001, then vote on it in the lower and upper houses of the parliament (Bundestag and Bundesrat) later that Fall. But the events of September 11 in New York City and Washington, DC derailed the political schedule of Germany's immigration reform. German public was shocked and officials embarrassed by the fact that two of the terrorists had immigrated to Germany before entering the United States. Similar to the public reaction in the United States, anti-Arab and anti-Muslim resentment increased significantly although most politicians, media, and public intellectuals cautioned against a simplistic equalization of Islam or Arabs with "terrorism."

To comply with political necessity and as a show of solidarity with the United States, in December 2001 the German parliament underwrote an antiterror legislation (limited to five years) that gave police and other government agencies new powers to investigate and prosecute persons or organizations involved in terrorism.

For political observers it looked as if the immigration reform had been sacrificed in the face of adverse events outside domestic control. But the Red/Green coalition was unwilling to give up an important part of their 1998 election platform and continued to push for a vote on the immigration bill. After some amendments and compromises, a close parliamentary vote in the Bundestag and a controversial voting procedure in the Bundestag (a review by the Federal Constitutional Court of the legality of the voting is pending), the new Immigration and Integration Bill (Zuwanderungsgesetz) was passed in March 2002. When German President Rau put his signature on the law in June 2002, the bill became law to be enacted in January 2003 (Schmidt-Fink, 2002).

As it stands now, the "Zuwanderungsgesetz" will streamline existing regulations, authorities, and procedures related to asylum and immigration of foreigners and ethnic Germans. And it creates new institutions and responsibilities, such as the Federal Migration and Refugee Office and the Federal Institute for Population Research. In addition it will provide substantial immigrant integration provisions such as language and training programs outlined above. The law makes Germany the first country in Europe actively recruiting immigrants on a broader base and officially defining itself as a country of immigration.

Although mainstream political parties reached a silent consensus to refrain from dragging the emotional issues of immigration and terrorism into the summer 2002 election campaign and using it for populist gain, the conservatives have not given up their opposition against some details of the new law. During the election campaign for the upcoming German national elections in September 2002, the conservative Bavarian opposition leader, Edmund Stoiber, vowed to delay the enactment of the law for one year and make amendments toward a stricter immigration policy if his party wins the elections. However, what is remarkable is that his conservative Christian Democrats (CDU) and the Bavarian Christian Social Union (CSU) no longer reject outright the definition of Germany as an immigration country nor do they pledge to abolish the immigration law completely. Rather, the conservative amendments promise to make the law "more efficient" and curb abuse or unwanted immigration, as feared by conservative voters. Stoiber also was silent about the "Leitkultur" debate triggered by his CSU party fellows in 2001 about the predominance of German identity, values, customs, language, and "cultural heritage," a debate targeted mainly against non-European and Muslim (Turkish) immigrants who often visibly stand out or are segregated from "mainstream" German society.

While it seems self-evident to a neutral observer that cultural assimilation cannot be simply politically prescribed, especially since the notion of a "lead culture" is elusive given the changing character of "culture," whatever its definitions, the debate (which has abated as of now) reflects a continuous rift in German political culture. The German Right still believes in the concept of ethnocultural dominance, the liberal center holds on the model of civic citizenship, and the Left prefers synergistic multiculturalism or even cultural relativism. While some aspects of the reforms of the 1990s are still contested, the character of the debate has changed significantly. A broad majority will no longer ask "if" but rather "how" Germany should incorporate millions of ethnic German and foreign newcomers and how far this requires a redefinition of identities and cultural boundaries.

Conclusion

As a result of changes in the character of immigration and of generational shifts in the German populace (expressed in a regime change from Center-Right to Center-Left), the 1990s altered fundamentally Germany's attitude and policies toward immigration and immigrants.

Slowly but continuously the new German republic dismantled or moved away from exclusive self-conceptions and citizenship regulations that date back to the heyday of European imperialism and nationalism at the turn of the nineteenth century. Germany overturned

> ethno-cultural provisions in the Basic Law and the Federal Expellee Law [that] were designed as a temporary remedy for the consequences of World War II, namely the division of Germany and the expulsion of ethnic Germans from territories under Soviet control. The temporary character of the law finds its expression in the fact that, after the end of the Cold War and with no apparent oppression of those ethnic Germans who remain in Eastern Europe, the central provisions granting citizenship rights were gradually being dismantled. (Levy and Weiss, 2002: 269)

The improvement of economic and political conditions in Eastern Europe and the former Soviet Union and the changes in the asylum and expellee laws significantly reduced the numbers of ethnic German resettlers and asylum seekers in the second half of the 1990s. And the temporary rise of Balkan refugees with temporary protected status in the mid-1990s abated after the pacification of the Yugoslav conflict. These developments reduced the attraction of right-wing populists playing on the fear of "Ueberfremdung" (foreignization, identity loss), labor market competition, xenophobic resentment, and ethnocentrist nationalism. Instead among the economic and political elite and the general population the multifaceted demographic, economic, social, and cultural benefits of immigration and pride in the maintenance of a cosmopolitan and more tolerant society gained ground. A growing consensus sees immigration as a solution rather than a problem.

In retrospect, the 1990s were the most important years in forming a new legal, political, and public mainstream consensus on immigration and citizenship in Germany. The feared political stagnation, blockade of reforms, or predicted ideological regression of Germany into the mindset of ethnic nationalism did not materialize. Instead inclusive immigration reforms toward civic citizenship came faster and more vigorously than most had expected, putting Germany, in many respects, ahead of its European neighbors without compromising central tenets of its liberal democracy.

It was German unification that finally undermined the fragile balance of the postwar arrangement that for forty years upheld elements of both universalism and ethnonationalist particularism in Germany's self-perception and practice of citizenship and immigration. This was most visible in the contradiction between ever-growing numbers of second-generation "foreigners" born and socialized in Germany and the quasi-automatic citizenship granted to hundreds of thousands of "ethnic Germans" born and socialized in Eastern Europe or the former Soviet Union. Faced with the task of integrating substantial numbers of non-German immigrants, the government was eventually forced to return to the much older territorial "ius soli" principle, to ease naturalization, and to tolerate dual/multiple citizenship. Once "nation" and Staatsvolk became increasingly decoupled, ethnocultural membership lost its importance compared to civic-territorial criteria (Joppke, 1999: 638), equal social and political citizenship rights, and the reality of increasing diversity and multiculturalism.

Consequently, the meaning of German nationhood also underwent a transformation that was already embedded in the universalist basic principles of the postwar constitution and enshrined in the historical lesson not to assimilate ("Germanize") foreigners against their will. As Joppke wrote in 1999, commenting and correctly predicting the reform underway in Germany, the ". . . German case thus carries a double message for citizenship theory. First, citizenship in liberal states is malleable. States are not slaves of their 'cultural idioms' (Brubaker) of nationhood, but may devise flexible citizenship policies in response to immigration pressures . . . . Secondly, national citizenship remains indispensable for immigrant integration" (Joppke, 1999: 645) in a world which is still governed by nation states and by rights as well as benefits which are distributed and controlled by territorial organizations. Third, Germany shows that within a framework of globalization and European integration, of growing interaction and interdependency, the immanent logic of regimes based on civic principles and universalistic liberties by necessity induces shifts in citizenship and ethnocultural identity toward a more pluralist and open society. Only if the global or regional framework and/or the regime type is reverting would one see again a movement toward more closure and a "re-nationalization" of societies.

Regardless of the progress made, in the political realm the conflict between the Left and the Right about details of implementation of the new immigration and citizenship law will not wither. Whereas the former focus prominently on the enriching cultural or positive economic and demographic aspects of immigration and stress the inclusive and universal character of secular political values of equality, liberty, and rule of law, the latter are more cautious and promote some form of acculturation or at least advanced integration. They also want to preserve the continental European and Western Judeo-Christian outlook of the country, and its traditions and lifestyles as much as possible, and they are skeptical about opening the "floodgates" to global immigration from non-Western cultures, civilizations, religions, languages, ethnic, and racial groups. Obviously the tension between post-nationalism/post-materialism and cultural nationalism will continue to dominate the political discussions.

Another reason why the debate will continue is the fact that the social, economic, and cultural integration of the first and 1.5 generation of the former guestworker immigrants and of ethnic Germans who arrived in the 1980s and 1990s, particularly those from the former Soviet Union, remains an unfinished task. Although Germany has made important reform steps, many details of how to control immigration and implement integration or to deal with the emergence of multiculturalism and ethnic diversity remain contested. Questions that will most likely dominate disputes in the future are (Muenz et al., 1999):

- How many immigrants from what areas with what profiles should be admitted? What requirements and criteria should be used to select and admit applicants? How to deal with visa overstayers and illegal immigrants? How to avoid that the raising number of foreign students become a brain drain for the sending countries?
- How can the cultural heritage of immigrants optimally fuse with that of the German mainstream? What policies, practices, and funds are needed to ease incorporation of newcomers? How can older immigrants' needs be accommodated? Does Germany need to expand its antidiscrimination legislation and implement equal opportunity policies to protect immigrants and newly naturalized citizens?
- How can the high unemployment rate of migrants, particularly second and third generation immigrant youth, be significantly reduced? (See table 9.1). What educational and training programs should be instituted to reduce the gap between native and immigrant educational achievements and the high drop-out rate (currently at 20 percent) of migrant children without secondary education degree?
- Should bilingual programs be implemented as early as preschool and kindergarten? What are the best means to improve German language reading and writing proficiency of elderly, women, and adolescents?

• How can local, state, national, and supranational European needs and interests efficiently and lawfully synchronized with universal rights and obligations as well as global and transnational pressures, developments, and demands?

But besides these questions and unfinished integration problems, there are also good reasons to be optimistic. Positive signs of incorporation are the increase of naturalizations, active participation of migrants on all levels of civil society, a strong identification of second and third generation immigrants with the German political and social system, rising entrepreneurial activity of migrants (see table 9.1), and an increase of native-migrant intermarriages from three to four percent of all marriages in the last decade, with 2 million persons now living in multiple or bi-national marriages (Fuecks, 2002: 80).

With the adopted path toward more inclusive politics toward minorities and immigrants, Germany has good prospects to develop in the twenty-first century a new pluralist, over time perhaps even a post-national and pan-European identity. Given Germany's geopolitical anchoring within Europe and the lack of external enemies, a parochial focus on national borders and exclusive ethnonational ideologies seems more than remote and unlikely. Yet, ultimately not only domestic but also global developments will determine a country's collective self-definitions, the predominant rules of its in- and exclusion, and the easiness of how its boundaries can be crossed.

Bibliography

Bade, Klaus J., and Rainer Muenz (eds.). 2000. *Migrationsreport 2000. Fakten-Analysen-Perspektiven.* Frankfurt/Main and New York: Campus.

Beauftragte der Bundesregierung für Ausländerfragen (ed.). 2002. *Daten und Fakten zur Auslaendersituation.* Bonn.

Braun, Karl-Heinz Meier-Braun. 2001. "Integrationspolitik," *Ausländer in Deutschland-AiD* v.17, n.2, pp. 17f.

Fuecks, Ralf. 2002. "Reform of the Citizenship Law: The Debate over Dual Citizenship in Germany," in *Challenging Ethnic Citizenship. German and Israeli Perspectives on Immigration,* edited by Daniel Levy and Yfaat Weiss. New York and Oxford: Berghahn Books, pp. 76–81.

Joppke, Christian. 1999. "How Immigration is Changing Citizenship: A Comparative View." *Ethnic and Racial Studies* v.22 (July 4): pp. 629–652.

Kurthen, Hermann. 1997. "Defining the Fatherland: Immigration and Nationhood in Pre-and Post-Unification Germany" in *Rewriting the German Past: History and Identity in the New Germany,* edited by Reinhard Alter and Peter Monteath. Atlantic Highlands, NJ: Humanities Press International, pp. 65–102.

Kurthen, Hermann; Werner Bergmann; and Rainer Erb (eds.). 1997. *Antisemitism and Xenophobia in Germany after Unification*. New York: Oxford University Press.

Lederer, Harald W. 1997. *Migration und Integration in Zahlen*. Bamberg: Europaeisches Forum für migrationsstudien (efms).

Levy, Daniel and Yfaat Weiss (eds.). 2002. *Challenging Ethnic Citizenship. German and Israeli Perspectives on Immigration*. New York and Oxford: Berghahn Books.

Motte, Jan; Rainer Ohliger, and Anne von Oswald (eds.). 1999. *50 Jahre Bundesrepublik—50 Jahre Einwanderung. Nachkriegsgeschichte als Migrationsgeschichte*. Frankfurt/Main and New York: Campus.

Muenz, Rainer and Ralf Ulrich (eds.). 1999–2002. *Migration und Bevölkerung*. Berlin: Humboldt University and Netzwerk Migration in Europa e.V. (monthly information brochure).

Muenz, Rainer, Wolfgang Seifert, and Ralf Ulrich. 1999. *Zuwanderung nach Deutschland-Strukturen, Wirkungen, Perspektiven*, 2nd edition. Frankfurt/Main and New York: Campus.

Muenz, Rainer. 2002. "Ethnos or Demos? Migration and Citizenship in Germany," in *Challenging Ethnic Citizenship. German and Israeli Perspectives on Immigration*, edited by Daniel Levy and Yfaat Weiss. New York and Oxford: Berghahn Books, pp. 15–35.

N. N. 1997. "German Citizenship and Naturalization," http://www.germany-info.org/consular/index.htm 11/1997.

Schmidt-Fink, Ekkehart. 2002. "Das Zuwanderungsgesetz," *Ausländer in Deutschland-AiD* 18(2): p. 3.

CHAPTER TEN

(RE)CONSTRUCTING COMMUNITY IN BERLIN: TURKS, JEWS, AND GERMAN RESPONSIBILITY

Jonathan Laurence

In Hungary we always said we were Hungarian Jews. Even in the concentration camps we would say, "that is a Hungarian Jew," "that's a Polish Jew" or "that's a German Jew." After the war, I felt like a Jew. Now, where I've been for nearly fifty years, I feel like a German Jew.[1]

When a Muslim has lived here for thirty or forty years, then he has become German—as have his kids. When he is constantly being reproached for not assimilating—that is, told he doesn't need a mosque that looks like a mosque, or that his kids do not have to learn about Islam in school like the other Christian and Jewish kids, then there is not really equality before the law in Germany.[2]

An immigration dilemma has confronted the Federal Republic Germany since the early 1970s. Postwar labor migrants from predominantly Muslim countries in the Mediterranean basin were officially discouraged to settle long-term, yet many stayed on after immigration was halted in 1973. Though these migrants and their children have enjoyed most social state benefits and the right to family reunification, their political influence has remained limited to the last quarter-century. Foreigners from non-EU countries may not vote in Germany, migrants are underrepresented in political institutions, and state recognition of Muslim religious and cultural diversity has followed a very cautious path. Since 1990, however, a much smaller but significant number of Jewish migrants from eastern Europe and the former Soviet Union have arrived in Germany. This population of 150,000 has been welcomed at the intersection of reparations policy and immigrant integration practice. Official readiness accept and incorporate these foreign Jews into a German religious community stands in contrast to religion and integration policies toward other non-German migrant populations. This paper compares the reception of Jewish and Turkish immigrants in the new Germany, taking into account the difference in historical relations between Jews and Germans from Turks and Germans.

In interviews, administrators and politicians use cultural preconceptions—rather than historical explanations—to explain these distinctions and administrative practices. Culture trumps history as a justification for special treatment of Jews. These officials could easily contend that Germany's responsibility to European Jewry is greater than to what, if anything, it "owes" Turkish Muslims who have settled in Germany. But today's migrant Jews are not European in the sense of holding citizenship of any European Union country. In the interviews cited below, the belief in migrant Jews' (and their non-Jewish family members) cultural ties to Germany supports the presumption that they will quickly adapt to and assimilate German ways (though this mythology has started to show some cracks). These frames construct a "useful fiction" similar to the logic allowing the immigration of ethnic German *Spätaussiedler*. In interviews with local officials, foreign Jews are viewed as cultural neighbors and their commitment to "becoming German" is portrayed as unassailable. Turks, on the other hand, because of presumed ties to their "fatherland" and Muslim customs, are often suspected of being less integration—willing or assimilable. "To return home" was cited in several interviews as a real possibility for second and third-generation Turkish immigrants. These cultural frames obscure basic commonalities of these two migrant religious minority groups. About 70 percent of Berlin's Turkish Muslim and Jewish populations of former Soviet Union were born outside of Germany.[3] The foreign-born Jews and Turks usually have no German ancestry and arrive with poor knowledge of the German language. Most do not give up their native passports whether or not they naturalize. The reticence to encourage community formation among non-German Muslims versus official sponsorship of a community-based Jewish identity among the mostly non-German Jews provides an interesting point of comparison.

Even though labor migration to the continent had mostly ended by 1973, immigrants did not stop coming. Over 600,000 non-German migrants legally migrated to Germany in 1999 alone.[4] Six policies in favor of family reunification, political asylum, and high-skilled labor bolstered foreign settlements and continued to diversify the national landscapes. Likewise, "church-state" relations were not engraved in stone with the emancipation of Protestants, Catholics, and Jews, respectively, in the nineteenth century. The political impulse to divorce nationality and religious belonging is as salient today as it was in the times of the Grand Sanhedrin or the Lateran Accords. Immigration scholarship in the 1990s has shown how the Marshallian progression of rights was disaggregated and reordered: the acquisition of social membership preceded political membership for non-Europeans residing in late twentieth-century Europe. Yet, as these populations age, reproduce, and make their lives in adopted countries, the challenge of politically incorporating migrants into representative institutions—especially religious representative institutions—is increasingly pressing. The holy grail of group integration, as a shared desire among migrant advocates and conservative political parties alike, may depend on micro-integration strategies.

With regard to the common goal of integration, association with religious institutions is seen as an aid to migrant Jews. So long as Islamic religious institutions are based abroad, they will be seen as a hindrance to the integration of Muslims. Corporatist arrangements such as those in place for the Catholic, Protestant, and Jewish communities set a participatory floor and ceiling. A minimum of rights and representation is guaranteed, while the upper limit of those groups' inclusion or voice is limited. Herein lies corporatism's mutually beneficial tradeoff. Elementarily viewed, the state grants citizenship status and full participatory rights, securing in return a group's acceptance of liberal democratic values and the rule of law. This consensus influences and legitimates refugee and integration policy decision-making at the federal level.

The granting of political rights and cultural recognition to two important religious migrant communities in German Turkish Muslims and former Soviet Jews—is striking in its incongruity. Divergences are most visible in preferential treatment of Jews in three policy areas: immigration, integration programs, and state support of religious activity. Germany's long-time exclusionary citizenship regime explains part of the disparity in its conferral of minority rights. Because of the different circumstances of their arrival in Germany, not all foreign groups are subject to the same laws. The three largest groups of immigrants among the 32 million foreigners who came between 1954 and 1999 are German repatriates, ethnic Germans asylum-seekers, and Turkish and southern European migrant laborers and their families. Different authorities (specifically for German immigrants, the Interior Ministry, and for non-German immigrants, the Commissioners for Foreigners) are responsible for implementing the different naturalization and integration policies. The logic by which the Berlin government internally distributes the labor of minority group support mirrors the citizenship-granting procedure of the Imperial and State Citizenship Law of 1913. That is, administration of subventions for Turkish associations occurs uniquely within the Senate's Commission for Foreigner Affairs.

As of the year 2000, this included matters of politics, culture, and religion. The Commission for Foreigner Affairs was supporting eighty organizations, 30–35 of which fall under the rubric "Turkish." When asked how many Jewish group received state subventions, the commissioner replied that the information must be gleaned from the culture senator, as the Commission for Foreigner Affairs "does not deal with German organizations." But of the 12,000 registered members of the Jewish Community of Berlin, 8,000 or 75 percent were born in the Soviet Union; the majority (5,000) of this immigrant group arrived in Berlin in years since unification, the rest beginning in the mid-1970s. More than half of the Turks were either born in Germany or have there for more than twenty years.[5] Manfred Becker, who is responsible for the Culture Ministry's religion office, stated: "we have close to zero contact with the Turkish communities. They speak first the Commission for Foreigner Affairs, even when religion is issue."[6] In the Culture Ministry's budget for Religious Affairs, are no expenses listed for the Islamic community that, unlike Protestant, Catholic, and Jewish communities, is not recognized as "corporation of public law."[7] Migrant Jews are appropriated as Germans, regardless of national origin, and they enjoy full political representation.[8] The nationality and citizenship status of Muslims in Germany apparently plays a decisive role in Islam's exclusion from state institutions. Corporation status grants groups "special rights which allow individual contact with bureaucratic offices."[9] And, even more importantly, "corporations have legal independence," may engage in self-administration and are allowed to negotiate as legal entities.[10] The Catholic, Protestant, and Jewish religious communities benefit from state-collected "church taxes" paid by members of their community—and these communities are politically represented at city, state, and federal levels. Because of the small number of Jewish taxpayers, the budget of the Jewish community is underwritten by the Berlin Senate. Religious status in the case of Jewish residents meanwhile outweighs national origin in the determination of support. This is partly a function of the guilt German governments have assumed for the crimes of the Third Reich and their desire to make reparations to Jewry as a whole. Jews also emigrate from countries where they may be considered *grosso modo*, a persecuted minority, whereas Muslims come as "economic migrants" from states where they constitute a majority. But neither postwar German respect for Jewish religious belonging nor the nationality status of community members sufficiently explains policy discrepancies with regard to the two groups. Cultural stereotypes prove far more decisive in explaining the local government's interaction with religious minorities.

On the basis of qualitative interviews conducted in 1998 through 2000 with three dozen German policy elites, bureaucrats, and religious community leaders, it will be demonstrated how differential treatment is justified by official claims of Jews' inherent proximity to German culture—regardless of their national origins—and by presumptions of the greater social "integrate-ability" (*Integrationsfähigkeit*) of (mostly Russian and Ukrainian) Jewish immigrants as compared to their (mostly Turkish) Muslim counterparts. Three million Muslims, all but 15 percent foreign nationals, form the third-largest national religious community after the Protestant and Catholic churches.[11] The number of Jews is less clear, but it is known that in the 1990s roughly 150,000 Jewish "quota refugees" from the former Soviet Union joined the 28,000 (one-third of them elderly) members of the Jewish community living in Germany.[12] Quota refugees include the immediate family members of former Soviet Jews, who may or not be Jewish. As of 2000, the Central Council of Jews in Germany represented 85,000 registered members. Since the Muslim and Jewish communities consist overwhelmingly of non-German permanent residents, a comparative study of their respective "church-state" relations provides a unique look at the development and operation of preferential policies toward migrant and religious minorities. It also demonstrates the selective flexibility of German administrative practice and "imagined community," especially noteworthy because of Germany's long-standing reputation among academics as a paradigm of ethnocultural exclusivity. Since 2000, German nationality is extended to individuals born in Germany to a parent who has resided in the country for more than eight years. This will lead to a dramatic advancement in immigrant rights, as foreigner law comes closer to matching the social reality of foreigners in Germany. The new law redraws the boundaries of national community; with this step, religious belonging may eventually be separated from national belonging for all immigrants. The German government currently insists upon "making it explicit that the homeland of Jews who live here, who are German citizens, is not Israel" and that "one must make a clean distinction between religious and national belonging!"[13] And, in a press release accompanying the Federal Government's answer to a Bundestag inquiry on "Islam in Germany," it is spelled out that "the theme of Islam in Germany should not any longer be seen as a topic for foreigners."[14]

Perhaps the single-most important catalyst for the organization of Islam in Germany was the discovery of Islamic fundamentalism in Hamburg following the September 2001 terrorist attacks. This led to calls that Islam itself needed to be "naturalized" and brought out of clandestinity in the words of the federal commissioner for foreigners. On the first anniversary of September 11, Interior Minister Otto Schily announced an Interministerial working group, which meets periodically to resolve familiar and new issues regarding the exercise of the Muslim faith. Schily insisted that the decisive factor for integration would not be the "legal position of religious communities" but rather the "spiritual and political attitudes of Muslims towards German society, and the behavior of natives towards new forms of religiosity." Though this is a kind of case-by-case, piecemeal solution, it is nonetheless

204 / JONATHAN LAURENCE

the true beginning of national "state-church" relations between Islam and the Federal Republic of Germany.

The automatic granting of citizenship to the children of Muslim foreigners will likely turn out to be a milestone in the right to equal religious representation. The national loyalty of Turkish Muslims may no longer be doubted once the coming generations become (and remain) German citizens; negotiating a statute for Muslim communities can only become less controversial when all discussion partners are nationals. The interviews conducted at the time of this field research show that Turks are often viewed homogeneously, without distinction among sub-groups or generations. Official impressions of their integration today, after three generations in Germany, reveal how much progress will need to be made, before they are considered to be at home in their adopted country.

These interviews shed light on the official motivations and, sometimes, personal justifications for minority policy directions. Elite actor perceptions of how much a given minority group "belongs"—the key to material resource allocation—are formed in subtle processes not always bound to strict legal interpretation. Elite bureaucrats and politicians may selectively interpret existing legislation. Interior ministry officials have discretional leeway in applying immigration, naturalization, and asylum law: a single signature can recommend deportation or "regularization" of residence status. Bureaucrats responsible for cultural affairs may pursue contacts more or less rigorously even with officially unrecognized religious communities. Politicians can author bilateral "policy contracts" between minority groups and the state. The analysis relies heavily on data gathered from the interviews with senior civil servants.

The frankness encountered in these semi-structured interviews about migrant religious minorities in Germany reveals under what conditions Germany has encouraged migrant groups to join a community of interests or, rather, left them to assimilate or segregate on their own. These bureaucrats' views of migrant groups' integration prospects and the place of minority groups in German society can influence their decision making as well as future directions of policy making and enforcement. The following issues will be discussed in turn: (1) nationality and legal status in Germany; (2) the renaissance of the Jewish community and the arrival of the Turkish *Gastarbeiter*; (3) the Berlin Senate's support of these two communities; (4) German national interest and the migration of Turks and Jews; (5) official perceptions of how easily these two migrant groups can be integrated into society; (6) the correspondence of official rhetoric on the motives behind Turkish and Jewish immigration motivation and their integration into society; (7) Jewish and Turkish/Muslim capacities to organize community interests.

"Native Foreigners and Foreign Germans"[15]: Nationality and Legal Status in Germany

Until 1999, Germany defined its citizenry, as Brubaker states, by "genealogical rather than territorial coordinates."[16] Unlike countries with *ius soli*, where birth on national territory assures citizenship, Germany adhered to *ius sanguinis*: citizenship was acquired solely through German ancestry. Out of a population of 80 million, roughly 9 percent have foreign nationality; many of these would have naturalized if they lived in a standard "immigration country," especially the more than one million "native-born foreigners." An impressive 16.2 percent of the current German population was born outside of today's borders. Even after the citizenship law reform, Germany will still produce foreigners: an estimated half of the 100,000 children born annually to foreigners will still not be eligible for German nationality. In migration studies the divergent treatment of ethnic German (*Spätaussiedler*) and Turkish immigrant groups, the country's largest, has served as an illustration of Germany's ethno-cultural policy bias. More than 3.5 million ethnic Germans from the former Soviet Union and eastern Europe have been immediately enfranchised, granted citizenship, and given linguistic and economic integration assistance by the state.[17] Turkish guest workers, their families, and German-born kin (totally 2.2 million) have limited political rights, wait eight to fifteen years for a German passport, and are left largely to integrate (or segregate) on their own. As elsewhere, dual citizenship is usually forbidden: non-German migrants must forfeit their former national identity card when naturalizing.

The perceived "pre-Germanness" of migrant group identity is closely tied to expectations of its members' eventual integration into society. The state-facilitated legal integration of ethnic Germans and the corresponding highly bureaucratized path to citizenship for Turks reflects these expectations. Ethnic German and non-German migrants alike are encouraged to fit in rather than maintain a "homeland" identity. Naturalization guidelines express that "commitment to Germany shall be judged from [the migrant's] fundamental attitude [toward] the German cultural realm. A permanent commitment is principally not to be assumed when the applicant is active in a political emigrant association."[18] "Multiculturalism" is a term often laden with negative connotations in Germany, and the danger of non-German "parallel societies" is forewarned against across the political spectrum. Multiculturalists' ideal of "plurality" is contrasted with the feared outcome of "particularism, [and] a totalitarianism of particular cultures."[19] Richard von Weizsäcker, who later became German President, for example, warned in the Berlin house of deputies in 1981 against the possibility that foreigners would spur "multiple cities to grow within our single city—and that must not be allowed to occur."[20]

Citizenship regimes, immigration law, and ethnic minority policy are the expressions and tools of national membership norms. Their combined national and local legal spheres delimit the social and political rights of minority groups. Yet juridical guidelines are not the only determinant of minority group status. German immigration and integration policy, like that of other Western democracies in the postwar and postcolonial period, is one founded on group preferences. Offering permanent residence and full citizenship rights to political refugees, for example, is favored over extending these rights to "economic migrants." The official line that "Germany is not a country of immigration" long meant that Turks, who first came for economic reasons, were not recognized as immigrants per se. German policy preferences for members of their "ethnic community" or for certain political refugees need not be viewed differently than, say, the Immigration and Naturalization Service's favoritism of Cubans over Haitians or the Israeli "law of return." Geopolitical interests, economic-conjunctural considerations, and humanitarian grounds subjective in each national context—all play a role in regulating migration. Acceptance and integration policy thus had a strong ethnocentric emphasis. But two important legal guarantees of political asylum also tacitly invited hundreds of thousands of non-German residents onto national territory each year. Like ethnic German status, asylum or refugee standing places migrants on a fast track to German citizenship and provides German language courses and six-months' start-up money. Jewish migrants should be viewed as a hybrid of political refugees and ethnic Germans. This is not just about reparations policy or even humanitarian measures. Unlike Bosnians or boat people, Jewish quota refugees are favored because of their presumed ties to German culture. And unlike Turkish Muslims, Jews are officially encouraged to join their religious brethren in a state-supported community. Jewish quota refugees are considered "well-integrated Germans" in the same way as are Romanian, Polish, or Russian ethnic Germans (*Spätaussiedler*): all enjoy legal and rhetorical treatment as Germans without any complaint that they form an immigrant block apart.

The Berlin Culture Ministry official in charge of religious communities stated: "We don't discuss the fact [that the Jews are Russian]. We simply don't discuss it . . . Once they make the decision to stay in Berlin, then they become Germans of Jewish persuasion."[21] The former federal commissioner for foreigners, Schmalz-Jacobsen, offered a comparison: When I go to a *Spataussiedler* settlement . . . I don't feel like I'm in Germany anymore, because everyone is speaking Russian . . . But we put a template over them and say, "These are Germans!" And we put the same template over the Jews. "God knows where these people were born, but somewhere there were German roots, and they must all be taken care of and financed."[22] When local officials do acknowledge integration problems for these groups, they maintain that their solution is only a matter of time or money. When justifying differential treatment of Turks, in contrast, officials emphasize the importance and entrenched nature of Turkish integration problems. One Interior Ministry official volunteered the following: "We don't really have in a pure sense 'a foreigner problem'. It is really primarily a Turkish problem."[23] In an article entitled "Immigration Problems: The Berlin Case," this same official writes about the most "visible" foreign group in Berlin: the 180,000 Muslims. "A significant portion of the post-war immigrants have a totally different civilizational, social and cultural background than the resident German population," and continues with the observation that "the largest group of foreign criminals last year was Turks, who accounted for 19.7 percent of foreigner crime."[24]

But how can one begin to assess the official political and financial arrangements of the Turkish and Jewish communities in a comparative light? There are, on the one hand, an infinite number of differences between the history, makeup, and interests of the Jewish and Turkish communities in Germany. Discussions on "German-Jewish" relations can ignore neither the unique burden of historical responsibility for the Holocaust, nor how this might skew any comparison of the treatment of Jews with that of other religious minorities. Indeed, current generous support of the Jewish community in cultural and religious domains is the outgrowth of the reparations policy begun by the federal government in 1952, which was complemented in the following years by local government contracts at the state level. Critical examination of the postwar evolution of the Jewish reparation package allows one to view German policy toward immigrant Turks with a new perspective. That cultural differences are allowed, even sponsored, in the Jewish community has long been feared and forewarned against in the Turkish one. The lubricant for successful incorporation—that is, state money for linguistic and social integration programs—is mostly withheld from the Turkish population. The integrative role to be played by a corporatist-style, local religious community is fully taken advantage of by the migrant Jewish population but not at all by the Muslim population. A close examination of the policy demands of, and responses to, these groups highlights surprising similarities between these two mostly foreign communities as well as important contradictions in German integration politics. There is a difference in German attitudes with respect to the state's responsibility—historical, in the case of Jews, and legal, with regard to Turks—for their active integration into society. But there is also a large gap regarding the perceived capacity for integration of one population compared to the other.

(Re)Constructing Community

The Jewish Community

In 1933 at least 170,000 German citizens of Jewish persuasion called Berlin home, roughly one-fifth of the pre–Third Reich German-Jewish population. This community, which had schools, libraries, synagogues, a museum, and community centers, was reduced through exile and genocide to 5,000 twelve years later. Its possessions, establishments, and cultural presence went the way of their previous owners, inhabitants, and participants. The early-1950s witnessed the introduction of a vigorously liberal immigration policy for foreign Jews and a reparations policy toward Jews living in Germany that would continue strong through the following half-century. The rebuilding of infrastructure and support of cultural and religious activities that could be achieved with taxpayer money was pursued. The reestablishment of Jewish life and community in Germany would be a test of regaining the faith of a group integral to German history, and also that of the anxiously onlooking world. General Lucius Clay, the US military governor, stated that Allied success in the democratization of Germany would be measured by how the country treated its Jews; from early on, the United States pressured Chancellor Konrad Adenauer's government to formulate an unambiguous policy toward Jews and Israel. High Commissioner John McCloy enunciated clearly in July 1949 that "the world will carefully observe the new West German state, and a decisive test will be its relationship with the Jews, and how it handles this."[25] In symbolic terms Germany was quick to recognize its own interest, both symbolic and economic, in repairing the rifts. One piece of advice offered to Adenauer by his adviser Herbert Blankenhorn in a 1950 cabinet meeting is particularly salient: "The new German state will only win back trust, esteem and credibility in the world when the federal government distances itself from the past with an impressive material reparation package . . . if we are able to manage the Jewish question in the world, then our economic life would reap the benefits." Receptive of cues from across the Atlantic, and genuine in its will to redress the wrongs of the past, the government would create a safe haven for Jews without historic precedent (with the exception of the newly founded state of Israel) in the deliberate hope of setting a new, positive tone in the fledgling Federal Republic.

The apologetic and restoration-oriented stance of West German authorities, which long safeguarded the means to practice Judaism in the Federal Republic, culminated in an open invitation to Jews and their family members to immigrate following the fall of the Berlin Wall.[26] They would be defined as quota refugees under the 1951 Geneva Convention: persecution would not have to be proven at an individual level, but rather membership in a persecuted group (Jews in the former USSR) would be grounds for refugee status. The idea behind the 1991 Quota Refugee Law (*Kontingentflüchtlingsgesetz*) was that these Jews could carry out their lives more freely in Germany than in Russia; as Manfred Becker of the Berlin Culture Ministry said, "they come to Germany to have a home, a spiritual home." Ignatz Bubis, the late president of the Central Council of Jews in Germany, described two factors in the mid-1990 negotiations between the Jewish community and the German government that led to the decision to classify Soviet Jews as quota refugees. "I said two things: first, 600,000 Jews used to live in Germany. Today, it is 28,000. It is not the Jews' fault that they became so few. There is a moral duty. Just before, Germany had accepted 30,000 Vietnamese boat people—so I said, that is a humanitarian gesture, with the boat people. That is already 2,000 more than there are Jews. Vietnamese never had any relationship to Germany. The second thing I said, was something Germany should view as important: if Jews want to live in Germany then that is something that today's Germans should appreciate and say Jews have trust in German democracy."[27] According to Bubis, Chancellor Kohl particularly agreed with this second point. On January 9, 1991 the state governors of all *Länder* approved the Quota Refugee Law. Jews arriving within eight months of the break-up of the USSR with only tourist visas could claim "immediate, unlimited right to residence, and federally financed integration facilitation such as language courses, job placement, enrollment for study, etc."[28] After February 1991, the proper application could be filled out by the Jew at the German consulate or embassy in his country of origin before departure (as is the procedure for ethnic Germans), and anyone arriving without proper permission would be subject to the same regulations as all other non-EU foreigners. But Jewish migrants continued to arrive well after the established date with only tourist visas (if any visa at all) and the senate found it impossible to treat them as just any foreigners. The *Jüdische Gemeinde* pressured the senate to allow Jews and their families who had any living relatives in Berlin to be accepted indefinitely as quota refugees. An internal brief from the Berlin Interior Ministry describes this move as "a regulation which was 'bought' by the political parties as a one-time exception, even though it was actually a group status regulation which would have required a special procedure by the federal Interior Ministry."[29]

The German government never imposed a ceiling on the number of former Soviet Jews who could benefit from this regulation. But though nearly 150,000 have come, including family members, the number of Jewish Community members nationwide is only around 85,000. Clearly, something went awry in the planning. While some German cities like Düsseldorf now have more Jews than even their pre-war population; others are seeing their age-old community structures tested by a population whose vision of Judaism is far less developed. The community leadership eventually sobered up; in June 2001, the new Zentralrat der Juden (ZJD) president Paul Spiegel began to gather consensus for a migration limit, noting that many of the migrants were not Jewish according to Talmudic law. Thus the ZJD itself asked the government, through its institutional position on an advisory migration panel (the Süssmuth Commission), to cap the number of arrivals at 25,000 over the next four years. (The largest number to come in one year was 19,000 in 1997, and about 16,500 arrived in 2000.) In contrast to the *Ostjuden* of the early twentieth century, who embarrassed their assimilated cousins in the interwar period, today's Jews from the East were actually seen to be accelerating the secularization of the Jewish population—and thus speeding its demise.[30]

The Arrival of Turkish Guest Workers

Turkish workers were invited to Germany beginning in the early 1960s as part of a mutually beneficial arrangement, whereby the guest workers could earn comparatively favorable wages to reinvest at home and Germany could meet its demand for labor. This was not an immigration policy, however. Though the program lasted only twelve years, it permanently changed the ethnic and religious makeup of postwar German society. What began as a seasonal labor recruitment program to support a booming economy's need for low-skilled workers in fact prefigured the westward migration of one million Turks (most of whom hailed from the southwest, Anatolian regions of Turkey)—even though a revolving-door system had been established in order to discourage it. In confluence with the oil crisis, German unemployment doubled to 2.6 percent, or nearly 600,000 between 1973 and 1974—up from around 150,000 at the height of the guest worker program. When the government ended the migrant labor program, many guest workers and their families—backed by a favorable ruling from the Constitutional Court—were already permanent residents. The rotation principle had shown its flaws as early as 1967, when notwithstanding negative economic growth rate most Turkish workers stayed in Germany. This trend would only increase in the six remaining years of the guest worker program, and the 1973 freeze in recruitment actually provided an incentive for non-EU workers to remain in the country. The Turkish population continued to grow through family reunification migration and, of course, through pro-creation and settlement. At the same time Soviet Jews began to trickle in to both Berlins, and by the dissolution of the USSR, a united Germany was committed to accepting any who chose to come. The non-German population grew from 3.5 million in 1973 to 4.5 million in 1980; in the years since, it has just less than doubled—to 9 percent of Germany's population.

Religion and Nationality

The massive influx of Jews that followed the Quota Refugee Law was matched by an increase in subventions aiding migrant integration into both the Jewish community (through cultural and religious activities in Russian) and German society (through special German language courses and professional training). But they are widely seen as highly "assimilated" Jews— (though, increasingly, as "visible" Russian immigrants). At this juncture, state support of the Jewish community merges with an activist integration policy toward non-German migrants. In addition, subsidized social occasions and Jewish education—including a good deal of Russian-language programming and publications—are organized by the communities, aiming to draw these former Soviet citizens to Judaism. There have even been stories told that the Community would hand out 100-Mark bills to new arrivals attending their first Chanukah or Rosh Hashanah parties. Officials in interviews repeatedly referred to the desire to "strengthen the Jewish community" in Germany when justifying the Quota Refugee Law.

Islam suffers for its recent implantation: Barbara John, the Berlin foreigners commissioner commented that "the privileges that [the Protestant, Catholic and Jewish] religious communities have are obtained through their recognition as a public corporation, and there is not this recognition for Islam . . . Islam is simply an existing world religion."[31] John also stated that the senate's policy toward the Jewish community is "a reparations policy . . . but out of this, a multicultural policy has emerged . . . Okay, this maybe does not have so much to do with German Jews. [But this is] because they were persecuted as Jews [during National Socialism], not as Germans."[32] Religious belonging, regardless of nationality, is the primary consideration in rights-granting. The federal culture minister views this as unproblematic and consistent with German-Jewish history: "a significant part of the Berlin Jewish community before the Nazi period was also of east European origin . . . The so-called German Jews also came sometime from somewhere!"[33] If Jews integrated once, then they can do so again: "the big Jewish minority that was here [before National Socialism] felt completely German, even to the point of being German nationalists," said the Federal Interior Ministry's secretary of state.[34] Foreign Jews in Germany, then, are recognized as transnational members of a community whose home and permanent destination is Germany. "It is a fundamental belief of the Berlin Senate to demonstrate a great readiness to accommodate [the Jewish settlers]," a Berlin Interior Ministry official stated.[35] But of Turks it is expected, as a Culture Ministry official phrased it, "that they will stop being Turkish."[36] The formalizing of Turkish or Islamic interests as a block apart, as such, is seen as a potential threat to German democracy—for such an articulation of group-specific interests would mean, in the words of Berlin's Interior Minister Werthebach, the "segregation from the value consensus of the majority culture."[37] Because of the historical experience of foreign Jewish populations in Germany, bureaucrats and politicians expect that also today's foreign Jewish community will be integrated without a problem.

Comparison of Support from the Berlin Senate

The Jewish Community

The opening paragraph of the present-day state contract governing the relationship between the Berlin government and the Jewish community captures the spirit of resultant postwar arrangements: Out of responsibility for German history, which is imprinted with the persecution and annihilation of German and European people of Jewish belief and origin, and in acknowledgment of the loss that Berlin and Germany have suffered as a result, Berlin affirms . . . that it will protect and secure the avowal and exercise of the Jewish faith for all time.[38] In practical terms, this investment amounts to dedicating a sizable portion of the state budget to the community for both determined and unspecified Jewish activities. Between 1997 and 1999, Berlin's Culture Ministry annually doled out DM 43 million for costs associated with Jewish prayer and education.[39] This figure constitutes nearly 30 percent of the ministry's DM 145 million religion budget for a group that accounts for 0.58 percent of the population. Even accounting for the one-time costs for the period from 1992 to 2002 for DM 165 million, the Berlin Senate has agreed to pay the annual costs of the Jewish community for DM 18 million per annum. Then there is the financial support of Jewish artists, cemeteries, Russian Jewish immigrant integration, community-building maintenance, security, synagogue programs, and so on.[40] As the state-recognized representative of a religious community (the only other two in Berlin are the Protestant and Catholic churches), the *Jüdische Gemeinde* also has 90 percent of personnel costs paid for its private school employees. "Nowhere in Germany does the Jewish community have so much financing as it does as in Berlin," claimed one culture ministry official proudly.[41] Since the total church taxes paid by community members is not sufficient, some estimate that the Jewish community receives up to DM 45 million of its DM 48 million annual expenses from the Berlin government.[42] This may seem like a lot of accommodation for a small group—the per capita allotment tallies to roughly DM 3,000 per Jewish resident of Berlin; Andreas Nachama, former leader of the Berlin's Jewish community, stated that "with respect to our smallness we get a rather considerable portion of state support." Ignatz Bubis put it in a different light: "One can't look at it per capita. One religion teacher can teach 60 children. But for three children you also need a teacher. That is the difference. Our small number doesn't mean we have different needs." As Hans Jakob Ginsburg observes in another context, the disproportionate financial support could be seen "not as the representation of a few thousand living, but rather that of millions of murdered Jews."[43] Until Berlin has 170,000 Jewish citizens again, some feel, there is a void that one must attempt, somehow, to fill.

The Turkish Community

Thirty of the 120 or so Turkish and Kurdish organizations in Berlin, which represent the 150,000 Turkish residents of me city, received a total of DM 89 million in the 1996 Berlin Senate budget for Turkish and Kurdish organizations; or, DM 550 per Turkish resident of Berlin. A Berlin Interior Ministry official observed: When you just look at the size of the population represented, there are about 10,000 Jews and roughly 150,000 Turks. Barbara John, Berlin's foreigner affairs commissioner, offered the following explanation: "We do not support other minority groups in the same way [as we do Jews] because the reparation aspect, luckily, does not exist with these other groups. That would have been horrible if the Germans had done to other minorities [what they did to the Jews—they would have certainly, given the chance— but luckily these other groups were not here."[44] But in the context of a de facto multiethnic society, some Turkish leaders have a hard time forgiving the extent to which different standards are applied. Representative are the remarks of the president of the Turkish Community of Berlin: "One must understand that the Jewish community has another situation, it's a question of history, and it is therefore somewhat different than with other foreigners. 10,000 Jews live here, but 180,000 Turks. The Jews get millions and millions, but as Turks we get DM 54,000 here. That's just rent and electricity, telephone . . . And for example we get DM 20,000 a year for social work. But the Jews get 350 social workers paid the whole day through."[45] The numerical logic at work in this response—accurate or not—demonstrates a recognition of injustice and hints at some envy. The president of the Turkish Parents Association, a small educational equality lobbying group, put it succinctly: "every time a Jew opens his mouth, he has money and all sorts of things poured into it."[46] The resources designated for ethnic minority cultural or religious activity are seen here as a common pool of funds—but the legal status of immigrant Turks precludes equitable distribution.

Germany's National Interest and Migration

"Something most welcome": Jewish Migration in Germany

The immigration allowance for Soviet Jews fits into the framework of reparations philosophy, which was to recreate a "blooming Jewish community," in Adenauer's words. "We only realized in the last few years that Jewish citizens could again play an important cultural role in German society," said the secretary of state of the Interior Ministry. "[Jews] can again be recognized as a group both in public life and also in the consciousness of many people, with a public role. This is a very good development. We already have one of die biggest Jewish communities in Europe again, which is something most welcome."[47] The Berlin Culture Ministry official stated similarly, that "[our treatment of the Jewish community] is a form of gratefulness. It is not self-evident that Jews would stay in Germany, organize themselves, or want to stay any longer. We thankfully recognize the fact [that they do]."[48] A combination of guilt and the projection of "German traits" onto non-German Jews allows the Berlin administration to privilege their social position. The sociologist Michal Bodemann views some aspects of this distinction, however, with suspicion. The special treatment of Jews in Germany today, he argues, serves both conciliatory and less noble political ends: "Although under different conditions, even today the Jewish minority as an incorporated group must carryout ideological labor [in Germany]. And in different ways it is instrumentalized by the German state for both internal and external political ends" (1986: 52). The implication here is that the special policy arrangements for the Jewish community are externally useful as a certification of German rehabilitation, and internally as indemnity against claims of cultural insensitivity for minority rights.

Historical responsibility aside, these positions can also be explained by the belief that, in generally supporting Jewish culture, one is indirectly supporting German culture. Commissioner Barbara John stated emphatically: "The cultural legacy of German Jewry is German!" "It is not Turkish or Rumanian or anything else!" Malte Krause, a top civil servant of Berlin's Interior Ministry, also supported this approach: "Germany sees the [present] fruition and construction of the Jewish community as the recovery of a part of its own historical culture. It is therefore also in our national interest to strengthen and support the Jewish community." An enormous amount of money is poured into the Jewish community in support of myriad activities both crucial and beneficial to presently flourishing Jewish life in Germany. Authorities maintain and protect a Jewish presence for the sake of both reconciliation with the Jewish community and the general reestablishment of trust in German democracy. The desecration of former Jewish community chairman Heinz Galinski's grave in fall 1998 inspired the following comment by a Berlin Interior Ministry official: This created a lot of worries in Berlin. It was evidence for how important it is to prevent such incidents for the sake of our system's political stability . . . Just imagine what kind of discussion would take place in Berlin, or maybe all of Europe or even worldwide, if anything happened to a member of the Jewish community that could have been avoided had the Berlin Senate handled things differently.[49] This official is acutely aware of Germany's political stability and the potential for damaging discussion at the expense of the country's hard-earned postwar reputation for tolerance. Public gestures of this tolerance are especially important, for obvious reasons, with regard to the Jewish community. Government officials wasted no time in appropriating funds for a large-scale public tolerance campaign following several antisemitic incidents in summer 2000. The Berlin Senate's determination to maintain a visible Jewish presence, through facilitated immigration, and cultural and religious subventions, represents the policy side of protecting physical sites like Galinski's gravestone and countless other buildings of the Jewish community.

"Ihre eigene Interesse": Turkish Migration to Germany

Speaking of postwar migration fluxes, a senior civil servant in Berlin's Interior Ministry said: "The greatest number of foreigners who came to Germany did not come here because we had defined it in our national interest, but rather as aftereffects of the guest worker program from the 1960s . . . This was not the expression of Germany's national interest."[50] An official in Berlin's Commission for Foreigner Affairs similarly observed that "the Turks have profited from the fact that they came to Germany; they were recruited as guestworkers, and stayed because it was useful and good for them."[51]

Turks could apply for naturalization only after eight years of residence (for minors) or sometimes as long as fifteen years (for adults). The disjuncture between residence status and nationality is due in part to the lack of provisions for double citizenship in German foreigner law. Naturalizations rose steadily between 1988–1998 but Turks were reluctant to give up their native nationality; rates have thus been historically low, hovering well below 10 percent. A "myth of return" on both sides meant that workers dreamed of retiring in their homeland and the German government avoided addressing integration questions. The actual rate of return to Turkey is also only around 10 percent, but the symbolic value of the Turkish passport is less easily quantified. Turkish governments have advocated double citizenship law in Germany and encouraged its citizens to hold onto their passports. Military duty was even reformed in 1995 in order that Turkish men living abroad could retain their nationality without needing to complete army service. The reticence to abandon the passport can be traced to questions of identity and pragmatism: one the one hand, the fear of losing inheritance rights in Turkey, and the feeling, summed up by one Turkish-German politician, that to give up one's native passport is the equivalent of giving up a family photo album.

In the absence of a national immigration policy, ad hoc measures providing for the arrival of family members were developed. But Germany had not explicitly planned for this eventuality, and the momentum of this unexpected immigration took on a life of its own.

It is hardly debatable that Turks came to Germany in their "own interest," but there seems to be a certain blindness with regard to the motivations for Russian Jewish migration. Economic reasoning would appear to have been at least as important as religious persecution—or the less plausible "desire to return home to Germany."

Nationality, Intelligence, and the Social "Integrate-ability" of Turks and Jews

Overall, Turks constitute less than three percent of the German population. Public opinion has not always been generous in their regard, with polls consistently reporting they are the foreigners "most difficult to integrate." This is due to linguistic difficulties of the first and second generations, to interpretations of Turks' reluctance to assume the German nationality and it is also related to their foreign religion. Adherence to Islamic rituals and Turks' perceived cultural differences have sometimes been characterized as incompatible with German national identity.

The question of a group's permanent destination—and status in the country of origin—is of key significance to local officials' attitudes toward the Muslim and Jewish populations. It is presumed that Jewish refugees are not likely to return to their countries of origin and will naturalize as soon as possible. Turks, in contrast, who as a group naturalize at an extremely low rate, reserve the right to "go back home"—even when born and raised in Germany. A former interior minister of Berlin stated that "Turks see themselves much more as a nation. But I don't know that the Jews who live in Russia feel Israeli, rather they feel like Jews! And that is also what differentiates them from the Turks."[52] National origin is therefore interpreted as a signal of the willingness to integrate into German society. This sentiment has also been expressed by the top civil servant in charge of foreigner affairs in the Berlin Interior Ministry, Hans Joachim Rose: I think that Russian [Jews] integrate more easily because there is no more option to return to Russia. With Turks one has the impression that there is still somewhere hidden, consciously or unconsciously, at least still in the second generation and maybe the third generation too, a certain option to return home. Perhaps it really is nicer to spend one's old age in Turkey, but for Russians that's not an issue. They say, "we're happy that we're out of there, we must now plan for our future here."[53] The migrants' national origin greatly influences the degree of state encouragement of formal religious representation and support of their native religion and culture; nationality is also taken to imply a migrant group's capacity to integrate. Those groups belonging to the majority in their country of origin and who came to Germany for "economic reasons" may be seen as a temporary presence or, at worst, as a fifth column. In the absence of state-organized, centralized "communitarist" initiatives for the Muslim population, their scattered organizational development has taken shape along national (and sectarian) lines. This retreat into their native culture—without any particular host country reference—is accompanied by a social, commercial, and political segregation of Turkish neighborhoods. Malte Krause observed that "there are strong differences between the Jewish and Turkish communities: in the Jewish community there is a group of people who, as Germans in Germany with a specific religious alignment, pose no problems either for security or religious tolerance. Insofar as there are questions of integration, they pose themselves of course only with the Turkish community." When pressed, Krause acknowledged that "for Russian Jewish immigrants, who perhaps cannot master the German language, and who lived for a long time under a dictatorship, there are integration problems of course. But the German state is ready to do anything necessary so that integration succeeds." A former interior minister of Berlin also conceded that "I know from talks with members of the Jewish community that there are difficulties in the community and, in part, with integration . . . but if the Jewish community looks for help, we help in any possible way." That these foreign Jews can be accepted and adopted immediately as Germans of Jewish persuasion—regardless of their original Russian, Ukrainian, or Bielorussian citizenship—reflects German assumptions about religious and national identity politics. Namely, they are expected to assimilate in a way that Turks are perceived as being incapable of doing.

The significance of national origin in official attitudes is compounded by more general assumptions about the influence of religious doctrine and level of education on the group's differing assimilability. The fact that most of the adult Jewish quota refugees are urban academics, and that the first generation of Turkish guest workers in the early 1960s were manual laborers from the poorest regions of Anatolia, influences these assumptions. But this does not distinguish between first and third generation Turks. The number two civil servant in charge of foreigners in the late 1990s Berlin Interior Ministry found that religious orientation of Turkish migrants did not facilitate their social insertion: "The more different the religion, the more the religious ideas make integration harder. And it is so that with the Muslim population, if I may say so, with their intellectually restricted background [*mit intellektuell einfach gestricktem Hintergrund*], especially hard, because they are so traditional, they don't even accept the role of women in the same way as we in our society do."[54] Additionally, the former federal culture minister warned that Islam "has not yet given up its dogma. Islam is relatively tolerant, but there are many different kinds of Islam and in certain regions it is not tolerant at all. . . . [T]he process of integrating Islam into German cultural life will take place over more than 50 years and will succeed. But it will depend on the readiness of Islamic leaders, religious leaders—and one must have some doubts about this—to allow an ecumenical form of religious belief. If they don't do that then integration will be made more difficult. This is not about Islamic scarves, this is about intermarriage."[55] It is hard to imagine German officials expressing concern about the orthodoxy of Jewish faith or recommending the dilution of the Jewish community through mixed marriages. The level of migrants' education has also been cited as a reason for segregationist tendencies on the part of Turks: "Most [of the Jews] are on average better educated and more intelligent people than the Turkish immigrants . . . And it is usually the case that, when someone has a particular intellectual background, it is clear to him that if he wants to have a role in society, has no other choice but to open himself to society and enter it." As becomes evident from these two quotations, there is a conflation between intelligence and level of education that pervades this official's discourse on the readiness of Russian Jews and Turkish Muslims to join German society. The level of education, however, is indirectly tied to impressions of migrant groups' ability to speak German, another key aspect of social integration: "When one speaks about language problems, one speaks almost always exclusively about Turks. Even with the former Yugoslav guest workers who lived here and became citizens, with them the language problem was never so virulent [as it is with Turks]."[56] From the small amount of data available, it is not clear that the positive integration balance in rhetoric corresponds with reality. Jewish quota refugees also have an average unemployment rate of 30 percent (in 1995). The director of Munich's employment office said in an interview, that "linguistic and professional deficits make it more difficult for Jewish refugees to find adequate employment. Unemployed Russians and Ukrainians in Munich tend to be the Jewish refugees."[57] "As a rule they arrive without German language abilities and less than half are able to pass a language test even after a six-month Interior Ministry language course."[58] But Bubis maintained that the difference between Turks and Jews is the question of willingness to leave their old identity behind: "we have Jews today from the ex-USSR who are not of German origin. But they come here to live and to become German. Ninety-nine percent of the migrants from the ex-USSR ask 'when can we finally become German?' Turks don't ask that. That is the big difference."[59]

As generations pass, the image of Turks as a hard-to-integrate population will likely soften. The federal government conducted a survey in 2000 that showed nearly 90 percent of children of Turkish origin have a good command of the German language. A 1995 labor ministry survey of media use among foreign workers and their families found that a third read German newspapers regularly—and an additional 45 percent sometimes do. For those under 25 years of age, 44 percent read German papers regularly where another 38 percent occasionally do. Another study in 2000 found that German television and radio are even more commonly consumed, with 88 percent of Turks tuning in.

More than 40 percent of the immigrants who arrived as guest workers or students articulate a desire to return permanently to Turkey, though only 17 percent of those born in Germany express the same. Nonetheless 60 percent of Berlin Turks visited Turkey annually or more often, with only 1 percent never having been, and 12 percent less often than every three years. In 1999, however, roughly 90 percent of Turks who died in Germany were repatriated to Turkey for burial. This is largely because Islamic law mandating burial without a coffin contravenes health regulations in most of the *Länder* and the requirement that Muslims be buried facing Mecca raises planning and space issues that need to be formally addressed by local authorities. There is a Turkish cemetery located on the Columbiadamm in Berlin (the only Muslim one in Germany, founded in the eighteenth century) but it is full. Only corporations of public law can charter new cemeteries, and Muslim associations mostly have the legal status of a "registered association." Pragmatic solutions in this area are likely to be forthcoming, as they have been in other European states with important Muslim populations.

Immigration Motives and Tendencies toward Segregation

But does rhetoric on assimilability and the motives behind immigration to Germany square with the experience of community leaders? The official justifications for the Quota Refugee Law are founded on a loose interpretation of these settlers' situation. As one Culture Ministry official said, "Although there are anti-Semitic voices in Russia, we all know there are no pogroms taking place."[60] Even their Jewishness is, to a large extent, inchoate. Many of the refugees are Jewish only to the extent that the so-called fifth point on their Soviet passports said they were. Barbara John said frankly, "most [of the Quota refugees] have absolutely no relationship with Judaism at all." Becker of the Culture Ministry acknowledges that "some of them have no knowledge at all of Judaism. They know nothing of Judaism. They don't even know a single Hebrew word." This is a rather limited understanding of the multiple ways to express one's Judaism, but the official's message is that the Russian Jews who choose to come to Germany, in sum, are those for whom religion is relatively unimportant. Berlin's former Interior Minister

Schönbohm has also spoken of the Russian Jewish immigrants as "returning" to Germany (*wiederzurückgekehrt*) to escape from "difficult conditions in Russia."[61] Like other politicians, Schönbohm has classified the immigration under a sentimental rubric, perhaps taking comfort in the idea that victimized Jews are being saved from persecution in another land: "Turks come here to participate in the German economy, to earn money . . . Jews come here because it was their home, or the home of their parents, and they want to live here. That is a different motivation [than for Turks], so to speak. Perhaps with some of them the economic situation plays a role. But there are above all differences in the motivation for why they come to Germany."

It is in this light that the Russian Jews can be seen as "returning" to Germany; the revitalization of the neighborhood of Jewish stores and community buildings in and around the *Oranienburger Straße*, where Hebrew, Yiddish, or Russian can be heard spoken, is charming—a stroll through a lost golden age—and a magnet for wealthy American and European tourists. But the Turkish equivalent concentrated at the *Kottbusser Tor* is widely denounced as a "ghetto" or "parallel society." As Bavaria's Interior Minister Beckstein (CSU) has commented, "we do not want Chinatowns and Polish cities [*sic*] like there are in the United States."[62] Officials insist that no comparable phenomenon exists in the Russian Jewish community. But one need only take a stroll through what has been termed "*Charlottengrad*" to question this formulation. One study of migrant Berlin described this community in terms one usually hears applied to "non-German" migrant neighborhoods: New urban spaces have emerged which are modeled on old preferences since many know no German or cannot read Latin characters . . . This desired segregation . . . the desire of a large number of migrants who want to stay among themselves is not just typical of this one neighborhood . . . marriage occurs almost exclusively among immigrants alone.[63] In the words of one Jewish organizer, the Jewish quota refugees were those who "didn't really want to go to Israel."[64] They are attracted by Germany's relatively attractive economy and generous state assistance. Irina Knochenhauer, a Jewish community leader from the former Soviet Union said that migrating to Germany "is a rather untypical step for older Jews from the former Soviet Union, who suffered very much during the war—it is actually an internal compromise." Economic and geographic considerations, she maintained, were of prime importance: "When their pensions are not sufficient anymore—because of the fall of the ruble—and then they hear that in Germany a minimum for survival is guaranteed, medical attention is guaranteed, burial is guaranteed, then that is quite important for a Jew . . . There is a choice among three countries: Israel, Germany, and America. America takes only certain groups of Jews who have familial relations of the first degree. Israel is, for many, myself included, too oriental.

That is the Orient, it's too hot, it's not European. And most Jews who come here, are from the European or east European origin. And for older people it's very hard to live in Israel. But here, it's just a two-hour flight from Berlin—maybe there are husbands' graves [in Russia], etc."[65] Knochenhauer also noted that many of "these people have as a rule no particular understanding of Judaism. As a whole they learned only that it was bad to be Jewish." With regard to their attitudes toward integration into German society, her impression of the Jewish quota refugees was altogether different than that of Berlin politicians and civil servants. Just as the reality of the Jewish situation may differ than the optimistic rhetoric of German officials, leaders of the Islamic community have insisted that Muslims do feel German: "Seventy-five percent of Muslims in Germany were born or grew up here. That is already a basis for integration . . . Most Muslims are not German [citizens]. But that does not mean that they do not feel like German Muslims."[66]

Capacities to Organize Community

Some interview respondents have contended that exceptions in immigration and citizenship law and ethnic minority policy are possible when small numbers of people are involved. Germany's 2.3 million Turks number more than twenty times the size of the Jewish population. Others posit that special recognition depends on group legitimacy and organization. If Turks had a unified central organization lobbying local governments, one argument goes, they might benefit to the same extent as do Jews from funding for religious and cultural activity. This could occur only if Islam, like Protestantism, Catholicism, and Judaism were recognized as a public corporation. As Cornelia Schmalz-Jacobsen, the former federal commissioner for foreigners, said: "That is only the half truth. It goes deeper: [Turks] are 'so foreign,' no? . . . You will have noticed, for example, that many people simply confuse Islam, the world religion, with religious fundamentalism." The Culture Ministry official cites the confused, diffuse state of Turkish representation in explaining the impossibility of providing Turks the same opportunities in a religious context. "Cooperation could exist . . . but the Turks are rather unorganized . . . Islam itself is a structure-poor religion . . . very diffuse and informal."[67] Nachama also stated that the "incalculable" number of Turkish communities and groups is their weakness—"when they build up one or two central organizations [like ours] then they will get the same help." Comparing the organizational evolution of the two communities, the secretary of state of the Federal Interior Ministry commented that the "Central Council of Jews in Germany is in a very fortunate situation right now, because it has a unified structure and clear leadership"; to gain equality, Muslims would need to learn to cooperate better together. But not all Muslim councils are of the same nature; in the absence of German sponsorship of Islam; though some of the 2,500 Islamic organizations in Germany have spent years cultivating their contacts with foreign government supporters, others have engaged local authorities. The spokesman for the Federal Commission for Foreigners Affairs lamented the fact that since so little was done for religious needs [of migrants], structures developed which have led in part to segregation and ghettoization processes. . . . We said that "we didn't need to pay attention to this because they were all going home anyway." We therefore missed the opportunity to open German institutions to immigrant groups and did not watch out for what kind of independent structures were developing. This makes today's dialogue and bilateral openness [between Turks and Germans] somewhat problematic. Those municipalities at the forefront of intercultural dialogue risk getting their fingers burned. The mayor of Bremen has organized an "Islam week" for five years, and recently gave an interview to the Islamische Zeitung in which he spoke of the necessity to engage Milli Görüs, saying they had some "excellent people." Werner Scherf even convinced the Alevites to cooperate with IGMG in this year's Islamwoche (but not the CDU). Scherf was rewarded with a television news program entitled "Naïve Tolerance" on the ARD channel, which asked why fundamentalists had found their way into the heart of Bremen's city hall? (It was later noted that ARD's 77-member board of directors included not a single Muslim.)[68]

It is estimated that slightly more than three-quarters of the 2.3 million Turks are Sunni Muslims while the remaining 400,000 are of the Alewite tradition. In a community where disagreements begin over the starting time of Ramadan, the perspectives for cooperation on a national level are perhaps slim. These nonetheless received a slight boost last April when two major organizations—the Islamrat and the ZMD—worked out common standards on ritual slaughter for Halal. There are now seven Länder with some level of internal Muslim associational cooperation—Hessen, Hamburg, Bavaria, Baden-Wuerttenberg, Schleswig-Holstein, Rheinland Pfalz, Niedersachsen. A voluntary Islamic council—the Schura—represents 85 percent of Hamburg's 120,000 Muslims and has acted as a quasi-official dialogue partner for the administration since 1999. Only 7 percent of the roughly 800,000 Muslim children in Germany are in private Koran schools. In several states, Islamic Religion courses on par with those offered to Christian and Jewish children are already underway. In Berlin, 53 out of 71 prayer spaces declared themselves represented by the Islamic Federation, which began the first religion courses for about 200 students in the Fall of 2001; Islamic instruction now offered in 15 Berlin schools. And for the first time, religion teachers will train in Germany—at the University of Muenster—beginning in fall 2003.

As much as Muslims need to make sacrifices and agree on certain ground rules in their interaction with German authorities, so is there is a need for consensus—free of drama and alarmism—within German political elites regarding who is dialogue—worthy. Even at the Local level, there remain, of course, certain objections of the host society, like the sticky issue of headscarves, the famous concern with the "equality of women" more generally, in addition to the fear that Muslim religious education is somehow less objective than Christian or Jewish lessons. The Berlin ministry for education, for example repeatedly rejected the Islamic Federation's curriculum proposals because of the way it handled gender equality and certain creationist issues.[69]

On the national level, several important umbrella organizations stand out. Each can claim a certain legitimacy but perhaps even the most "representative" association can only speak for small percentage of Germany's Muslims. Politicians have found individual fault and are skeptical about any possible cooperation. Nadeem Elyas, head of the Central Council of Muslims in Germany (*Zentralrat der Muslime in Deutschland—ZMD*) has said that

> we must be able to work even without the status of public corporation . . . It is not such a dominant or existential question for us. Because such a status would bring internal strife, which would be more damaging than useful . . . Some kind of organizational structure must exist that binds us to the state. But this structure must not necessarily be the same structure as there is for the churches . . . this hierarchical structure . . . which says what one must believe and what one may not believe, what is right and what is wrong, is rejected by Islam.

In 2002, the ZMD proposed a charter that would found the basis of corporation status, which included the explicit recognition of the German constitutional order; but oddly enough the organization waited a full year before translating it into Turkish. But some view the ZMD as too close to Saudi Arabia. The Turkish-Islamic Religious Union (*Türkisch-Islamische Anstalt für Religion—DITIB*) is the foreign arm of the religion ministry of the republic of Turkey. DITIB pays for rent and prayer accommodation in 800 local offices throughout Germany (its Imams are state employees of Turkey, and its programs in Germany run out of Turkish consulates). DITIB and the lay-state oriented Alewite community sometimes refuse to take part in discussions because of their philosophical distance from these competing associations. On the local level, DITIB has even tried to block the development of German-language religious education.

As part of the post–September 11 fight against terrorism, parliament amended the law on associations to remove the "religious privilege" that limited the authority of the government to ban religious organizations. With the amendment, the "Caliph State" Islamic organization in Cologne was banned, and its leader was deported to Turkey in addition to the organization Hisb el Tahrir el Islami, an anti-Israel organization with ties to the far-right NPD.

Conclusion

"On the one hand, Germany's openness towards the Jews makes our life easier and facilitates our interaction with German society," said Elyas, the head of the Central Council of Muslims in Germany. "Here we have a model, an ideal, of character and relationship with the state. We can say, for example, in the same way that you treat Jews, with openness, tolerance and acceptance, so should you interact with every religious community."[70] The reparations arrangements for Jews in Germany are remarkable and historically unique. As a result, Germany has the fastest growing Jewish presence in the world outside Israel. But can political trust operate on purely bilateral terms between former perpetrator and former victim, or does the desire to recreate political community require the pluralistic extension of special rights to maximize, within limits, democratization? Can the reestablishment of political trust in postwar Germany rest squarely and uniquely on the revival of the Jewish community? Werner Nell writes how debates over "the recognition" of the "immigrant situation" pitted "the partly catastrophic history of German nationalism [against] a cosmopolitan-oriented alternative."[71] The state secretary of the Federal Interior Ministry corroborated this sentiment: "I believe that we in Germany still have the image of a homogeneous society. What we learned from the horror of the Nazi period is that we must be especially attentive and rigorously fight any racist or xenophobic action. Other peoples also have this responsibility, but we especially so . . . I believe that a certain cultural colorfulness is really good for us."[72]

The political energy in the first fifty years of the Federal Republic that might have been expended on reforming the nationality code focused on generous asylum policy and reparations arrangements. Reparations policy is targeted and limited: the welcoming, acceptance, and promotion of Jews as a form of repentance and rebuilding of trust is the end in itself. The measures for their insertion in German society have been introduced without public controversy or debate—perhaps in part because of the small numbers involved, but largely because of the symbolic value that a new Jewish presence lends to Germany. The mood, tone, or philosophy of the policy is not extended to other groups, regardless of their size or need to be integrated and supported in German society, such as the Turkish population living in Germany. Barbara John referred to this contradictory situation "the terrible irony of history": The former generation of Germans persecuted and killed Jews because they had the impression they were somehow foreign. Which is ridiculous. Now they have 3 million Muslims who really, definitely are foreign . . . Now the Germans are democratic and bear this burden. The question is how long they will stay democratic. I think that they will stay democratic because they have—thank god—learned their lesson. Most of them, anyway.' Until this "lesson" is made concrete—and Muslims are fully integrated into German society—the Jews may be seen as Germany's albatross and its license. Ever remorseful for the senseless murder in its past.

Germany courageously assumes the burden of showing all who will look that it did wrong and hopes to redeem itself. But the Ancient Mariner who shot the albatross only understands his error—and is finally freed of its burden—in appreciating what lessons to draw from his action: in Coleridge's maritime terms, appreciating "the beauty" of all "happy living things" of the sea.[73] One senses that the self-flagellation over the mistakes of Nazi Germany focuses exclusively on reviving the albatross and fails to apply its lessons to the greater goal of reestablishing domestic and international political trust.

There have been some hopeful signs. Upon the German Constitution's fiftieth anniversary in May 1999, the newly inaugurated President Johannes Rau made a point in his inaugural address to say he would represent all Germans, "especially those still without a German passport." He made a small historical step by being the first head of state to extend a fixed invitation to the head of the *Zentralrat der Muslime in Deutschland* to many official state receptions. All political parties have come out in support of the right of Muslim children to equal religious education. During the summer of 2002, a large subsidy granted to a Turkish organization (DOMiT) for an exhibition on the history of Turkish migration, which may eventually lead to the construction of a migration museum.

The new citizenship law may orient these organizations' constituents toward Germany and away from their country of origin. But this will take a great commitment on the German side to extend the institutional "welcome mat"—in terms of state funding and political and religious representation—to the same extent as they have done for Jews.

The difference in state support will be made in how a German Islam is encouraged to emerge. This will likely lead to an institutional opening with regard to state financing and political representation as it occurred for Jewish migrants. Migrant Jews from the former Soviet Union have been "converted" into Germans for many legal and rhetorical purposes in a process not unlike that undergone by ethnic German immigrants. This is often based on the presumed unproblematic integration of the Russian

226 / JONATHAN LAURENCE

Jews. Concrete problems of linguistic and professional integration are countered with financial solutions unavailable for Turkish migrants.

The relatively recent interest of German government in helping organize Islam and the absence of political negotiating partners has meant that Turks in Germany relied on the Courts for the acquisition of practical religious equality. This is reminiscent of the late 1970s, when labor migrants avoided deportation attempts by European governments and won the right to family reunification thanks to the intervention of constitutional courts. Some of religious demands are new issues, like demands for prayer breaks in private sector jobs or the right to wear a headscarf as a teacher or in a driver's license photograph. But Muslim communities also desire simple religious equality in policy areas where the German state has extensive precedent of religious accommodation, and religion is allowed to play a larger role in public life than in many other European countries: cemetery sections, religious education, ritual slaughter of animals (like Kosher regulations), the call to prayer (akin to church bells), the presence of Muslims on advisory councils of television and radio stations, university professorships in Islamic theology and religious chaplains in the military, prisons, hospitals.

The goal of such a political process is to firmly root religious practice in national context, and minimize external, transnational "threats" to the secular state mainly, by retaining some influence over who *finances* clergy and prayer space; who staffs representative organizations; it co-opts the moderates and enlists them in the task of internal consensus building—for example, by substituting state-recognized clergy for potentially fundamentalist Islamic proselytism. As Interior Minister Schily observed in a speech last fall, it is the government's role

> to distinguish between violent fanatics and those peaceful citizens who happen have a different religion—"the state cannot afford to ignore the . . . dynamics and potentially explosive nature of religious questions . . . integration can only succeed when we are able to take account of the new religious needs."[74]

As it stands, Turkish and Muslim communities are not yet voters and thus are mostly at the mercy of local administrations—and find themselves and rather everyday issues regarding religious communities instrumentalized in daily political life, as issues from mosque construction to religious education are debated in newspaper columns instead of political assemblies. Although these communities have been a feature of the local landscape for over two generations, few permanent solutions have been developed. The state's motivation and timing in the institutionalization of *communal religious ties* with "outsider" minority populations. Religious community serves as civic glue for the religious population and thereby facilitates the group's integration into society. Communities can provide the basics of integration: social welfare functions, internal policing, even language instruction.

Chancellor Gerhard Schröder met with Jewish Central Council President Paul Spiegel on the anniversary of Auschwitz's liberation in January 2003 to sign a state contract (*Staatsvertrag*) with Germany's largest Jewish umbrella organization, the *Zentralrat der Juden in Deutschland*. This agreement tripled the funds made available to the *Zentralrat* and designated it as the sole representative of Jews in Germany (which immediately provoked a lawsuit from the Liberal Union of Progressive Jews). One explanation for why more than fifty years had gone by without formalization of the Central Council's relationship with the government is that the Constitution assigns competence over religion to the local level of the *Länder*. But Catholic and Protestant organizations had long ago signed similar national-level contracts through the Interior Ministry, and the lack of a contract for the Jews was an odd exception to the government's otherwise meticulous treatment of the postwar Jewish community. The *Staatsvertrag's* preamble seems to have been paraphrased from one of the local state contracts that for decades have governed local Jewish Community relations with the *Länder*:

Cognizant of the special historical responsibility of the German people for Jewish life in Germany, in view of the immeasurable suffering that the Jewish Population experienced between 1933–45 . . . [the government states its commitment] to maintain and care for the German-Jewish cultural legacy . . . and to the building up of the Jewish community and the Central Council's *political integration and social duties*.[75]

This is the first time that a Chancellor has acknowledged the important immigrant integration role the Central Council has to play since the government acquiesced to the Central Council's request to invite Soviet Jews to settle in Germany in 1990–1991.[76] In the wake of the relatively large-scale Jewish migration that took place, the contract does not state outright that the "German-Jewish cultural legacy" is being carried forth by the remains of Soviet Jewry. But the fact that the increase in funding is intended to pay for "integration" work by the Central Council marks the end of an informal myth about the former Soviet refugees who have quadrupled Germany's Jewish population, to a total of about 120,000 in the last ten years; their position of prominence and their integration problems are no longer taboo. And their estrangement from Judaism is also being addressed; Spiegel spoke at the press conference of the need to make "familiarize the persecuted Jews from the former USSR with the rites and customs of Judaism"—a difficult task when only thirty rabbis are covering Germany's eighty-three communities. The €3,000,000 federal promise to the *Zentralrat* was largely symbolic—it amounts to a tiny fraction of the Berlin Senate's annual budget for Berlin Jewish Community. But for a country whose every move with regard to Jews is scrutinized at home and abroad, the public relations value of a Chancellor embracing the Jewish community was not lost on the government: in addition to the press conference and signing ceremony, the interior ministry put a photograph displaying a Star of David literally engraved in stone on the cover of its January 2003 magazine, with the headline "A Sign of Trust—the Contract with the Central Council of Jews in Germany." This deliberate projection of an image of permanence and unity stands in stark contrast to the computer-printout photograph taped to the wall in the Interior Ministry's sub-department for Islam—where three men are featured in the candid shot, the chairmen of Germany's three largest Muslim umbrella organizations.

With the State Contract, the Federal Government has strengthened the *Zentralrat der Juden in Deutschland*'s hand. Mostly, though, the government has in a sense recognized that Germany's "gift" of "new blood" to its Jewish community may have been akin to a poisoned chalice—or at least a double-edged sword. The dual need to inculcate a German and a Jewish identity: necessity to *integrate* on the one hand, and to strengthen religious community identity, on the other. Symbolically, the usefulness of the illusion of *Einheitsgemeinde* has been reaffirmed; but it can hardly be said to describe the reality of Jewish life in Germany: The exclusion of the Liberal Jewish community, whose lawyers are currently preparing to challenge the government's decision to grant monopoly status to the ZJD.

This chapter has aimed to show how elite consensus with regard to who "belongs" undergoes change and thus how minorities come to receive material support for their cultural, political, and religious activities. The coming years will show to what extent the change in citizenship law will radically alter the organizational experience of "non-German" minorities.

Intercommunity relations between Muslims and Jews actually pretty good, compared to other countries. The vice-president of the ZJD, Michel Friedmann, has come out in support of Turkish membership of the EU, which he called "geostrategically essential."[77] And the number of anti-Semitic incidents actually decreased in German 2001—even while Palestine was in a phase of full-blown Intifada, there was almost no spillover violence.[78] Germany is growing into its status as a multicultural democracy. Community interests will increasingly come to the fore, and governments will have to reckon with this. The new citizenship law's effects will likely accomplish most of the most difficult tasks simply through electoral means. A more symbolically self-conscious approach to the Turkish community will likely develop on its own. The lessons that have been learned in the Jewish case, historically, that communities can provide integration help, a social network, a safety net and interlocutors are slowly being internalized and adapted.

Notes

1. An interview subject named Laszlo, quoted in Judith Kessler, "Eine Kaleidoskop von Meinungen," in Van Aiynberg bis Zaidelman: Jüdische Zuwanderer aus Osteuropa in Berlin und die Jüdische Gemeinde heute (Berlin, 1997).
2. Nadeem Elyas, Central Council of Muslims, chair, interview by author, June 14, 2000.
3. It is estimated that there are 180,000 Muslims in Berlin, including 137,000 Turks. For official statistics from Berlin's Interior Ministry, see Bericht wr Integrations-und Ausländerpolitik des Senats von Berlin 1996/1997 (Berlin 1998) and Hans-Burkhard Richter "Probleme der Zuwanderung am Beispiel Berlins," in Aus Politik und Zeitgeschichte, B 46/97 (November 1997). It is estimated that there are more than 16,000 Jews in Berlin, three-quarters of whom are dues-paying community members. Thirty percent of the "foreign" Turkish population were bom in Berlin (40,510 out of 137,111) and another 23 percent (31,830) have lived in the city for more than twenty years; "Nichtdeutsche nach ausgewählten Herkunftsgebieten und Aufenthaltsdauer am 31.12.1997" in Bericht des Senats (Berlin, 1998); Sabri Adak, Turkish Community of Berlin, chair, interview by author, December 14, 1998.
4. National Foreign Intelligence Board, "Growing Global Migration and its Implications for the United States," NIE 2001 02-D (Washington, 2001), figure 2.
5. Barbara John, interview by author, December 7, 1998 (see note 3). This may also have to do with the reluctance of German authorities to meddle with Jewish affairs: the money is transferred to the Community, which is then responsible for administering integration programs, etc., on its own.
6. Manfred Becker, Berlin Ministry of Science, Research and Culture, Referatsleiter Kirchen, Religions-und Weltanschauungsverbande, interview by author, February 11, 1999.
7. In 1998, the Islamic Federation in Berlin was recognized as a "religious commu-nity" in a ruling by the upper administrative court; see Oberverwaltungsgericht 7 B 4.98, November 4, 1998, and survived a challenge in the Federal administra-tive court (see Bundesverwaltungsgericht 6 c.5.99, February 23, 2000). The Jewish communities receive their subsides from the Berlin House of Deputies (Abgeordnetenhaus) budget under the title of "Church Subsidies"; Vorabdruck zur Beratung im Abgeordnetenhaus September 17, 1999 (Berlin House of Deputies, 1999).
8. Andreas Nachama, former chair of the Jewish Community in Berlin, described his contact with local government offices: "the individual senators who are responsible for us, in particular the Senator for Cultural Affairs, with whom we meet every four to six weeks . . . and naturally also the Mayor . . . and we also of course have good relations with the Senator for Public Works"; interview by Ruud Koopmans for MERCI project, February 19, 1999.
9. German Bundestag Document, Bundesdrucksache 14/4530 (Berlin, 2000).
10. This status is described in Article 137, paragraph 5, sentence 2 of the Weimar Constitution and in Article 140 of Basic Law (German Constitution).
11. Of this number, there are 2.3 m Turks, 180,000 Bosnians, 123,000 Iranians 105,000 Moroccans, and others. Only 370,000 to 450,000 are German citizens;

Antwort de Bundesregierung auf die Grosse Anfrage Islam in Deutschland, German Bundestag Document, Bundesdrucksache 14/2301, draft from June 25, 2000 (Berlin, 2000).

12. Statistics as of July 31, 2000, obtained from Bundesverwaltungsamt, department III 4.K-1.04.50/03. Only about 70 percent of the emigrants will become members of the community, and non-Jewish family members are included in the number o arrivals; Beni Bloch, Central Welfare Agency of Jews in Germany, director, tele phone interview by author, August 3, 2000.
13. Cornelia Sonntag-Wolgast, former Parliamentary Secretary of State, Federal Interio Ministry, interview by author, July 3, 2000.
14. German Bundestag Publishing Office, Heute im Bundestag, December (Berlin 2000).
15. This formulation is borrowed from Ruud Koopmans's article "Deutschland und seine Einwanderer: ein gespaltenes Verhältnis," in Max Kaase and Günther Schmid, eds., Eine lernende Demokratie (Berlin: Edition Sigma, 1999).
16. Rogers Brubaker, Citizenship and Nationhood in France and Germany (Cambridge, 1992), p. 119.
17. Migrationsbericht 1999, Mitteilungen und Beauftragten der Bundesregierung für Ausländerfragen (Berlin, 1999).
18. K-U. Hailbronner and G. Renner, Staatsangehörigkeitsrecht: Kommentar (Munich 1998), p. 864.
19. Werner Nell, "Multikulturelle oder transkulturelle Gesellschaft?" in Anto Escher, ed., Auslander in Deutschland. Probleme ciner transkulturelkn Gesellschaft a geographischer Sicht (Mainz 2000), p. 14.
20. Richter, "Probleme der Zuwanderung am Beispiel Berlins."
21. Becker, interview by author, 1999.
22. Sonntag-Wolgast, interview by author, 2000.
23. Hans-Burkhard Richter, Berlin Interior Ministry, Regierungsdirektor fur Auslän-derfragen, interview by author, June 16, 2000.
24. Richter, "Probleme der Zuwanderung am Beispiel Berlins."
25. Y. Michal Bodemann, "Staat und Ethnizität" in Micha Brumlik, ed., Jüdisches Leben in Deutschland seit 1945 (Frankfurt, 1986), p. 62.
26. This was actually a policy of the interim government of the GDR which was adopted by the FRG with the accord of the governors of all federal states; Jeroen Doomemik, Going West: Soviet Jewish Immigrants in Berlin since 1990 (Avebun 8, 1996).
27. Ignatz Bubis, Central Council of Jews in Germany, former chair, interview with author, May 13, 1999.
28. Internal memorandum, Berlin Interior Ministry, Referent fur Auslanderrechgae Senatsverwaltung fur Inneres, Vermerk, IV A4–0345/2446, November 10, 1998.
29. Ibid., p. 2.
30. Erik Kirschbaum "German Jewish leader urges immigration clampdown" Reuters, June 6, 2001 BERLIN "We have often discovered that many of the refugees are not Jews according to halachic rules," Spiegel said, referring to Jewish law based on the Talmud. "In the future there has to be more scrutiny to ensure that the refugees are in fact Jews and not just people with some distant Jewish origins," Spiegel told the weekly Allgemeine Juedische Wochenzeitung newspaper Wednesday.

31. John, interview by Ruud Koopmans for MERCI project, March 11, 1999.
32. Barbara John, Commissioner for Foreigner Affairs, Berlin Senate, interview by author, June 20, 2000.
33. Michael Naumann, former Minister of State in the Federal Chancellory and Federal Commissioner for Cultural and Media Affairs, interview by author June 30, 2000.
34. Sonntag-Wolgast, interview by author, 2000.
35. Malte Krause, Berlin Interior Ministry, Grundsatzangelegenheiten der InneiSt^ politik u. Planung, Leiter, interview by author, January 27, 1999.
36. Becker, interview by author, 1999.
37. Unpublished position paper, Berlin Interior Ministry, Positionspapier Auslander- politik in Berlin, Senatsverwaltung fur Inneres Berlin, Grundsatzangelegenheiten der Innenpolitik/Planung, December 8, 1999, p. 6.
38. Berlin House of Deputies Document, Gesetz zum Staatsvertrag liber die Beziehungen des Landes Berlin zurJudischen Gemeinde zu Berlin, Ges.Nr.94/61/3B, February 8, 1994 (Berlin, 1994).
39. €1 is slightly less than DM 2.
40. Berlin Ministry for Science, Research and Culture internal document, "Leistungen an die Kirchen."
41. Becker, interview by Ruud Koopmans, April 20, 1999.
42. Cited by Y. Michal Bodemann "Galut 2000-Aufbruch zu einer europaischejüdischen Identitat," Kolloquium im Centrum Judaicum Berlin, December 6, 1998. Only DM 9.8 million are considered as official reparations payment; Nachama, interview by author, February 23, 1999.
43. Hans Jakob Ginsburg, "Politik Danach—Jüdische Interessenvertretung in der BRD" in Brumlik.
44. John, interview by author, December 17, 1998.
45. Sabri Adak, Turkish Community of Berlin, chair, interview by author, December 14, 1998.
46. Kasim Ayden, Turkish Parents Association, President, interview by author, December 16, 1998.
47. Sonntag-Wolgast, interview by author, 2000.
48. Becker. This echoes former Chancellor Kohl's 1988 Rosh Hashanah address to the Jewish Community in Berlin: "we appreciate with thankfulness and great respect for every Jewish citizen, that today there is again an active Jewish Community in Germany. It is a great encouragement that you are able to recognize in Germany your home"; Bodemann, Gedachtnistheater, p. 175.
49. Krause, interview by author, 1999 (see note 65). Galinski's grave was then assigned a 24-hour police guard (Der Tagesspiegel, February 16, 1999); also, Ignatz Bubis later declined burial in Germany for fear of similar attacks.
50. Krause, interview by author, 1999.
51. John.
52. Jörg Schönbohm, interview by author, 2000.
53. Hans-Joachim Rose, Berlin Interior Ministry, Senatsdirigent und LeitilBS3 Abteilung IV (Staatsangehorigkeit, Auslander), interview by author, June 28, 2000.
54. Richter, "Probleme der Zuwanderung am Beispiel Berlins."
55. Naumann, interview by author, 2000.

232 / JONATHAN LAURENCE

56. Rose, interview by author, 2000.

57. Interview with Erwin Blume, "Bildung und Beruf," June 10, 2000, *Suddeutsche Zeitung*. See also Otto Romberg and Susanne Urban-Fair, eds., *Jews in Germany after 1945: Citizens or 'fellow' Citizens?* (Frankfurt, 2000).

58. Report by Brandenburg Commissioner for Foreigners' Affairs, 53 Zuwanderer aus der ehemaligen Sowjetunion 'Judische Emigranten und Familien.' "

62. See "Union befurchtet 'Chinatowns,' " Der Tagesspiegel, February 5, 1999.

63. Renate Amman and Barbara von Neumann-Cosel, eds., Berlin: Eine Zeichen der Migration (Berlin, 1997).

65. Irene Knochenhauer, Jewish Community of Brandenburg, managing director, interview by author, June 28, 2000.

69. Interview, Verwaltung für Schule, Jugend und Sport, January 2002.

72. Sonntag-Wolgast, interview by author, 2000.

73. Samuel Taylor Coleridge, The Rime ofthe Ancient Mariner (London, 1836).

74. Otto Schily "Soziale Integration in der deutschen Gesellschaft als politische Aufgabe" Symposiums "Religion Kirche Islam" am September 9–10, 2002 (http://www.bmi.bund.de/dokumente/Rede/ix_90559.htm

75. (author's emphasis), Federal Ministry of the Interior, "Vertrag mit dem Zentralrat der Juden in Deutschland," <http://www.bmi.bund.de/dokumente/Artikel/ix_91415.htm>; compare to Berlin House of Deputies, "Gesetz zum Staatsvertrag liber die Beziehungen des Landes Berlin zur Jüdischen Gemeinde zu Berlin," Ges.Nr.94/61/3B, February 8, 1994 (Berlin, 1994): "Out of responsibility for German history, which is imprinted with the persecution and annihilation of German and European people of Jewish belief and origin, and in acknowledgment of the loss that Berlin and Germany have suffered as a result, Berlin affirms . . . that it will protect and secure the avowal and exercise of the Jewish faith for all time.

76. "Staatsvertrag mit dem Zentralrat," die Tageszeitung, November 15, 2002.

77. "Saarbrücker Zeitung", January 15, 2003.

78. Bundesinnenministerium, January 18, 2003. Demnach wurden 2002 insgesamt 1478 Übergriffe auf Juden oder jüdische Einrichtungen und Fälle antisemitischer Hetze registriert. Im Jahr 2001 habe die Zahl der antisemitischen Straftaten noch bei 1629 gelegen.

CHAPTER ELEVEN
PERPETUAL IMPOSSIBILITY?
NORMALIZATION OF GERMAN-JEWISH
RELATIONS IN THE BERLIN REPUBLIC

Ruth A. Starkman

In a May 2002 article in one of Germany's leading newspapers, the *Frankfurter Allgemeine Zeitung*, German Foreign Minister Joschka Fischer offered two seemingly contradictory concepts of "normality" concerning Germans and Jews in post-unification Germany. Referring to the *"Antisemitismus-Streit,"* a tense public debate over the "second Intifada" in Israel, which broke out in the spring of 2002, Fischer argued both for "normalizing" relations between Jews and Germans, but against "normalizing" Germany history. As the anti-Semitism debate exacerbated tensions between Germany's German and Jewish populations in the spring of 2002, Joschka Fischer first attempted to assuage the fears of the Jewish community, asserting:

> . . . each and every instance of anti-Semitism is not only a threat to Jews in Germany, but also to our society and our democracy as a whole. "Is it right to stay in Germany?" The ease or difficulty with which our Jewish compatriots are able to answer yes to this question depends crucially on whether they can live perfectly "normally" as Jews in Germany and as Germans.[1]

Fischer maintained that the growing "normality" of German-Jewish relations depends on the ability to assure German-Jews of their belonging while also promoting discussion about Israel and Germany. The very openness of this discussion would signify the "normalization" of relations between Germans and Jews and German and Israeli democracies. A few paragraphs later, Fischer, however, concluded with a negative assessment of "normality" with

234 / RUTH A. STARKMAN

respect to German history:

> ... those who wish to dispose of German history, as it were, by a detour to the Middle East ... must be opposed by all those who perceive German unity as freedom to accept responsibility and not as an escape into a supposedly harmless "normality."[2]

Here, "normality" referred to conservatives' efforts to draw a line under Germany's Nazi past and reinstate a positive German national identity. This essay examines the tensions between the two concepts of "normality" in the context of public debates about Germany's memorial practices and shows how the term remains unstable in post-unification Germany. Viewed both as an ideal rendered impossible by Germany's destruction of European Jewry in World War II, and as a conservative will to move on from the past, the perpetually elusive German "normality" remains open to debate. If perhaps agreeing on nothing else, most observers would concur that the "normalization" of Germany and German-Jewish relations has long been underway, and that the increasing frequency of public debates on the topic indicates nothing less than an agonizing struggle between German Jews, whose self-understanding has been shaped by their status as victims of a formerly murderous, fascist Germany, and the Germans, who, after near fifty years of stable constitutional democracy, seek a more positive national self-image.

Some of the confusion arises from Germany's doubled usage of the term "normalization" lies in the wide array of other uses of the concept. Seen as a philosophical concept, "normalization" refers to rationalization and control of human knowledge and existence, a standardization of behavioral norms that arose in the West in the era of industrialized modernity. French social philosopher Michel Foucault outlines a notion of "normalization" in his famous book on the modern penitentiary, *Discipline and Punish*, in which he describes the evolution of norms as the means by which bodies can be disciplined "subjected, used, transformed, and improved."[3] In a disciplinary system, bodies are individually and minutely observed, their activities measured, and their measurements compared and averaged. Those individuals falling outside desirable values are subjected to reform. The result is a process that Foucault notes is both individualizing (in that it describes particular characteristics in minute detail) and homogenizing (in that it is used to help the individual conform to the given "norm").[4] German social philosopher, Jürgen Link elaborates Foucault's notion of "normalization," presenting it as the dominant form of social integration in modern societies, one in which "normalization" demands overwhelming conformity in the public sphere.[5] While Foucault and Link view normalization as a force of coercion, other theorists of modernity, notably Frankfurt School theorists Theodor W. Adorno and Max Horkheimer, as well as social philosopher Jürgen Habermas, have emphasized the dialectic between coercion and democratization. For Habermas, especially, the evolution of norms in modernity is a positive condition of possibly for democracy. Distinguishing between "normativity" and "normality," Habermas describes the former as the "categorical norm of western democracy," and derides the latter as the deformation of "normativity," its "ideological façade."[6] In the context of debates over Germany's efforts at normalization, Habermas refers to German "normality" as "the second existential lie (*Lebenslüge*) of the Federal Republic: we have become *normal* again."[7]

In addition to these formal conceptions of the terms "normality" and "normalization," a more popular notion of the term often appears in the context of international relations. Widely used as well in political terminology, "normalization" often refers to the opening of diplomatic channels with countries previously considered hostile to Western democracies. Because of its use as a measure of conformity to Western standards, it also frequently appears in conjunction with "globalization," another highly debated term, which has been variously described as the concomitant acceleration and strengthening of the dominance of a world capitalist economic system, the supplanting the primacy of the nation-state by transnational corporations and organizations, and eroding local cultures and traditions through a global culture.[8] For its detractors, "normalization of relations" and its attendant globalization means the intervention of imperialist capitalism, which destroys local cultures. To proponents, both concepts represent the continuation of modernization and a force of progress, increased wealth, freedom, democracy, and happiness.

Germany, long considered a belated state that followed a "special path" (*Sonderweg*) to modernity, has always debated its relation to "normal" cultural and political conditions vis-à-vis the rest of Europe.[9] The Andenauer era strove for the "normalization" of Germany and its integration in the West at the expense of scrutinizing its role in World War II. While westward-looking, such normalization was also culturally conservative as far as German historiography was concerned. The student movement period of the late 1960s and 1970s revolted against the Federal Republic's early efforts at conservative "normalization," as a younger generation of Germans began to confront its parents and grandparents about their involvement in National Socialism. By the mid-1980s, however, the student movement encountered reaction from conservative historians, most notably, Ernst Nolte, whose efforts to "relativize" and "normalize" the Nazi past resulted in *Historikerstreit*.[10] During the debates on unification in 1989–1990, "normalization" still connoted mostly conservative visions of Germany's past. In the context of Germany's

236 / RUTH A. STARKMAN

euphoric nationalism, critical observers like Habermas saw efforts to "normalize" Germany identity, that is, conceive of a positive national self-understanding, as a threat to the Federal Republic's democratic achievements as "post-national" state.[11] Indeed for Habermas, a truer, more historically reflective "normativity" in German self-understanding stands in direct opposition to "normalization" in the conservative sense. "Normativity" means not shoring up some new German identity, but rather embracing formal and legal norms, taking pride in the state's successes as a constitutional democracy, a *Verfassungspatriotismus*.[12]

Since the mid-1990s, however, and especially with the election of the Social-Democratic/Green Government in 1998, "normalization" has come to mean not merely a conservative historical revisionism, but the positive stability of German democracy, its westernization and Europeanization. In 1998 German Chancellor Gerhard Schröder referred to unified Germany as a "normal state" in that it now shares the same values as other western countries. Part of this transformation in the usage of the terms "normalization" and "normality" reflect a historic generational shift. For the first time, the Federal Republic of Germany is now governed by a generation that has no personal experience of the Nazi period. At the beginning of unified Germany's second decade, seven-tenths of all Germans were born after the war and in the recent elections there were 3.3 million first-time voters.

In this context of a new era, "normalization" has a special meaning for Germany as a nation. Indeed, many of its relations on the international scene point to "normality," such as the Kosovo conflict, in which Germany participated in military operations for the first time since 1945. American Jewish Studies and Holocaust memorial scholar, James E. Young, viewed Germany's intervention in Kosovo with much enthusiasm:

> No longer paralyzed by the memory of crimes perpetrated in its name, Germany is now acting on the basis of such memory: it participated boldly in NATO's 1999 intervention against a new genocide perpetrated by Milosevic's Serbia; it has begun to change citizenship laws from blood- to residency-based; and it is about to dedicate a permanent place in Berlin's cityscape to commemorate what happened the last time Germany was governed from Berlin. Endless debate and memorialization are no longer mere substitutes for actions against contemporary genocide but reasons for action.[13]

Young's positive assessment of Germany's participation in Kosovo suggests that taking part in an international political effort itself is the hallmark for "normality." To be sure, Germany has arrived as a democracy, free (though not without much public debate) from its longtime political paralysis, but domestically, and especially culturally, Germany's view of itself, its minorities and its past exist in a state of perpetual contention. Some observers remain wary of Germany's efforts at "normalization," viewing these not as part of a larger progressive transformation, but rather as a continuity in conservative efforts at political and cultural redemption. Stefan Berger examines how Germany's extreme right after unification has endeavored to reestablish a nationalist historiography and detects an equally conservative search for normality among the liberal-conservative mainstream of German historiography.[14]

Whether shaped by continuity or transformation, Germany's efforts to be a "normal state" were dramatically affected by unification. Onlookers wondered whether the new Germany would, in the words of Thomas Mann, impose a "German Europe" on the rest of the continent, or become a "European Germany." More than a dozen years later, the new Germany has become increasingly Europeanized, a sign most visible in its (grudging, regretful) adoption of the euro.[15] Unification has also transformed the character of Germany's Jewish population, which has more than doubled since 1989. Jewish immigrants from the former Soviet Union, who were granted preferential status after 1990, increased the number of Jews living in Germany to some 70,000 (some estimate that it may actually be as high as 100,000). The current German-Jewish community consists of a "veteran" Jewish population (primarily made up of former displaced persons from Eastern Europe and their descendants) and the newcomers.[16] There are also several thousand Israelis and Iranian Jews, many of whom came in the 1960s.[17]

This growth and change in the character of Germany's Jewish population can be seen in three studies, American sociologist Lynn Rapaport's *Jews in Germany After the Holocaust: Memory, Identity, and Jewish-German Relations*,[18] Canadian sociologist Y. Michal Bodemann's edited volume, *Jews, Germans, Memory: Reconstructions of Jewish Life in Germany*,[19] and American Jewish Studies scholar Sander Gilman, *Jews in Today's German Culture*.[20] Rapaport's study, which concluded in 1990, clearly demarcates earlier, long-standing attitudes toward Germans in the German Jewish community, one in which there was little desire to normalize relations with the Germans. On the contrary, her research shows Jews defining themselves as morally and culturally superior to the Germans. According to Rapaport, the vast majority of Jews whom she has interviewed refuse to identify with the national state, the cultural tradition or with the German people. German-Jewish historian Micha Brumlik's introductory essay to Bodemann's book begins with a similar perspective, namely that Jews in Germany view themselves not as German-Jews, but rather as *Jews* who live in Germany.[21] Given this rejection of identification with Germany, Bodemann's collection goes on to ask how was it possible that a new and sizeable Jewish community developed after the Holocaust in Germany and posits the idea that a "veteran" Jewish community and the new arrivals will ultimately strive for closer integration into German society.[22] Gilman's book, meanwhile, asserts that Jews in Germany today are marked by a particular "visible invisibility." That is, because they have become so integrated into German culture, Jews can choose the degree to which they wish to be visible as an "Other" to the Germans. Today, the Other is more clearly represented by the Turks, Gypsies, Pakistanis, and Vietnamese. Such relative "invisibility," however, has not led to greater normalization.

Indeed, though the Jewish population has greatly changed, efforts toward greater integration continue to constitute what German historian Dan Diner has described as a "negative symbiosis," a systematic reversal of the "German-Jewish symbiosis" so optimistically anticipated by the Age of Enlightenment.[23] Some contemporary German Jews have even rejected the idea of a positive symbiosis altogether, echoing Gershom Scholem's denial "that there has ever been such a German-Jewish dialogue in any genuine sense whatsoever, i.e., as *a historical phenomenon*. It takes two to have a dialogue . . ."[24] Salomon Korn, member of the Central Council of Jews in Berlin elaborates Scholem's famous assertion anecdotally in an essay entitled "The Often-Conjured German-Jewish Symbiosis is Just a Myth:"

> Recently I asked a prominent German businessman how long it took for him to be able to say the word "Jew" without his heart racing. His answer: "Honestly, I can't even do that today."[25]

Korn doesn't say whether the businessman's heart raced because he didn't like Jews, or because he feared them, or because the confrontation with an "Other" remains uncomfortable, or simply because he suffered the tension of being a perpetrator, who has to face his former victim. Rather, Korn leaves the anecdote unexplained, because all of the above emotions are characteristic of the "negative symbiosis." For Joschka Fischer, it is only complete acknowledgment of this "negative symbiosis" that will lead to a normalization of relations between Germans and Jews: "Only on this basis could a chance for new coexistence emerge from what historian Dan Diner called the 'negative symbiosis.' "[26] Bound together by the past, while also guaranteed the rights of open democratic exchange, Germans and Jews, Fischer asserts, should be able to "normalize" relations, criticize each other, and criticize Israel: "Criticism is possible only on the firm foundation of indelible solidarity."[27]

In reality such solidarity remains elusive, and every effort to "normalize" contemporary Germany has led to bitter debate. From the Walser-Bubis Debate of 1998, to the Holocaust memorial debate, and most recently to the *Antisemitismus-Streit*, the tensions over Germany's efforts at normality have arisen for two reasons: First, it remains unclear whether the "normality" in question refers to the transformative, progressive variety that has emerged in the last decade, or whether it simply reinvents an effort at "normalization" harkening back to the *Historikerstreit* of the 1980s. Secondly, and perhaps most discomforting to observers and especially the German Jews, who have grown accustomed to their "negative symbiosis," no one is certain, what exactly a "progressive" normality would look like.

After a decade of wrenching debate over the place of memory in the new Germany, the German Parliament approved a plan in June 1999 for the building of a vast memorial in the center of Berlin to the six million Jewish victims of the Holocaust. The monument will be situated near Brandenburg Gate and designed by the New York architect Peter Eisenman. It will combine a field of more than 2,000 stone pillars with a building that will serve as an educational center. In his recent book, *Facing the Nazi Past United Germany and the Legacy of the Third Reich*, British Germanist Bill Niven reflects on the ways in which this debate helped to raise awareness of the centrality of the Holocaust in German culture.[28] At the end of the debate, pronouncements in German parliament endeavored to grasp this centrality. Wolfgang Thierse, the speaker of Parliament, declared in June 1999:

> We are not building this monument solely for the Jews . . . . We are building it for ourselves. It will help us confront a chapter of our history.[29]

This plan, which led to architect Peter Eisenman's final reworking of the memorial in July 2000, embodied many of the problems with Germany's struggle for "normalization." Immediately prior to its conception, a compromise plan arose that was dubbed "Nausenman," a somewhat comic name for the Frankensteinian combination of Eisenman's plans and State Minister of Culture Michael Naumann's request for a learning center attached to the memorial. Nausenman was to contain a multidimensional complex, the first Leo Baeck Institute in Germany, a large library with all the available books on the holocaust as well as books on German-Jewish history, and a Genocide Watch center to educate against future genocides.[30] Niven comments that Naumann's library concept suggested a kind of "bureaucratic gigantomania,"[31] which also implied mastery of the past:

> The library's stress on post-holocaust intellectual and moral reflection would, moreover, have implied that the Germans had "moved on" and were now enlightened, in all senses of the term.[32]

Niven accounts for Minister Michael Naumann's presumptions of mastery as characteristic of a "government with no experience of the war . . . . Instead of looking back with regret, Germans look forward in moral determination to resist future genocide. This is part of the new German 'normality.' "[33] For Niven, Naumann's efforts at normality were "overstated, but in some respects interesting,"[34] perhaps all the more so because these efforts demonstrated the extent to which the process of attaining normality remains still in progress. In an address following the dedication of the monument, James E. Young also identified Germany's evolving approach to the past:

> Now that the parliament has decided to give Holocaust memory a central place in Berlin, an even more difficult job awaits the organizers: Defining exactly what it is to be remembered here in Peter Eisenman's waving field of pillars. What will Germany's national Holocaust narrative be? Who will write it and to whom will it be written? The question of historical content begins at precisely the moment the question of memorial design ends. Memory, which has followed history, will now be followed by still further historical debate.[35]

In the midst of public discussion of the Holocaust monument, another debate raged in response to the remarks of Martin Walser on Germany's practices of Holocaust memorialization. The highly publicized debate not only influenced a positive decision for the Holocaust monument from the then newly elected SPD government, which had hitherto been lukewarm about the project, it also showed once again the degree to which Germans continue to struggle to define and attain normality. In Waler's 1998 acceptance speech for Germany's prestigious literary award, the *Friedenspreis des Deutschen Buchhandels* (the Peace Prize of German Booksellers), he questioned the increasing emphasis on the Holocaust in the 1990s, saying that he had begun to "look away" when constantly subjected to media images of Germany's shame. Declaring that the Holocaust should not become a "routine threat, a tool of intimidation, a moral cudgel or just a compulsory exercise,"[36] Walser criticized the Holocaust monument as "a monumentalization of shame"[37] and rejected the "instrumentalization of our shame for present purposes."[38] Stating that he himself could never imagine leaving the side of the guilty, Walser nevertheless favored the idea of a private conscience rather than a constant public preoccupation with Germany's past.[39] As he saw it, the combination of public obsession and media appropriation of the Holocaust undermined Germany's very effort to achieve normality sixty years after the beginning of the extermination of European Jewry. Attempting to demonstrate how Germany's Holocaust reception has rendered German "normality" taboo, Walser posed the rhetorical question: "But under what suspicion one comes, if one says, the Germans are now a completely normal people, a regular society."[40]

At the end of the speech attended by Germany's most famous politicians and intellectuals, the great majority of the audience members stood up and applauded. A notable exception were the head of the Central Council of Jews in Germany, Ignatz Bubis and his wife, who had sat stony-faced through the speech. A few weeks later at a commemoration of *Kristallnacht*, Bubis declared:

> This shame [the Holocaust] was in fact once there and cannot disappear from a will to forget, and it is "intellectual arson," (*geistige Brandstiftung*) for some-one to see in [such remembrance] an instrumentalization of Auschwitz. These are the kind of claims that usually come from extreme-right "Party Leaders" (*Parteifuehrern*).[41]

In the context of a day of remembrance for Germans and Jews, Bubis asserted that Walser's efforts at critiquing the role of the Holocaust in German life amounted to an anti-Semitic assault. Walser's speech, mean-while, was more complex than Bubis's critique would suggest. Written in a highly self-conscious, ironic, the speech reflects Walser's awareness of the volatility of his topic for a German audience. Ultimately, the debate left uncertain what exactly riled Walser's critics, Germans and Jews alike. Whether it was Walser's rhetoric, or fear of a reactionary response, or merely the fact that a German had questioned Germany's memorial practices at all, remains still in question.

Despite Walser's efforts at subtlety, there was indeed considerable right-wing appropriation of Walser's speech, as well as "more pedestrian efforts at historical revisionism."[42] Much of the German public sympathized with Walser, but responded to his words with widely varying agendas. Many wrote letters to the editors of the major newspapers and to Walser himself, thanking Walser for stating opening what they felt, but were afraid to say publicly. Meanwhile, observers close to both Walser and Bubis, like famed Suhrkamp editor Siegfried Unseld, defended Walser on the basis of his left-ist credentials and past efforts on behalf of German-Jewish understanding.[43] Some intellectuals, including Rafael Seligmann, a member of Germany's younger generation of Jewish writers, saw the speech and ensuing debate as a long overdue confrontation of the tensions between Germans and Jews.[44] Others, including some politicians like Hamburg major Klaus von Dohnanyi and intellectuals like former East German writer Monika Maron took the debate as an occasion to correct the moral imbalance with the Jews as beneficiaries of German guilt. Dohnanyi questioned whether the Jews would have not acted just as the Germans had they not been persecuted alongside the Sinti, Roma, homosexuals and communists in the 1930s.[45] Maron suggested a kind of public censorship in debating the Holocaust at all. She defended Walser: "I too shake a little, when I defend him, Why? Where do I live that I am afraid to say what I think?"[46]

Shaking from fear of public reprisal, Monika Maron suggests that in such a state, where one has to watch one's own speech so carefully, Germans are a far cry from a modern, democratic normality. Such a rhetorical inversion of contemporary Germany with its dictatorships of the past, encapsulates the problems of the debate per se. For, comments like Dohnanyi's and Maron's showed that Walser's criticism of memorial practices could not simply exist in an ahistorical, politically disinterested vacuum.

Seen outside the context of Germany and the Walser debate, the question of the increasing instrumentalization of the Holocaust remains contested, but nevertheless a historical fact. Few observers will doubt that the Holocaust has gained a certain commercial aspect since NBC's 1979 series *Holocaust* and Steven Spielberg's commercial blockbuster *Schindler's List*. Some scholars, like British historian Tim Cole view Holocaust memorial sites and museums, as a new kind of tourist venture,[47] others, like American historian Anson Rabinbach question whether all the efforts at memorialization erode rather than promote memory of Germany's past.[48] Surely debates about the Holocaust in England and the United States, where one of the most discussed books of 1999 was American Historian Peter Novick's *The Holocaust in American Life*,[49] take on a different character than those in Germany. There is little doubt of the difficulty in debating the instrumentalization of the Holocaust in Germany, where the subject remains entangled in quasi-religious taboos. When Walser asserts that Holocaust memorialization practices in Germany threaten to become a routine lipservice, or in German, "Lippengebet,"[50] he exposes the tacit dialectic between a postwar German *mea culpa* reflex and its concomitant resentment.

Part of the difficulty of Germany's foiled path to "normality," as Walser articulates in his speech, and subsequently developed in the course of the ensuing debate, lay in what Walser saw as the mendacity of public discussions about the Holocaust. In a broadcasted discussion organized by Frank Schirrmacher, entitled "We Need a New Language for Memory," that included Walser, Bubis, Salomon Korn, and Schirrmacher, Walser maintained that Holocaust "the most difficult problem of our history," had developed a particular "slumbering routine language usage"[51] that scarcely coincided with the kinds of thoughts Germans were only able to express with "family and friends" in the private sphere.[52] Such a disjunction between everyday experience and the ability of Germans to really say what they feel about Jews and the Holocaust, Walser argued, undermined the process of normalization itself. Korn and Schirrmacher and many others supported Walser on this point. Bubis retracted his "intellectual arson" charge and comparison to right-wing extremists, but asserted that the very disjunction between public and private discussions of the Holocaust indicated the necessity for public norms to guide the Holocaust discussion. This exchange made clear that Walser's desired German "normality," had to exist outside of norms for public discussion because these, according to Walser had lost meaning through routinization.

The problem with Walser's speech therefore lay less in his efforts to assess Holocaust reception in Germany, than in his aesthetics and rhetoric. First, his aesthetic of private memory as opposed to routinized public discussions, was contested by Micha Brumlik, who saw Walser's will to private reflection as a retreat from collective reflection on the past.[53] British Germanist Stuart Taberner[54] and German-Israeli Germanist Amir Eshel[55] locate Walser's aesthetic of private memory in the context of his autobiographical novel *Ein springender Brunnen*, for which he had received the *Friedenspreis*. Both Taberner and Eshel remark on the novel's rejection of public memory in favor of private individualized perceptions and discuss how Frank Schirrmacher, the champion of the end of politicized literature during the 1990 *Literaturstreit*, framed Walser's speech with a similar rejection of politicization. Taberner and Eshel also both identify Walser's efforts at self-reinvention as an apolitical writer as a sign of the author's move to the right. While Taberner sees the Walser-Bubis debate as simply a continuation of the *Historikerstreit* of the 1980s and the *Literaturstreit* of 1990, Eshel views Walser's efforts as less a critique of the instrumentalization of the Holocaust than an occlusion of memory; an attempt, in Walser's words to "free" a "conscience" of its historical burden.[56]

Indeed, Walser's rhetoric suggests a strategy of hibernation in an idealized individuality; a kind of naïve reception of Max Horkheimer and Theodor W. Adorno's analysis of the routinization of culture in modernity, as well as their notion of a redemptive individuality. For Walser, Germany's contemporary society suffers at the hands of its modern democracy, not because as Horkheimer and Adorno would have it, routinization is part and parcel of modernity—part of the very "normalization," for which Walser longs—but rather because of coercive public language that has come to stifle "individual feelings" about the Holocaust. Likewise, Walser's notion of "freedom" from routinized Holocaust discussions in contemporary Germany bears little resemblance to Horkheimer and Adorno's miminalist redemptive individual. Decrying the "language-usage" that predetermines how people should think about Auschwitz, Walser expresses his notion of individualized memory:

> I will not allow myself to be told how I have to remember. Perhaps I did not
> make it clear enough that [I think] there should be public memory. But how

every individual feels and what kind of conscience he and his family and children have, that must be left up to him.[57]

Walser offers no reflection on how this notion of a private conscience would correspond to public acts of memory. Only that they should be private in a way that rejects Germany's often uneven and opportunistic postwar approach to the public, that is, collective Enlightenment. Even so, Walser's notion of a private conscience might not have drawn such resistance from his intellectual detractors, had it not coupled with Walser's tone of victimization. For the speech, as well as the debate, tended to project German persecution onto those unnamed promoters of the Holocaust industry. In Walser's and his supporters' case, the desire to establish a positive national identity distanced from the past, transforms Germany's Jews and Germany's Holocaust culture into the persecutors.[58] When Walser describes his response of looking away from the "constant presentation of our shame" he positions himself as a victim of a media campaign. His, as well as Maron's rhetoric constructs a German victimhood, by suggesting a bodily suffering. Walser's ears ring, he looks away, he shakes. Maron shakes a little too.

This kind of projection undermines Walser's plea for German "normality," especially a German nation in which Germans and Jews could discuss and criticize Holocaust reception with the open exchanges that are ideally characteristic of a "normal" modern society. "Normality" for Walser seems to consist in an effort to undo collective reflection on the past. In the spring of 2002 Walser went on to break more taboos with his book, *Tod eines Kritikers*, which was withdrawn from publication after *FAZ* editor Frank Schirrmacher denounced it as anti-Semitic.[59] This debate, accompanied by an appearance with Schroeder on May 8 in which Walser intoned his longing for a more positive German identity, seemed to cement Walser's image as a revisionist. Above and beyond what this political designation might mean for Walser himself, his public positions have elicited a larger discussion about Germany's evolving self-image. For Walser a "normal" Germany would be one that would be once again allowed to "feel" pride rather than settle for the anemic, formalist notions of "constitutional patriotism" "*Verfassungspatriotismus.*" He is also seen now as a "taboo-breaker" in an era, when Germans are beginning to test the limits of the old taboos of the "negative symbiosis." As for the rhetoric of Walser's speech and the initial debate it opened, it unleashed a resentment so strong that it allowed some observers to project upon the victims of the Third Reich the role of the perpetrators.

The aftereffects of the Walser-Bubis debate can be seen in the *Antisemitismus-Streit*, which broke out during the German election campaign. The deputy leader of the Free Democrats and former Kohl cabinet member Jürgen Möllemann publicly criticized Israel, accusing Israel and

Prime Minister Ariel Sharon of "trampling international law" with its interventions in the West Bank. This criticism itself may not have had the same resonance elsewhere as it had in Germany. But as if in an effort to dispose off German taboos, Möllemann not simply criticized Israel but identified himself with the victims of Israel's military campaign, tacitly condoning Palestinian suicide bombers, saying that if his country were occupied, "I too would resist, indeed violently, not just in my own country but also in the aggressor's."[60] Not alone in his position toward Israel, Möllemann, recruited a prominent Syrian-born German, Jamal Karsli, who had left the Greens after they threatened to expel him for his anti-Israel statements. Karsli attacked the Israelis for their "Nazi methods" and granted an interview to an extreme right-wing publication, *Junge Freiheit*, in which he criticized Germany's "Zionist lobby."[61] Möllemann accused the Jews themselves of provoking anti-Semitism, saying, "Hardly anyone makes the anti-Semites, who unfortunately do exist in Germany, more popular than Mr. Sharon—and in Germany, Friedman, with his intolerant and spiteful manner."[62] Michael Friedman, the deputy at the Central Council of Jews and an acerbic talk-show host, accused Möllemann of flirting with anti-Semitism and called for his expulsion from the party. Instead, FDP leader Guido Westerwelle engineered Karsli's resignation.

Having appropriated Palestinian suffering to both ameliorate Germany's Nazi past and illustrate German victimhood in the present, Möllemann opened the door for other right-wing sympathizers. The Austrian far-right politician, Jörg Haider, has praised Möllemann, while the embarrassed FDP party leader, Guido Westerwelle, in Israel on a previously arranged trip, endeavored to present the Free Democrats as supportive of Jews and the state of Israel. Other leaders of the Free Democrats, clearly embarrassed by the publicity, denounced. Möllemann's effort "to collect far-right votes, calling it a catastrophe" for the party, which spent thirty years in government until 1998.[63] Mr. Sharon told Mr. Westerwelle that he found "very disturbing the things being said about the Jewish community in Germany." Paul Spiegel, the leader of the Central Council of Jews in Germany, called Mr. Möllemann's comments "the worst insult a political party has delivered in the history of the Federal Republic since the Holocaust."[64]

Reflecting on the fact that the FPD's ratings rose in the polls after this exchange, New Republic journalist John B. Judis remarked:

> If more mainstream politicians follow . . . Möllemann's example of stoking ethnic resentment and right-wing nationalism for political gain, the implications will be felt not merely in Germany but across Europe. In a sense, after all, it is precisely German "political correctness"—its leaders' inhibitions about the pursuit of narrow and exclusionary national self-interest—that has made Europe what it is today.[65]

Here Judis bemoans, that Germany's move toward "normalization," understood as the increasing frankness of discussions between Jews and Germans, would lead to a demise of a cultural inhibition Judis feels is necessary to keep Europe from openingly embracing anti-Semitism and racism. Jews in Germany also expressed anxiety about the German loss of inhibition. Deidre Berger, director of the American Jewish Committee's office in Berlin, described the *Antisemitismus-Streit* as a "change of paradigm," remarking "that the discussion could get this far is a sign of a growing feeling in Germany that it's time to have a normal relationship with Jews and Israel . . . But the problem is that there's nothing normal about this relationship."[66]

As the *Antisemistmus-Streit* broke many of the taboos about Germany's ability to criticize Israel on a large public scale—the German left has always been critical—Jews in Germany are becoming more politicized and more vocal. Like Bubis's response to Walser, Germany's Jewish cultural leaders are strenuously resisting the breaking of public taboos, partly out of fear of losing the moral high ground among the Germans, but largely because for them, "normalization" of German-Jewish relations means accepting public norms that inhibit what they feel to be a latent anti-Semitism disguised in other forms, such as political criticism of Israel. In short, they seek a public discourse that would be "normative" in Habermas's sense.

Salomon Korn stated publicly during the debate in the spring of 2002 that "there is no new anti-Semitism, the already existing one has simply been revealed" and that he felt "uncomfortable" in Germany.[67] For him, there is still no German Jewish dialogue. The only solution Korn sees is the continuation of the unfinished, previously "one-sided dialogue" of the Enlightenment era. Korn's claims about Jewish cosmopolitan identity, however, unltimately reveal the Jewish perspective of this dialogue and its disjunction with the German:

> Only when the Jews no longer function as a "complete Other" in the collective consciousness of Germans . . . only then can talk of a pragmatic "normality" begin. But in order for this to happen the Germans must first find themselves. This difficult path leads from a not completely mastered ethnic-influenced German national consciousness, past still-present black holes in their national soul, to a national consciousness shaped by a German-Europeanism—that is, towards where some of the German-Jews already were a hundred and fifty years ago.[68]

Notes

1. Joseph (Joschka) Fischer, "Deutschland, deine Juden. Wider die neue Sprachlosigkeit im deutsch-jüdischen Verhältnis." *Frankfurter Allgemeine Zeitung*, May 11, 2002 in English: "Can We Criticize Israel?" *Frankfurter*

Allgemeine Zeitung, English Edition, May 13, 2002. This article also appeared in the International Herald Tribune, May 14, 2002.
2. Ibid.
3. Michel Foucault, *Discipline and Punish: The Birth of the Prison*, trans. Alan Sheridan (New York: Vintage Books, 1979, ca. 1977), p. 136.
4. Ibid., p. 184.
5. Jürgen Link, *Versuch über den Normalismus. Wie die Normalität produziert wird*, 2nd ed. (Planden/Wiesbaden: Westdeutscher Verlag, 1999).
6. Jürgen Habermas. *Die nachholende Revolution* (Frankfurt am Main: Suhrmap, 1990): p. 209. See also Jürgen Link's discussion of Habermas, *Versuch über den Normalismus. Wie die Normalität produziert wird*, 2nd ed., pp. 15–18.
7. Jürgen Habermas, "Die zweite Lebenslüge der Bundesrepublik: wir sind wieder *normal* geworden" *Die Zeit*, December 11, 1992 (48). The first Lebenslüge was Germany's postwar effort to exorcize National Socialism as an aberration, rather than part of modernity, and to deny its persistence after 1945.
8. Attempts to chart the globalization of capital, decline of the nation-state, and rise of a new global culture include the essays in Mike Featherstone, ed., *Global Culture: Nationalism, Globalization, and Modernity*, special issue of *Theory, Culture & Society* (London; Newbury Park: Sage Publications, 1990); Anthony Giddens, *The Consequences of Modernity* (Stanford: Stanford University Press, 1990); Ann Cvetkovich, Douglas Kellner, eds., *Articulating the Global and the Local: Globalization and Cultural Studies* (Boulder: Westview Press, 1997).
9. Cf. David Blackbourn and Geoff Eley, *The Peculiarities of German History: Bourgeois Society and Politics in Nineteenth-Century Germany* (Oxford; New York: Oxford University Press, 1984). Blackbourn and Eley have argued, that this version of the German "Sonderweg" used to explain the events of the 1930s and 1940s, was based on an idealized model of British "normality."
10. *Historikerstreit: die Dokumentation der Kontroverse um die Einzigartigkeit der nationalsozialistischen Judenvernichtung*, 2nd edition (Munich: R. Piper, 1987). Literature on this Historikerstreit is enormous for one of the best studies see Charles S. Maier, *The Unmasterable Past: History, Holocaust, and German National Identity* (Cambridge, MA: Harvard University Press, 1988).
11. Jürgen Habermas, "Yet Again: German Identity—A Unified Nation of Angry D-mark Burghers," *When the Wall Came Down*, pp. 86–102.
12. Ibid.
13. James E. Young, "Reflections on the dedication of Berlin's Memorial for the Murdered Jews of Europe," The Stockholm International Conference on the Holocaust, 2000.
14. Stefan Berger. *The Search for Normality: National Identity and Historical Consciousness in Germany since 1800* (Providence: Berghahn Books, 1997).
15. "Kohl's Legacy," *Time International* v.155, n.4 (January 31, 2000): p. 28
16. Only as recently as January 2003 did the German government sign an agreement with the country's leading Jewish organization, putting their relations on a formal legal footing and giving the organization the same legal status as the predominant churches. The signing of the accord by Chancellor Gerhard Schröder and Paul Spiegel, above, head of the Central Council of Jews, came on the 58th anniversary of the liberation of the Auschwitz death camp. Mr. Spiegel called the treaty a milestone for the 100,000 Jews in Germany, and

Mr. Schröder said it was a sign of the Jewish community's trust in German society. The government will provide $3.3 million annually to help train rabbis and teach Jewish rites. *The New York Times*, January 28, 2003, World in Brief.

17. World Jewish Congress Policy. *Dispatch* n.33, October 1998.
18. Lynn Rapaport. *Jews in Germany After the Holocaust: Memory, Identity, and Jewish-German Relations* (Cambridge: Cambridge University Press, 1997).
19. Y. Michal Bodemann, *Jews, Germans, Memory: Reconstructions of Jewish Life in Germany* (Ann Arbor, MI: University of Michigan Press, 1996).
20. Sander L. Gilman, *Jews in Today's German Culture* (Bloomington: Indiana University Press, 1995).
21. Micha Brumlik, "The Situation of Jews in Today's Germany," *Jews Germans, Memory*, ibid., pp. 1–18.
22. Y. Michal Bodemann, *Jews Germans, Memory*, ibid., pp. 19–46.
23. Dan Diner, "Negative Symbiose: Deutsche und Juden nach Auschwitz." *Babylon* 1, 1986, pp. 9–20.
24. Gershom Scholem, "Against the Myth of the German-Jewish Dialogue," *On Jews and Judaism in Crisis*. Werner J. Dannhauser, ed. (New York: Schocken, 1976), p. 61.
25. Salomon Korn, "Die viel beschworene deutsch-jüdische Symbiose ist bloß ein Mythos," *Frankfurter Rundschau*, June 15, 2000.
26. Fischer, "Deutschland, deine Juden. Wider die neue Sprachlosigkeit im deutsch-jüdischen Verhältnis."
27. Ibid.
28. Bill Niven, *Facing the Nazi Past: United Germany and the Legacy of the Third Reich* (London and New York: Routledge, 2001).
29. Roger Cohen, "Berlin Holocaust Memorial Approved." *New York Times*, June 26, 1999.
30. Niven, *Facing the Nazi Past*, p. 230.
31. Ibid.
32. Ibid.
33. Ibid., p. 231.
34. Ibid.
35. Young Speech, "Reflections."
36. *Die Walser-Bubis-Debatte: eine Dokumentation*, Frank Schirrmacher, ed. (Frankfurt: Suhrkamp, 1999), p. 13.
37. Ibid., p. 13.
38. Ibid., p. 12.
39. Ibid., pp. 13–14.
40. Walser, p. 13.
41. Ingatz Bubis "Rede des Praesidenten des Zentralrates der Juden in Deutschland am November 9, 1998 in der Synagoge Rykerstrasse in Berlin," *Walser-Bubis Debatte*, ibid., p. 111.
42. Niven, *Facing the Nazi Past*, p. 181.
43. Siegfried Unseld, Brief an Ignatz Bubis, *Walser-Bubis Debatte*, ibid., pp. 36–37.
44. Seligmann, *Walser-Bubis Debatte*, ibid., p. 198.
45. Dohnanyi *Walser-Bubis Debatte*, ibid., p. 146.
46. Monika Maron, "Hat Walser zwei Rede gehalten?" Walser-Bubis-Debatte, p. 182.

47. Tim Cole, *Selling the Holocaust: from Auschwitz to Schindler: How History is Bought, Packaged, and Sold* (New York: Routledge, 1999).
48. Anson Rabinbach, "From Explosion to Erosion: Holocaust Memoiralization in America since Bitburg," *History and Memory* v.9, n.1/2 (Fall 1997): pp. 226–255.
49. Peter Novick, *The Holocaust in American Life* (Boston: Houghton Mifflin, 1999).
50. Walser, *Walser-Bubis Debatte*, ibid., p. 12.
51. Wir brauchen eine neue Sprache für die Erinnerung, p. 446.
52. Ibid., p. 445.
53. Micha Brumlik, *Walser-Bubis Debatte*, ibid.
54. Stuart Taberner, A manifesto for Germany's 'New Right'? Martin Walser, the past, transcendence, aesthetics, and *Ein 'Springender Brunnen'.German Life and Letters* v.53, n.1 (January 2000): pp. 126–141.
55. Amir Eshel, "Vom eigenen Gewissen: Die Walser-Bubis Debatte und der Ort des Nationalsozialismus im Selbstbild der Bundesrepublik," *Deutsche Vierteljahresschrift für Literaturwissenschaft und Geistesgeschichte* v.2 (June 2000): pp. 333–360.
56. Ibid., pp. 359–360.
57. Ibid., p. 446.
58. The term "projection" here encompasses both in the psychoanalytic concept of perceiving others as having traits that one inaccurately believes oneself not to have or, as Anna Freud described it, a defense mechanism, and, as well the more recent understanding of projection as a cognitive bias that influences one's self-concept. Freud, *Instincts and their Vicissitudes*, in J. Strachey, ed. and trans, The standard edition of the complete works of Sigmund Freud v.14, pp. 111–142. London: Hogarth Press (Original work published in 1915) Anna Freud, *The Ego and the Mechanisms of Defense* (New York: Hogarth Press, 1936). Baumeister, Roy F., Dale, Karen, Sommer, Kristin L. "Freudian defense mechanisms and empirical findings in modern social psychology: reaction formation, projection, displacement, undoing, isolation, sublimation, and denial,"*Journal of Personality* v.66, n.6 (December 1998): p. 1081.
59. Frank Schirrmacher, Offener Brief in der Frankfurter Allegemeine Zeitung, "Der neue Roman von Martin Walser: Kein Vorabdruck in der F.A.Z.," May 29, 2002.
60. Steven Erlanger, "Specter of High-Level Anti-Semitism Taints German Campaign," *New York Times*, May 29, 2002, p. 4.
61. John B. Judis, "Can Europe Survive German Nationalism?" *The New Republic*, June 24, 2002.
62. Erlanger, "Specter of High-Level Anti-Semitism."
63. Ibid.
64. Ibid.
65. Judis, "Can Europe Survive?"
66. Ibid.
67. Salomon Korn, "Ende der Schönzeit.Es gibt keinen neuen Antisemitismus— der vorhandene wird entlarvt," *Frankfurter Allgemeine Zeitung*, May 6, 2002.
68. Salomon Korn, "Die viel beschworene deutsch-jüdische Symbiose ist bloß ein Mythos."

INDEX